Marian Prince was born in North Vancouver BC, Canada. Starting her family at a young age, she married and had two children by 18. Her husband moved her to the deserted end of Lasqueti Island, often leaving her stranded during long tug boat trips. She had to learn to hunt and garden, to feed her young family. As life moved on, she remarried having two more children. No longer an urgent necessity, she continued to garden on the sunshine coast to supply healthy organic produce for her growing family. She went on to earn a horticultural certificate in 1990 after moving to the interior of BC. She has years of experience in growing and preserving and is honored to share this information with you so that you too can provide the best produce for you and yours.

Marian Prince

A GARDEN BUILT FOR YOU

AUSTIN MACAULEY PUBLISHERS™

LONDON ∗ CAMBRIDGE ∗ NEW YORK ∗ SHARJAH

Ordering Information
Quantity sales: Special discounts are available on quantity purchases by corporations, associations, and others. For details, contact the publisher at the address below.

Publisher's Cataloging-in-Publication data
Prince, Marian
A Garden Built for You

ISBN 9781647508265 (Paperback)
ISBN 9781647508272 (ePub e-book)

Library of Congress Control Number: 2021917402

www.austinmacauley.com/us

First Published 2021
Austin Macauley Publishers LLC
40 Wall Street, 33rd Floor, Suite 3302
New York, NY 10005
USA

mail-usa@austinmacauley.com
+1 (646) 5125767

Introduction

My name is Marian Prince and I have loved gardening for as long as I can remember. Some of it is probably genetics, as my grandfather worked in greenhouses in Burnaby, B.C., from the time he immigrated to Canada from Britain in the early 1900s. When my mother was old enough to work in the greenhouses, it was her favorite place to go as well.

As a child, we always had a backyard garden. I probably wasn't the best help to my mom, but it always gave me a peaceful feeling to be in our garden plot, learning to differentiate the weeds from the garden plants.

At the ripe age of 12, my mom gave me my own garden space. I chose to grow pumpkins, and what a success they were. I was a little disappointed with their shape, as they were the elongated variety, not the round variety as I had hoped for. However, that was the true start to my desire to be involved in horticulture.

As an adult, my very first home-gardening attempt was a complete flop and deflated me for some time. I was living on Lasqueti Island, a tiny island in the Gulf of Georgia, at the time. I had carefully chosen the garden site, making sure it was near the house and near a good water source. It also had excellent sun exposure, so I got down to digging, raking, and preparing the soil. I had my seeds in hand and started the planting process. I was using the in-ground row-planting method and had my markers at each end of the rows, you know, with the seed packages turned upside down on the wooden stakes. I had hills nicely mounded for the squash and pumpkins, with three seeds in each hill as per the planting instructions. My seed potatoes were nicely hilled and everything looked perfect. A lot of work and it was planted. I just had to sit back and watch it grow, or so I thought. The day after all of my excitement and hard work, I got up to have a look at my beautiful garden plot only to see that it had been completely destroyed. The free-range cows had decided to pay me a visit overnight and trampled the whole thing until nothing was left. What a bitter disappointment that was. Next time round, I would have fencing around the garden plot and no free-range cows anywhere near!

My next garden was very successful. I was now living in Sechelt on the Sunshine Coast and had a large garden plot area on 1/3 of an acre. It was close to the backdoor in a sunny spot, and the water source was right handy to the entire area. I went to local sawmills to pick up the ends and seconds of rough-cut boards in order to build a fence around my garden. There weren't any free-range cows in the area, but I now had four children, a couple of dogs, and was horse sitting 'Rosy' for my brother-in-law. No chances taken; my garden needed protection! I used Rosie's manure (composted of course) and had the most awesome peas and cucumbers ever. During this time, I discovered 'square-foot gardening.' This changed my whole outlook on gardening and I adopted this method wholeheartedly. I don't recall how I ended up with the book, *SQUARE FOOT GARDENING*, written by Mel Bartholomew, but it was a complete game changer for me. I highly recommend the book for any and all gardeners alike.

Years later, I moved to the Okanagan Valley in South Central British Columbia and received the Practical Horticulture Certification at Caribou College in Kamloops, B.C. (now Thompson Rivers University). I have worked in the forestry industry doing silviculture surveys and timber cruising. I have had a career as a landscape designer, landscape estimator, nursery worker, and landscaper for over 15 years. And I never gave up my love of being an active home gardener and food preserver, giving me over 45 years' experience in this field.

I am writing this book now to share some of my successes and failures with gardening enthusiasts everywhere. Whether you are new to gardening, a beginner gardener, or a seasoned gardener, you will find some little tidbits of helpful information throughout these pages.

Chapter One
Planning Your Garden

So, how many of you have planted a garden in the past? Do you get all excited in the spring with many seed packets and nursery seedlings in hand? Have you been able to get all of your seeds and seedlings planted? Have you been able to find the time to maintain that garden? What happened? Did you lose interest in it because it became too time consuming, or did it become overrun, becoming a forest where you could no longer distinguish the plants from the weeds?

How many of you have been able to harvest the crops from the garden you planted? Did you find you had too many of one crop and not enough of another? Were your plants overcrowded and becoming spindly with little to no fruits? Did you have one crop overtaking the rest of your crops?

Did you know what to do with the remainder of your harvest, or did it fall to the ground and rot away?

After your initial build, which will take some time, effort, and a bit of expense, this book is designed to make gardening easy, practical, productive, fun, and not a chore. You will be amazed at how a few practical steps will change the way you are used to gardening. 'After all, the final harvest is the main goal for having a garden, right?'

➢ Choosing the Best Site for Your Garden

- **Sunny Location:** Most plants, especially the warm weather crops, like at least eight hours of sunlight per day but will still do okay with six hours. Root crops will do okay with four–six hours of sunlight, and the cool weather crops are fine with three–four hours of sun. Sun is the key ingredient for plant photosynthesis, a process that gives the plants their energy. Try to plan your garden running east to west for the best sun exposure. Also, be sure to shelter your crops from strong winds without shading them from overhead trees. Oh, and don't forget to have a nearby water source.

- **Secure Area**: Keeping your garden close to your house or entrance walkway will be a regular reminder for you and your family that you have a thriving garden. You will feel the pride as you walk by it on a daily basis. You also want to keep it away from children's play spaces and bounding dogs. This will prevent trampling of your crops. Keeping your garden within eyesight will reveal any weeds that are popping up, soil drying out, and the ripening of your crops. Children will be thrilled to see their food developing, especially if they have played a part in the planning and planting process. Avoid planting over septic tank field lines, buried utility cables, or water lines.

- **Size**: The size of your garden will generally be dictated as to the size of your yard. If this is your first garden, go small, see how much time you devote to the garden. If you find gardening really is for you, expand it the next year. You also don't want a garden larger than what your family can use. If you have little to no room, try using some pots, or think about renting a garden plot in a community garden.

- **Level**: Try to choose a relatively level site for your garden with good drainage. This will prevent water erosion and water runoff. You will want your soil to remain evenly moist, especially during the seed-germination process. If your site is not level, the water runoff could wash out the little seeds and seedlings that you have lovingly planted. Your garden will require daily watering for good seed germination and plant establishment. A level site will keep the water where you want it, helping you to become water-wise.

➢ Choosing the Type of Garden, You Will Have

- **Summer Salad**: Are you looking to have a summer salad garden with various lettuces, greens, maybe a couple of pepper plants, a plum or cherry-tomato plant, cucumber, radish, green onions, possibly a zucchini plant, and a few herbs?

- **Culinary Herbs**: Possibly you only want to have a culinary herb garden with flat leaf and curly leaf parsley as well as French, English, lemon, nutmeg, and caraway thyme. And how about sage, you can have pineapple sage, regular sage, or multicolor sage. Let's not forget rosemary, oregano, and basil. Oh, and all the mint varieties, flavors of chocolate, spearmint, peppermint, lemon, orange, and apple mint. There is also marjoram, tarragon, cilantro, dill, lavender, borage, and chives. All of these herbs dry and freeze beautifully for long-term use.

- **Medicinal Herbs**: You might want to grow a medicinal herb garden with valerian, angelica, chamomile, Echinacea, verbena, rue, lavender, feverfew, St. John's Wart, calendula, and catnip. Or a combination of culinary herbs and medicinal herbs. But beware, most of these herbs will reseed in abundance, taking over your garden space the following season.

- **A Couple of This and a Couple of That:** You may want to have a space with only one or two types of plants with a lot of varieties of each. For instance, five–ten types of tomato plants and two four types of corn.

- **Fruit Gardening**: Possibly you don't want any vegetables or herbs but only a fruit-bearing garden, in which case you will have strawberries, raspberries, rhubarb, blueberries, currants, possibly blackberries, grapes, and gooseberries.

- **The Most Common Garden**: Most of you will want to have this most common backyard garden which is a little bit of everything. You will want to grow small fruits, herbs, and vegetables in order to have some good summer feasts and to also preserve some for winter use. In this case, you will be planting more of everything, using a larger area. A few herbs, some lettuce, radish, green onions, potatoes, garlic, carrots, beets, spinach, chard, beans, corn, tomatoes, cucumbers, squash, onions, and peppers.

➢ Choosing Your Gardening Method

- **In-Ground, Row Gardening**: This is a method as old as the hills. People used to have large spaces and could afford the area for row planting with a two–three-foot (one meter) walking area between rows. For this method, all you need to do is rent a rototiller for a few hours, till up the area you have chosen for your garden, and throw in your amendments. This method is great if you have the room, the time for maintaining it, and a free or cheap water source for irrigating. This is by far the most economical method, as there is very little construction required, well, possibly a fence surround to keep out deer, pets, and free-range cattle. However, there is generally more weeding and bending required to plant, thin, maintain, and harvest. Because there is such a large space between your planting rows, I would suggest laying a good-grade landscape fabric on your walking space and placing a layer of mulch, hay, or even crusher chips on top. This will greatly cut down on the time you will spend hoeing and weeding. However, a lot of the water you use for irrigating will be wasted by watering these walkways needlessly. Because the purpose of this book is to make gardening easier, practical, and economical, I will primarily be focusing on the square-foot gardening method.

- **Square-Foot Gardening**: This is a newer method of gardening, designed for smaller areas, and this method can be used in ground or in raised beds. As mentioned previously, this method of gardening was designed and written about by Mel Bartholomew. If you choose this method for in-ground planting, you will still have to create a walking space using planks, stones, concrete, etc. in order to plant, maintain, and harvest. If you choose the raised garden-bed method, you will have to decide on the material that you will use to build your raised garden with (concrete blocks, poured-in-place concrete, rocks, cedar planks, or steel frame). Or you can purchase a pre-fab garden frame available at most garden-supply stores. Without going into too much detail at this point, the idea behind square-foot gardening is that it is space saving, water saving, and work saving. Garden plots can be four feet (1.2 meters) wide with a walking area on both sides, making it easy to reach two feet (.6 meters) in on either side. The ideal situation is to have raised beds at least one foot (.3 meters) deep. So, if you choose to go with the ideal, more than likely you will be importing soil at this stage. You can have a premixed, good quality growing medium delivered to your garden site for a relatively economical price. Remember that the garden frame and growing medium are onetime purchases or long-term purchases and will last you a lifetime or a long time of gardening pleasure. I will go into more detail regarding these two gardening methods when we discuss the BUILDING PROCESS in CHAPTER TWO.

➢ Creating Your Garden on Paper

- **Metric or Imperial**: Do you use the metric system or the imperial system? I am more comfortable with the imperial system, and because I have used this method for years, that is what I will talk about mostly. That is not to say that the metric system can't be used the same way for laying a garden out. The scale I use on the grid paper is two squares = one foot. So, let's get started with the enclosed grid paper.
- The top of your paper should always be the north point, so if your garden is wider than longer, turn your paper to the side. (Remember, east-to-west planting gives you maximum sunlight exposure.)
- Next, in pencil, draw out the boundaries of your garden and mark the location of trees, structures, walkways, fences, etc. in their general area and approximate distances from your garden site. Don't worry if

some of your garden space is in a shady area, as some plants like a little cooler temperature.

- Mark the location of your water source.

- **Decision Time**: Now is the time to decide what plant material you want to grow. Get out some seed catalogues (I use West Coast Seeds and Stokes Seeds; both have some very valuable information and a wide range of seed types and species). Besides your drawing or on the back of your grid paper, jot down the types of seeds, seedlings, and/or plant material you want in your garden. Place your order and wait for those seeds with gardening anticipation.

That is as far as we will take this process for now. In future chapters, I will talk about how much room is needed for each specific plant. You will then be able to completely design your garden on paper. Refer to the examples that I have provided of my garden areas. My planting varies from year to year. The reason for that is because different plants use different minerals and micro nutrients in the soil, so crop rotation is pretty important. Keeping a record of where you have planted from year to year will stop the depletion of these minerals and micro nutrients. I try to do a four-year rotation, so in the fifth year, I go back to the first-year planting scheme.

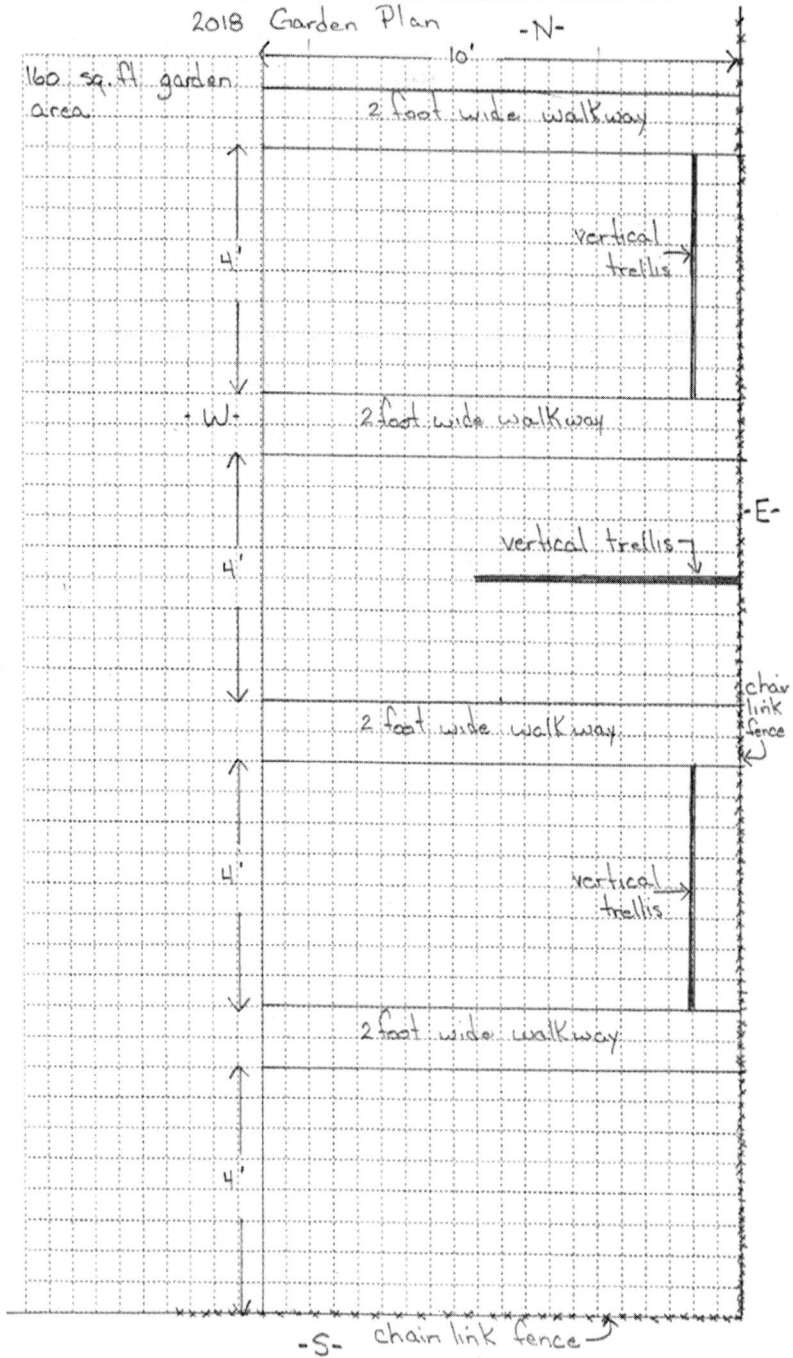

2018 Garden Plan   -N-

160 sq. ft garden area

10'

2 foot wide walkway

vertical trellis

4'

-W-

2 foot wide walkway

vertical trellis

4'

-E-

chain link fence

2 foot wide walkway

vertical trellis

4'

2 foot wide walkway

4'

-S- chain link fence

2018 Garden Plan

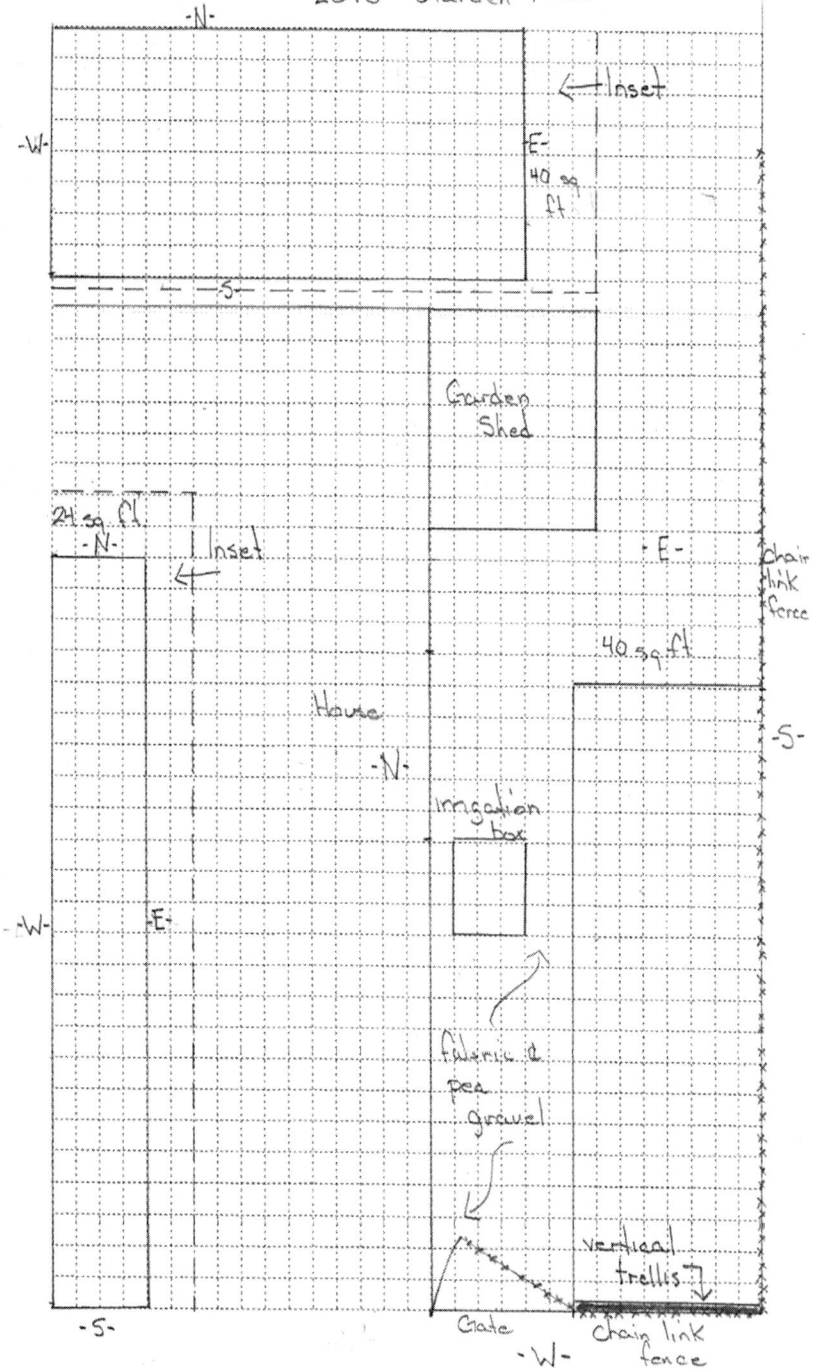

-N-
-W-
-E-
40 sq ft
Inset
-S-

Garden Shed

24 sq ft
-N-
Inset
-E-

Chain link fence

-E-
40 sq ft
-S-

House
-N-

irrigation box

fabric & pea gravel

vertical trellis

-W-
-E-
-S-

Gate
-W-

Chain link fence

Chapter Two
Building Your Garden

➢ In-row Planting

As previously mentioned, the purpose of this book is to make gardening easy, practical, and economical. The 'in-row' gardening method is not a practical method of gardening in small spaces and it requires more work. I therefore will be focusing on the easier method of gardening, which is raised beds. If you do choose the 'in-row planting method' and plan to use an existing lawn area, a practical measure is to rent a turf cutter to strip the lawn. If you simply rototill the lawn into the soil, you will continually have grass growing in your garden. Throw the stripped lawn into a pile and allow it to compost for later use.

➢ Raised Beds

We will now go into a little more detail regarding raised beds. Raised gardens have many benefits over in-ground tilled spaces. Some of those benefits are:

- If you have a bad back, a raised garden doesn't require as much bending for planting, weeding, or harvesting.
- A raised garden heats more rapidly in the spring, which allows for earlier planting. In some climates, you can sometimes squeeze in a second crop during the growing season.
- In a raised garden, you can fill it with a good-quality soil that has the right nutritional values and drainage qualities.

- You can also use the square-foot gardening method in raised beds, reducing thinning and weeding work by a bunch.
- Raised beds keep path weeds away from your garden soil.
- They prevent soil compaction, because you don't walk in them.
- The sides of the beds keep your garden soil from being washed away during heavy rains and irrigating.
- Raised garden beds are available in a variety of different materials, or they can be built without a lot of effort.
- It is usually easy to install vertical-growing frames in raised beds.

➢ Material Used for Building Raised Beds

- **Wood**

Pressure-Treated Wood: Many people, including myself, for years, used pressure-treated garden ties for building raised beds. The industry used to use chromated copper arsenate (CCA) for residential use. That is a preservative with a track record of decay resistance going back to the mid-1940s. There were health concerns about the chemical and so the industry stopped using this product back in 2003. Now several preservatives are used in the pressure treatment of wood. Some include Alkaline Copper Quaternary (ACQ), Copper Azole (CA), and Micronized Copper Quaternary (MCQ). These all are less toxic than the CCA treatment used years ago, but they contain higher levels of copper and so are much more corrosive. Manufacturers recommend using gloves and safety goggles when handling the product. Some treated wood is recommended for above-ground use only because of its poor life expectancy. The pressure-treated wood that is cured with Alkaline Copper Quaternary is considered by the EPA (Environmental Protection Act) safe for food crops, but until the safety of pressure-treated wood is proven conclusively, I recommend you use another type of wood product for your build.

Spruce, Fir, and Pine: Common and economical woods are spruce, fir, and pine. The pros to wooden raised beds are:

- They are easy to install.

- The material is readily available at most building supply stores.
- They work nicely for any type of garden, depending upon the design and construction.
- They are a perfect project for the do-it-yourselfer.

However, wood doesn't last forever, so you will at some point have to replace it. You can extend the life of your wood by treating the dry raw planks with water-soluble borate chemicals. Boron is an effective wood-rot prevention that is dissolved in water and either sprayed or painted onto the lumber. The best application method is to soak each board in a trough of heated dissolved solution for a minute or so to allow the solution to soak into the entire board. Once the lumber is treated, allow it to dry in a shady area. Be sure to keep each piece separate from the others, giving them good air circulation. Once dry, you can do your build and paint all surfaces with a lead-free paint. You can make your own solution by combining by weight:

- 20% Borax (20 Mule Team Borax washing soda purchased at grocery and hardware stores)
- 15% boric acid (purchased at drug stores)
- 65% water

Heat the solution until it is dissolved; the boric acid is slow to dissolve. Once dissolved, it can be stored in the fridge. Apply at temperatures no lower than 40° F. (4.5° C.). Another safe product available to us is 'Lifetime Wood Treatments' which can be purchased in a powder form at Home Hardware Stores.

Cedar: Western Red Cedar is a tree native to the west coast of North America. It contains natural preservatives that resist moisture, decay, and insect damage. It has the ability to lay flat, stay straight, and hold any fastenings tightly. Cedar has twice the stability of most commonly available softwoods and also has high thermal insulating properties. The downfall to using cedar for your raised garden bed

is it is not as readily available as fir, pine, or spruce and is considerably more expensive.

- **Concrete**

Poured in Place: The use of urban landscape elements like poured-in-place concrete has increased in recent years. What used to seem ordinary and humble can now be chic and even trendy, making concrete a very flexible and desired addition to most types of gardens. Some of the benefits to using poured-in-place concrete is it will last indefinitely when installed properly. It can be tinted with a color to blend, match, or contrast with your home and other structures. However, concrete can be expensive and, in some cases, is not a project for the do-it-yourselfer. If you choose to use this product, once it's there, it cannot be easily moved or dismantled.

Masonary Rock or Brick: These products used for raised beds can easily fit into nearly any style of garden, depending upon the type of rock you use. But, unless you are a mason or are training to be one, I would not tackle a project like this. Once again, this is a permanent fixture, unmovable, and hard to dismantle. Having a mason do the work for you would be a very pricy proposition. Also, the materials are quite expensive, heavy to handle, and need a truck to deliver.

Cinderblocks: Apart from wood, I would say that using cinderblocks is the next most common raised-bed-construction method. Raised beds made from this product can be constructed in a number of different ways.  They can simply be stacked to the desired height of the bed, or they can be mortared in place. This method is easy to construct, the material readily available, and the product very durable. It has a rustic appeal and is relatively inexpensive. If you wanted to have a more elegant finish with a surface treatment and capped tops, it will naturally be pricier. As the picture shows, vertical-growing treatments are easy to place in the holes of cinderblocks, but don't simply build this form of construction for the vertical benefits. I will be pointing out other vertical-growing methods later on.

- **Steel Studs**: I got this idea after looking at all of the above options after my pressure-treated ties completely rotted out. I really didn't want to go back to the pressure-treated option because of the negative

health risks. This is my garden area. I have two raised beds each 10' x 10' (three meters x three meters), with a two-foot (60 cm.) walking space between the 4' x 10' (1.2 x 3 meters) gardening surfaces. Steel

studs come in six-inch (15.25 cm) and four-inch (ten cm.) heights and can be screwed together with self-tapping screws to make a one-foot (30 cm.) high garden or higher if you choose. The four-inch (ten cm.) height studs makes for double

the work of inserting the self-tapping screws. I happened to get them very cheap and opted to spend less money in exchange for more time spent on the build. These raised beds give me 160 square feet (15 sq. meters) of growing space and I get almost all I can use of harvested product. I also have a couple of in-ground planting areas. I do a lot of freezing, dehydrating, and canning that lasts well into the next growing season. This method is a little time consuming to put together but is relatively inexpensive to build and only requires a drill. Each stud costs around $4.00, so by building it ten feet x ten feet (three m. x three m.) with a two-foot (60 cm.) space between, you will require 12 six-inch (15.25 cm.) studs. This will only cost you around $50.00, and because they are steel and will not rust or rot, they last forever. They don't release any nastiness into the soil. They heat the soil up way before the in-ground growing method, giving you an extended growing season. It is easy to install vertical-growing units and to cover with frost protection or shade fabric. If you move and want to take the garden with you, it is not impossible to do so. Just unscrew, dismantle, and way you go. So, while you are still in the planning stage, keep in mind most garden planting is done in mid-May. That will give you a good weather window to get your garden construction finished in time for planting.

➢ Vertical Growing

Raised beds provide a limited amount of growing space, but you can easily add vertical space by building a trellis for climbing plants. A trellis can be built from PVC pipe, wood, metal, wire, and netting. I built mine from stuff I had around the yard. One is made from an old chain-link fence, another from an old dog run. I did one with netting on half inch (12 mm.) PVC. It works but would be more stable if make from one-inch (25 mm.) PVC.

The benefits of vertical growing are:

- Gives you additional growing area.
- Keeps plants off the ground and protected from slugs and other hungry pests.
- Allows for better air flow, preventing fungal disease.
- Keeps the fruits suspended so they are clean and not muddy when picked.
- Makes harvesting easier, as the fruits are more visible.
- They can act as a shade covering for those plants and herbs that require a little extra cooling.
- Can act as an attractive or privacy screen and can hide untidy areas in your yard or your neighbors' yard.

Chapter Three
Your Growing Medium
and Amendments

So, you have chosen the site for your garden. You have determined the boundaries of your garden on paper. You have chosen your gardening method and even picked out and ordered the plant material you will be growing. You are well underway with the construction of your garden bed, so what is next?

Soil is the base for all outdoor gardening. Whether you are using your existing soil or whether you are using imported soil, it will need some amendments. Now we have to see how we are going to fix the soil in your garden site to grow the best crops. Don't let this topic scare you off. Many books like to make the subject of soil far more complicated than it really is. As a matter of fact, when I went to college and took the practical horticulture program, the textbook on soils that we used was well over 700 pages long, just a little overkill, except for the individuals practicing in soil management.

Remember, our main goal for gardening is the 'harvest'. In saying that, the better the quality of your soil, the healthier your plants will be, hence a larger and better harvest.

➢ Soils

The perfect soil is a well-drained, fluffy, friable, rich in organic matter, high in nutrients mixture. I can

guarantee that you do not naturally have this type of soil, but we can fix whatever type you have in a few easy steps. Basically, there are only three soil types.

- **Sandy/Gravelly:** soil is composed largely of gritty and angular-shaped pieces or particles. It feels rough and gritty when rubbed between the fingers. It can also have large rocky particles in it. This soil has a lot of open spaces between the particles; the benefit of this is for air movement and a lot of room for the roots to grow. The downfall is that water passes very quickly through these same open spaces. This is fine in wetter, spring weather, but later on in the hotter season, the soil dries out very quickly and the nutrients and moisture disappear. Having a sandy soil requires constant watering and fertilizing.

- **Clay:** At the opposite end of the soil scale is a clay soil. Heavy clay soils are very difficult to work with. They are slippery when wet and like concrete when dry. I doubt any of you have a full heavy clay soil. A lighter clay soil, when rubbed between the fingers, feels a little slippery and mildly gritty. This soil consists of very fine, heavy particles that lay together, allowing for little space. It is extremely difficult for water, air, and plant roots to penetrate this soil. Clay soil drains very poorly and dries out slowly, but when it does dry out, it becomes hard. Generally, a clay soil has good nutrients, but the plants aren't able to access them.

- **Loam:** The third type of soil is the best. It is called a loam and has sand, clay in particle size and structure as well as having a lot of humus in it. There are enough air spaces between the particles to allow air, water, and plant roots to penetrate. The soil is lighter and more easily worked. Loam drains well but holds moisture and nutrients long enough for the plant roots to absorb them.

The better the quality of your soil, the healthier your plants will be, hence a larger harvest. After all, the main goal to having a garden is for the harvest at the end. Hardly anyone starts out with the perfect soil, and it takes seasoned gardeners years to create a really good-growing medium, but luckily for us, most plants are very forgiving and will produce relatively well with the basic amendments. In a nutshell, an overly sandy or gravelly soil will not hold moisture or nutrients. A soil heavy in clay holds too much moisture and there are no air pockets for healthy root growth. The solution to both problems is to add organic matter.

If you are starting from scratch and have never had a garden in your yard, you will have to put in a little more work and effort to get your garden going. You are also going to need some tools for the preparation. These tools are also important to have for the continued maintenance of your garden. However, a quick fix for digging and aerating your soil is to rent a rototiller and let it do the work for you. Sifting is also a very good idea, as it will eliminate old roots and debris as well as aerate your existing soil.

Here is a list of tools you will need:

- Wheel barrow
- Screener
- Round-point shovel
- Square-end digging spade (will also act as an edger)
- Good quality work gloves

If you have a gravely/sandy soil that has never been worked before, you probably have some larger rocks in it. Smaller rocks can be a benefit to a garden because they warm up in the sun's heat throughout the day and they hold that heat at night, but you will want to get rid of the larger rocks. If you are like me, you'll get rid of the smaller, up to one-inch (two cm.) size rocks too. If you have a clay-type soil, not a full-fledged clay soil, you will want to break it up, so for all types of soil, I recommend using a garden screener. It takes a little time to build and a wee bit money, but making a small garden screener is a really good idea. As you dig your soil, put it through the screener. A screener is an apparatus constructed of a wooden frame and covered with a wire screen. You can have a fine wire screen or a coarser wire screen. You can have a manual screener or a motorized screener. There are many plans for both types on the internet, but this one is really very simple. Here are the step-by-step instructions for building this screener.

The List of Things You Will Need

- Six feet of 1"x1" lumber
- Ten feet of 1"x2" lumber
- Five feet of 1"x4" lumber
- 16 feet of 2"x4" lumber
- 14-16 1½" wood or deck screws
- 8-12 2" wood or deck screws
- 8-12 3½" wood or deck screws
- One 24"x36" piece of hardware cloth with either ½" or ¼" mesh
- Metal staples
- Two metal handles
- Wood glue
- Candle wax
- Paint, stain, varnish, or water sealer (optional)
- Saw, jig, or circular
- Drill and drill bits
- Staple gun
- Tin snips or metal cutters
- Sandpaper

Frame Construction

1. Cut two 36" long pieces from the 2"x4" lumber.
2. Cut two 27" long pieces from the 1"x4" lumber.
3. Cut two 36" long pieces from the 1"x1" lumber.
4. Screw the two 1"x4" cross pieces to the bottom of the 2"x4" (pre-drilling will help prevent splitting).
5. Glue the two 1"x1" pieces to the inside of the two 2"x4" pieces, where the four pieces meet at each corner.

The frame should be 24" wide measuring from inside to inside, just above the 1"x1"s so that the screened tray can ride on top of the 1"x1"s

Tray Construction

Screw the tray's 2"x4" side and end pieces together using three half-inch screws.

Cut the hardware cloth screen to match the width and length of the 2"x4"s that were screwed together, but not right to the edge. Secure it to the bottom of the 2"x4"s with metal staples. You only need to put in enough staples to hold it in position tightly.

Screw the 1"x2"s to the tray's bottom.

Attach/screw a handle to each end.

The tray should be 24" wide, outside to outside, to fit on top of the 1"x1"s of the frame.

Sand the wood surfaces and seal with stain, water sealer, paint, etc. If you desire, rub a candle on the bottom of the tray and the tops of the frame 1"x1"s so the tray slides easily.

You will find that you will use this screener a lot in your garden. It is great for breaking down compose, manure, and other clumps.

You really only need to dig down a foot in your garden space. One foot is plenty of room for all crops, even the root crops; not many carrots are over a foot long.

So now you have a large amount of beautifully sifted soil to work with. The solution for a light clay soil at this point is to mix it with sand. You can use a lot of sand depending on the amount of clay in your soil. You can add sand bit by bit and watch it disappear, but you will also notice your soil texture changing. For all soils though, even the toughest clay soil, a must is the addition of ORGANIC MATTER.

➤ Organic Matter

Organic matter can come from plants or animals. It can be composted manure from cows, horses, chickens, sheep, goats, rabbits, llamas, or alpacas. It can also be from a compost pile consisting of grass clippings, leaf mold, and kitchen scraps.

*I cannot say enough about the importance of adding organic matter to your soil.

So where does this magical product come from? How do we get our hands on it? Well, it is sold in most garden centers. You can purchase composted steer manure, composted horse manure, worm castings, and other products. They are rarely mixed together, so you don't get the same benefit of the various nutrients and micro nutrients unless you purchase an assortment and mix them together yourself. They are also quite costly. If you are lucky enough to live near a farm that raises sheep, goats, rabbits, chickens, horses, cows, llamas, or alpacas, you can usually purchase the manure at a low cost. You can use sheep, goat, and rabbit manure without composting it. Chicken manure needs to be composed because using it straight will burn the roots of the plants. Horse and cow manure need to be composted to destroy weed seeds. However, you can have your own wonderful **Organic Matter** in your own backyard, allowing 'Mother Nature' to do the work for you. The cost? Nothing, except for purchasing or making a holder for it.

➢ Composting

Composting is the process of manufacturing this amazing product called compost. I am sure you have all heard the terms, compost heap, mulch pile, compost pile, and humus maker. These terms are all for the same thing, the ORGANIC MATTER produced. First, you will need a holding container. The average-sized container holds about one cubic yard (one cu. meter). Start with that and more can always be added if you find you need it.

- The Heap: If you want to get going right away, you can use a small corner tucked away from the house. No construction is necessary. Just keep piling leaves, grass clippings, a bit of mulch, and some kitchen scraps (no meat or bones) on the pile. Water it down several times and turn it over a few times, and in a few months, you will have awesome organic matter that you will want to screen into your garden.

- Chicken Wire: You can build a simple compost bin yourself by using fencing material, either chicken wire or snow fencing. It is cheap and very easy to set up. If you want to turn the pile, you can remove the fence, set it up beside the first pile, and turn the compost into the newly set-up bin. Simply make a circle or square out of the fencing and tie it with metal wire to four posts.

- Pallets: Another simple easy and almost free technique is to use shipping pallets. They are very easy to come by and companies are usually happy to see them go into a recycling project. Nail or wire four pallets together to make a four-sided bin at least three feet x three feet x three feet. The bin is ready to use. A fifth pallet can be used as a base to allow more air to get into the pile; it will also increase the stability of the bin.

- Garbage Can: A plastic or metal garbage can may be used as a compost bin. They require very little space in your backyard and are cheap and easy to set up. Remove the bottom of the can and puncture holes throughout. You may want to raise the can off the ground for additional ventilation. My two Rubbermaid cans lost their lids, so I flipped them upside down, cut out the bottom, and cut slits in the sides for air circulation. I bought foil pizza pans from the Dollar Store for lids and weighed them down with a rock.

- Barrel: If you want to get really creative and are the handyperson type, then you'll find this composting unit suited to your building needs. The barrel, an old 45-gallon drum that has been well-cleaned out, is rotated several times whenever new materials are added. It is

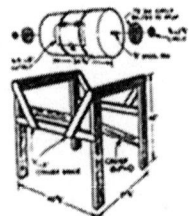

constructed with a minimum of hand-powered tools and, for some of us, is not too difficult or time consuming to build.

- The Tumbler: Or you can purchase a readymade tumbling composter from most gardening supply stores or go to **www.YimbyHomeAndGarden.com**. This composter has two separate chambers with built-in paddles that mixes the material as you turn the tumbler and holds about five cubic feet of fine finished product.

- Cinderblocks: Or bricks may be used to build a compost bin. It is easy to set up and can be constructed with two sections to facilitate the turning of the pile from one section to the next.

- Plastic: Or you can simply purchase plastic compost bins from most building supply stores, garden centers, or your local regional districts and city halls. They come in various colors and styles.

- The Cadillac of all composters is the home-build rodent-resistant three-bin compost system. Plans provided by the Greater Vancouver Regional District.

THE LIST OF THINGS YOU WILL NEED

- 2x4's: eight at 42" for posts and six at 34" for top rails
- 2x2's: six at 36" and six at approx. 27½" for base rails
- 1x6's: 35 at 36" and 12 at 30" for sides and tops and two at 32 ½" for front slider guides for center box
- 1x4's: four at 36", six at approx. 30", 12 at approx.16 7/8", two at approx. 32½", and six at 27"
- 1x2's: six at approx. 31" and three at approx. 30"
- 12 feet of 2x2 for lid support

- Nine feet of 1x4 for back and top
- Nine feet of 1x6 for back and top
- Nine feet of 2x4 for front cross piece
- Six boxes of bell wire insulated staples (5/8"-100 box or 5/8" poultry staples)
- Two pounds 2½" galvanized nails
- One pound 3¼" galvanized spiral nails
- 80 1¼" galvanized brass or stainless-steel screws
- 3–3" strap hinges
- 31 feet or ¼" wire mesh 36 inches wide
- Measuring tape
- Drill
- Bit for screws
- Hammer
- Tin snips
- Hand or circular saw
- Carpenter's square

CONSTRUCTION

- Build the Back: Cut nine feet of wire mesh. Lay out the 1x6's at nine feet long on a level surface with an inch between each board and then add the 1x4 at nine feet long to the bottom. Staple the mesh to the boards.

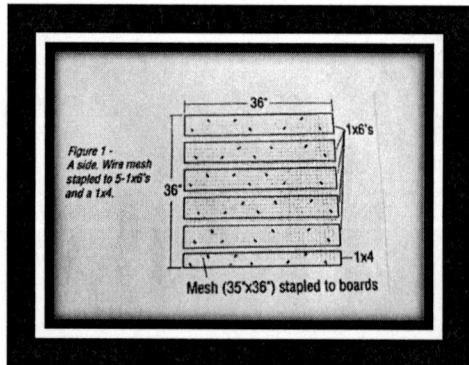

Figure 1 -
A side. Wire mesh stapled to 5-1x6's and a 1x4.

36"

1x6's

36"

1x4

Mesh (35"x36") stapled to boards

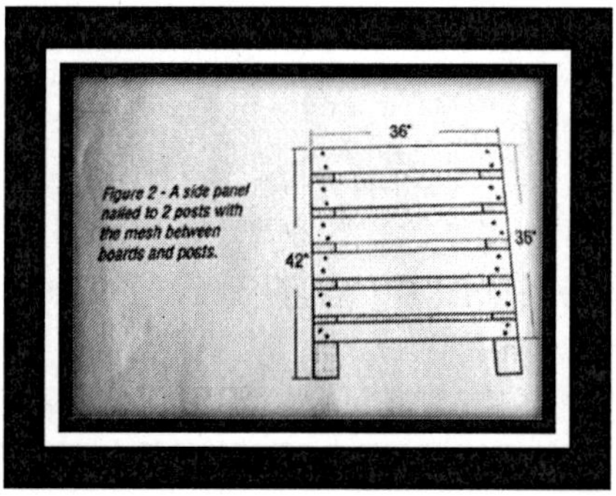

Figure 2 - A side panel nailed to 2 posts with the mesh between boards and posts.

- Build the Four Sides: Cut 20 1x6's 36 inches long. Cut four 1x4's 36 inches long. The four sides are identical. Lay five 1x6 with a 1x4 at the bottom on a level surface with approx. one inch between each board. Lay the piece of wire mesh on top. Ensure everything is square, and staple the mesh to the boards (Figure 1). Repeat for other sides. To build the sides, lay two 2x4 posts on a level surface 36 inches apart. Lay the mesh and board panels on top with the mesh between the boards and posts. Ensure that everything is square and nail the posts with 2¼" nails. Repeat for three other sides (Figure 2).

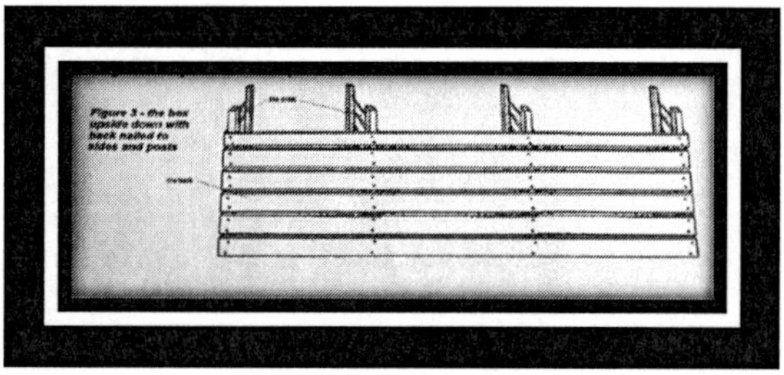

Figure 3 - the box upside down with back nailed to sides and posts

- Attach Back Two Sides: Stand the two sides on a level surface facing each other and leave 36 inches between all sides. Stand the other two sides facing each other with the six inch of post shown in Figure 3. Ensure everything is square before nailing the back panel with 3¼" nails.

- Install Supporting Rails and Bottom: Set boxes on posts (Figure 4). Front Cross Piece – Ensure the boxes are square in all planes and nail 2x4 at nine feet to front posts at the bottom.

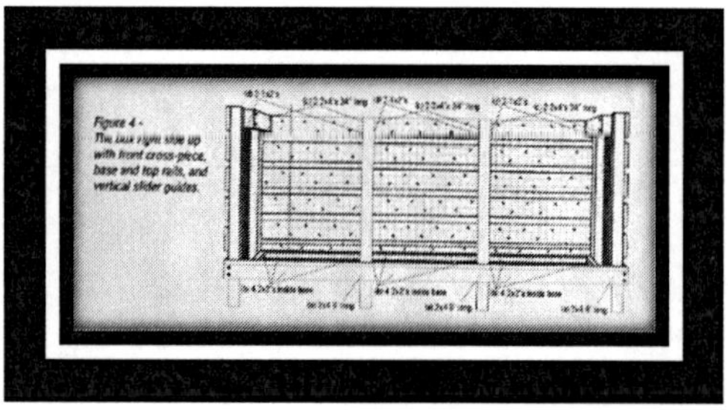

Figure 4 - The box right side up with front cross-piece, base and top rails, and vertical slider guides

31

a. <u>2x2 Base Rails</u> – Cut six 2x2's at 36 inches long and nail to the inside of posts at the base of the box. Measure for other six 2x2's (approx. 27½ inches long) and nail.

b. <u>Top Rails</u> – Cut six 2x2's 34 inches long and nail from back of box to front posts. Note that they will end two inches from the front edge of front posts to allow for sliding front.

c. <u>Vertical Slider Guides</u> – Measure vertical from top to 2x2 base to bottom of 2x4 rail (approx. 31 inches). Cut and nail 1x2 to post two inches back from front of post to guide removable front sections. Repeat for other two box sections.

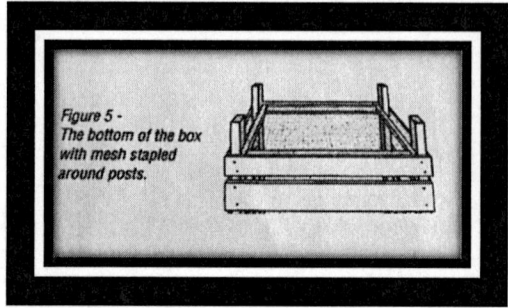

Figure 5 - The bottom of the box with mesh stapled around posts.

d. <u>Bottom</u> – Turn boxes upside down. Cut mesh 39 inches long. Lay mesh with 39-inch length running from front to back. Cut 2x4 holes in mesh for the posts in both end boxes but leave the center piece without the holes. Staple mesh to base. (Figure 5)

- <u>Install Three Fronts:</u> The front is made with two front guides nailed to the front posts and two removable front panels. Each removable panel should be approx.

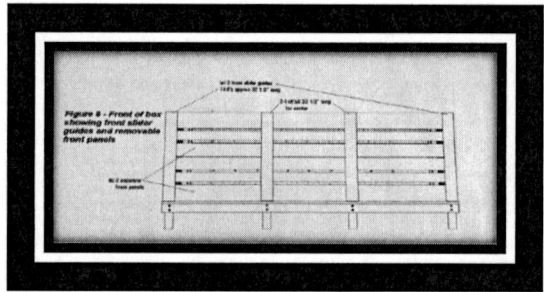

Figure 6 - Front of box showing front slider guides and removable front panels

30 inches wide and 16 7/8 inches high and is built to slide in and out of the top of the box. For the front slider guides, measure distance between the top to base and top of post (approx. 32½") and cut two 1x4's to fit on either end and two 1x6's for the center slider guides. Nail to front posts with two ¼" nails. For the three front

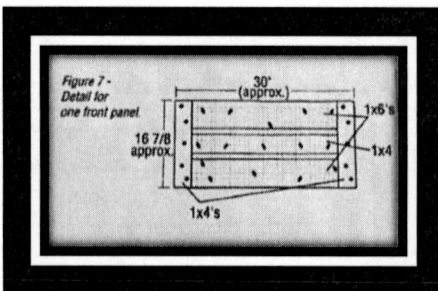

Figure 7 - Detail for one front panel

30" (approx.)

16 7/8 approx.

1x6's

1x4

1x4's

sections, measure the distance between the inside of the two front posts which are on the either end of the three box system (approx. 30¼ or ¼" less than the distance between the posts). Cut 12 1x6's and six 1x4's to fit. Cut mesh to fit each section (six at 29 inches and 16 inches) and staple to two 1x6's and one 1x4. Repeat for the other five front sections. Cut 1x4f bracing to fit (approx. 12 at 16 7/8). Screw 1x4 bracing to front sections.

- Build and Install Tops and Lids: The top is formed from two sections – two boards fixed at the back and three removable lids. For the fixed section, cut a 1x4 and 1x6 nine feet long and nail to the box across the back. For the

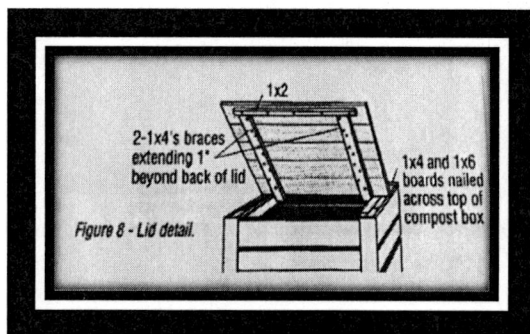

Figure 8 - Lid detail.

removable section, cut five 1x6's 36 inches long and lay them edge to edge across the top of box. They should end up flush with the front of the box. If they don't because of varying board widths, add a piece of 1x2 or trim to fit. Lay these five boards edge to edge on a flat surface and staple mesh cut to approx. 36"x27". Cut 1x4 braces 27 inches long and attach to the mesh side with screws. These braces should fit inside the 2x4 rails at top of box and extend approximately one inch out the back of the removable lid to control the lid pivot. Cut a 1x2 approx. 30 inches long and attach with screws as shown so that it fits directly over top of the front panel and inside of front posts. Repeat twice more for the other lids. Make the lid support with three 2x2's (an arm, a support for arm, and a block guide) and a three-inch strap hinge. The arm is 14 inches long and screwed up to a strap hinge 16¾ inches from front of lid. When the lid is lifted, the arm drops into V-notch on the 2x2 support for arm. Attach safety-gate hook to lid and front section. Select a location for the three-bin compost system and dig eight holes each six inches deep. Set the compost-box posts in the holes, fill holes with leftover dirt, and the compost bin is ready for work.

USING THE THREE-BIN SYSTEM

The method described below is a fast, hot active system that requires more management. The work is turning or mixing the organic material. Regular turning once a week ensures that bacteria get the air; they need to breakdown the material.

This composting method is most efficiently accomplished in batches. Stockpile organic material until there is enough to fill the compost bin, usually a cubic meter or 3'x3'x3'. Kitchen waste can be saved and stored in a sealed plastic garbage can and covered with sawdust or soil to control odors and pests. Chop or shred all material to maximize surface area. Add the material in layers from two to three inches thick. Moisten layers as necessary. Alternate layers of carbon-rich material (browns) with nitrogen-rich material (greens). Fill the compost bin full with material.

Within 24 hours, the temperature will rise to 60 to 70 degrees C. This is the hot composting system and you should monitor the process. These temperatures are maintained for four–seven days. When temperatures drop, it is time to aerate the materials. This is done by turning the materials into the second bin. Try to get material from the top into the bottom and center of the unit to achieve complete destruction of weed seeds and pathogens.

This temporarily interrupts the heat cycle, but the temperatures will quickly rise for another four–seven days. The material will cool and can then be added to the third bin. Compost managed this way should be left to mature for three months.

FIVE EASY STEPS TO MAKING FAST COMPOST

As previously mentioned, making compost is probably the single most important thing you can do for your organic garden. The success of your garden depends on the soil, and the health of your soil depends on the compost you give it. And making compost isn't difficult. With very little effort on your part, you can turn throwaway materials into this sweet-smelling, nutrient-rich, no-cost soil conditioner. This is how we start this easy composting process.

There are many approaches to making compost, but the fastest way to get finished compost for this year's garden is to make an active, or 'hot,' compost pile. By providing a steady supply of water and air to the pile, you'll encourage the microorganisms that drive the composting process to work faster. Here are the five key steps for making compost in about 30 days. (Summer heat, not winter.)

- Shred or chop materials as finely as you can before mixing them into the pile. For example, you can chop fallen leaves by running your lawnmower over them. The same strategy applies to kitchen scraps. Keep a small bin under your sink or in your fridge to keep your chopped scraps and crushed eggshells in. 'The smaller, the better' is the rule for quick composting ingredients.
- The two basic types of ingredients for making compost are those rich in carbon and those rich in nitrogen. Carbon-rich materials, or 'dry browns,' include leaves, hay, and straw. Nitrogen-rich materials, or 'wet greens,' include kitchen scraps and grass clippings; these work best when used sparsely and mixed in well so they don't mat down. Your goal is to keep a fair mix of these materials throughout the pile.
- Build the pile at least 3'×3'×3' so materials will heat up and decompose quickly. (Don't make the pile too much bigger than that, though, or it will be hard to turn.) Unless you have this critical mass of materials, your compost pile can't really get cooking. Check the pile a couple of days after it is built up – it should be hot in the middle, a sign that your microbial decomposers are working hard.
- Make sure the pile stays moist but not too wet. (It should feel like a damp sponge.) You may need to add water occasionally. Or, if you live in a very wet climate, you may need to cover the pile with a tarp to keep it from becoming too soggy.
- Moving your compost adds air to the mix. You can open up air holes by getting in there with a pitchfork. Even better, shift the entire pile over a few feet, bit by bit, taking care to move what was on the outside to the inside of the new pile, and vice versa. Or consider using a compost tumbler, a container that moves the materials for you when you turn it.

MATERIALS TO COMPOST
ORGANIC MATTER

Coffee grounds

Spoiled greens or other produce

Vegetable and fruit peelings

Teabags and tea leaves

Eggshells

Straw

Sawdust (no cedar)

Hay

Corncobs

Leaves

Grass clippings

Shredded twigs

Shredded bark

Pine needles

Hedge trimmings

Wood shavings

Old sod

Garden prunings

Spent annual and vegetable plants (no insects or diseases)

Barn and stable manure

Blood meal

Bone meal

MATERIALS TO AVOID IN THE COMPOST

Invasive weeds

Diseased or pest-laden materials

Meat, bones, grease, eggs, cheese

Seeds and fruit pits

Cat or dog manure

NOTE: Things like meat, bones, and grease slow down the decomposition rate and can attract animals and rodents. Seeds and fruit pits attract rodents to your compost. Household pet manure can transmit parasites that are harmful to humans.

However, that being said, available to us avid gardeners and composers are indoor electric composters. These are quite pricey, running between $300.00–$400.00 but can be used year-round. They are easy to use and handle up to four gallons of food scraps per week AND allows you to compost meat, fish, and dairy products, breaking them down using air circulation and electric heat in a two-week time span. They fit compactly on your countertop, taking up a 20-inch x 12-inch space.

Okay, so now looking back:

- You have drawn your garden site out on graph paper and identified the surrounding structures.
- You have determined your soil type and know how to amend your soil.
- You know that no matter what your soil type may be, you should sift the soil with a screener.
- You have chosen your gardening method.
- You have learned the importance of adding organic matter to any and all soil types.
- And you should have a pretty good idea as to what type of holding unit you will use for composting. You have a list of what good compost materials are and what to avoid.

➤ Soil Texture

Scientists can make this a very complicated topic, and if you were to look this up on the internet, you would probably be scared away. For our gardening purposes, we have already dealt with soil texture without actually calling it by name. When you have added sand to clay soil, you have adjusted the soil texture, and when you add organic matter to soil, you also have adjusted the soil texture. What we are going to talk about now is simply an improvement to your already-adjusted soil texture. These items are readily available and very economical to add to your existing soil. Once you have your sifted, amended soil placed in your garden bed, you can then mix all or any of these products into your soil prior to planting.

- Vermiculite is mica rock that explodes like popcorn when it is heated. It becomes very light weight, holds water like a sponge, and provides air pockets in the soil. It is a soil amendment for textural purposes only, having no nutritional benefits at all. It helps the friability and moisture-holding content for both sandy and clay soils. Vermiculite never breaks down, lasting forever, so it is a very good investment for your garden. You can mix it into your garden soil at a rate of 25 percent. (In college, we mixed our own soilless mixes at a rate of 1/3 peat moss, 1/3 sand, and 1/3 an equal amount of vermiculite/perlite combination.) Vermiculite can however become compacted if it is trod on. Vermiculite can generally be purchased at building supply stores such as Rona or Home Depot. Be sure you purchase the coarse grade in the largest size bag you can find to make the product more cost effective. The price varies but is usually around $20.00–$25.00 for a two-cubic-foot bag, but it also comes in a four-cu.-ft. bag. Vermiculite has a pH level of 7.0.

- Perlite is the white Styrofoam-looking pellets you see in potted indoor plants. It is a non-crystalline volcanic-glass product which occurs naturally. The many benefits of using Perlite are, it improves aeration and drainage, it makes moisture and nutrients readily more available to plants, it is inorganic, and it doesn't break down. It also serves as an insulator to reduce extreme soil-temperature fluctuations. Used as an amendment, it helps prevent soil compaction, and as with vermiculite, it has no nutritional benefits. It is a sterile product free of weeds and disease, clean, odorless, lightweight, and safe to handle (but wearing a face mask is advisable, as it has a certain amount of dust to it). It is also anti-caking, so it is very good to use in clay soils. It can be found in most big box store garden centers for $15–$20 for four cu. ft. Perlite has a pH level of 7.0.

- Peat moss is the decomposed remains of prehistoric plants that have been compressed for thousands of years at the bottoms of bogs and swamps. It is a natural organic soil conditioner that regulates moisture and air around plant roots. It can retain 20 times its weight in moisture and releases water slowly as plants need it. It allows for proper root growth by loosening and aerating soils, and by adding it to sandy soils, it will help to retain moisture. It will also help to keep your soil from hardening. It does however decompose over the years and so will have to be replaced. It can be purchased at garden centers everywhere for about $10.00 for a four-cu.-ft. bag. Peat moss has a pH level of 3.4–4.8 so is a little on the acidic side and again does not have any nutritional value.

➢ Soil pH

The topic of soil pH can also be a scary subject, but I am going to simplify it for you. In all the years that I have been gardening, I have never worried about the pH of my soil. Basically, the lower the number is, the more acidic your soil. The higher the number is, the more alkaline it is. A very acidic soil can lock the nutrients in the fertilizer and prevent them from being used by the plants. On the other hand, a highly alkaline soil won't allow plants to use the micronutrients that they need. As vegetable and fruit growers, most of our plants fall into the mid-pH range on the scale. Soil-testing kits are available at gardening centers and are not very expensive. To fix an acidic soil, add some ground-up limestone at a rate of five lb. per 100 sq. ft. or wood ash at a rate of two lbs. per 100 sq. ft. If your soil is a little on the alkaline side, add pine needles, shredded leaves, sulfur, sawdust (not cedar), or peat moss.

PH TOLERANCE OF POPULAR FRUITS AND VEGETABLES

5.5–6.0	6.0–6.5	6.5–7.0	7.0–7.5
blueberry	bean	Beet	cabbage
crabapple	Brussels sprouts	broccoli	cauliflower
potato	carrot	gooseberry	celery
raspberry	collard greens	grape	cucumber
rhubarb	corn	leek	mint
	chives	lettuce	strawberry
	garlic	marjoram	thyme
	lima bean	melon	
	parsley	onion	
	peas	parsnip	
	peppers	peach	
	pumpkin	pear	
	radish	rhubarb	
	rosemary	spinach	
	rutabaga	Swiss chard	
	sage		
	squash		
	sunflower		
	tomato		
	turnip		

➢ Fertilizers

- **Natural Fertilizer:** If you have followed along and done all that we have previously talked about, you will have your compost to use as a fertilizer as well as a soil builder and soil-texture changer. This is considered to be a natural fertilizer which is organic. There are enough nutrients and micronutrients in most decayed organic matter to sustain all of the plant growth in our gardens. This wonderful humus matter is food for the plants. To garden in soil that is rich in organic matter but contains no added fertilizer is not only possible but very practical. A natural compost fertilizer contains beneficial soil organisms that help to fight off disease and pests. This is an organic method of gardening. The organic matter also attracts earthworms which are hugely beneficial for keeping the soil loose and light, providing air and water pockets. However, if you don't have the space or are not inclined to have a composting system, you can purchase compost material at garden supply stores, although it is more expensive than creating your own. You cannot overfeed plants with well-composted material, and it will not burn the roots of plants.

- **Chemical Fertilizer:** Plants tend to use natural fertilizer and chemical fertilizer in the same manner, but chemical fertilizers don't do anything favorable to the soil. As a matter of fact, they can damage the soil with constant regular use. They can also damage your plants, as these fertilizers are of a high concentration level and can literally burn the plants roots and kill beneficial microorganisms. Chemical fertilizer will also drive earthworms away, so you lose the benefit of the worm castings and the tunneling that worms provide for air pockets in your soil. The only real benefit to using chemical fertilizer is that the manufacturing process has been done for you and you can use it instantly. If you use this product, use it sparingly; more is not better. So, this would be considered non-organic gardening. Over the years of chemical-fertilizer use, there has been a harmful buildup of these nutrients in our lakes and rivers. Chemical fertilizers can also contain fillers, some of which can be harmful to your health.

In most cases, good gardening practices such as aerating and composting are much better than using chemical fertilizers. Chemical and organic fertilizers show their nutrient content with three bold numbers. These numbers represent the three different compounds in the fertilizer. These are **N** for nitrogen, **P** for phosphorous, and **K** which is for potash or potassium. The three numbers listed on the fertilizer labels represent the percentage of these compounds found in the fertilizer.

A. **Nitrogen** compound helps plant foliage to grow strong, so things like lettuce, cabbage, Swiss chard, and kale will use slightly more nitrogen than they will the other two compounds. But, be aware that high nitrogen levels will make for quick growth and weaker plants which are more susceptible to diseases and pests.

B. **Phosphorous** compound helps roots and flowers grow and develop, so the flowering and fruiting plants will use a tad bit more of this compound, as will the root crops such as potatoes, carrots, beets, and turnips.

C. **(K) Potash** compound is important for overall plant health. However, there are many other elements that are essential to healthy plant growth such as sulfur, hydrogen, oxygen, carbon, magnesium, copper, cobalt, sodium, zinc, boron, and molybdenum.

So, to sum up once again, go natural (organic), not chemical.

Use this natural fertilizer at full strength for your initial soil preparation, then at half strength for monthly feedings.

INGREDIENTS	N	P	K
THREE PARTS BLOOD MEAL	45.0	3.9	2.1
TWO PARTS BONE MEAL	8.0	42.0	0.4
THREE PARTS WOOD ASHES	_____	4.5	21.0
FOUR PARTS LEAF MOLD	2.4	0.8	1.6
TOTAL: 12 PARTS	55.4	51.2	25.1
NPK VALUE OF ONE PART HIGH NITROGEN MIX	4.6	4.3	2.0

Chapter Four
Designing Your Garden

You can choose either the metric or imperial method for your design layout. I recommend using a pencil until you are happy with your planting scheme.

➤ Choosing Your Crops

- **Your Climate Zone:** You should naturally plant crops that you and your family will use and that will grow in your climate. For instance, certain nut trees or citrus fruit trees won't grow in a climate with cold winters. Celery is difficult to grow in a hot, dry climate. Most vegetables are annual plants, which means they need to be planted yearly. A lot of herbs will seed themselves for the next year, although some are perennials and shrubs. And fruits are either trees, shrubs, or perennials and will return year after year. Pretty well, any crops you are going to have in your backyard garden will grow in air temperatures between 70–90° F (20–32° C.) and soil temperatures between 65–75° F. (18–24° C.). There are crops that prefer cool weather and crops that prefer hot weather. Some vegetables, such as tomatoes, peppers, some cabbage family, and eggplant, need a very long growing season, so if you don't have a setup to start your own seeds with heat and light, it is best to purchase a few of these from a garden center. Some are heavy feeders and need fertilizing monthly, and some are light feeders, so the initial compost you use is enough to see them through the growing season. Some plants like to grow with their companions and will grow poorly if planted by others that they dislike. This is called companion planting. I have provided a list of companion plants later on in the chapter.

- **Seeds or Seedlings:** It is practical and economical to purchase seeds for some types of vegetables, especially the ones that don't transplant well, but not for others. When purchasing seeds, you generally get quite a few in each package. That doesn't mean that all of them should be planted at once. For example, six tomato plants give me enough tomatoes to eat fresh, to preserve 24 pints of stewed tomatoes, eight pints of tomato-salsa sauce, eight pints of marinara sauce, four small jars of sundried tomatoes, etc. In the information section for each garden plant, I have included a section on the yield of each plant. Of course, this is just general and will vary based on weather and other growing conditions. Seeds are generally viable for three years, so I pay roughly $3.49 for one package of seeds that last me three years. I throw out any that remain after three years, knowing I have saved a bunch of money by not purchasing nursery stock. But that is me, always looking to be thrifty. I also love the time I spend out in my little greenhouse in early spring. If you don't have an area for seed starting, a good rule of thumb is to purchase seedlings for the veggies that can't be directly sown outside in the spring from a garden center in mid-May.

- **Heirloom or Hybrid:** At this point, we need to talk about the difference between heirloom plants and hybrid plants. Heirloom plants are plants that were grown by gardeners from as far back as the 18th, 19th, and early 20th centuries. Heirlooms are open pollinated, meaning the seeds that are collected one year will have the same characteristics as the parent plant. They are true to their form, the genetics remaining and they have not been altered in any way. The seeds from these original plants have passed down from generation to generation over the centuries. Amazingly, many of these cultivars still exist today. Heirloom plants are making a huge comeback for home gardeners. Heirlooms are ideal for backyard gardeners, as they often taste better, are more tender, and produce better than hybrids. You can save your seeds from these heirlooms from year to year, and you will find your vegetables will be more reliable because the plants have adapted to their local environment, making them more disease and insect resistant. One very large benefit to growing heirlooms is the seeds can be collected and planted the following year. Because heirlooms are making such a comeback, groups of seed collectors are forming throughout the world. These dedicated heirloom gardeners will often share seeds and information with one another, keeping these original plants from becoming extinct. One summer, I grew only heirloom plants. I found most had diverse deep colors, the patterns and the flavors were intense, bright and juicy that will never be found in hybrids. Heirlooms come with a lot of history behind them too. I highly recommend the Heritage Harvest Seed Catalogue for a wealth of information including history and origin of these marvelous plants. This catalogue can be found on the website at www.heritageharvestseed.com. Hybrids on the other hand have been intentionally cross pollinated by plant breeders using two or more varieties and aiming to produce seeds with the best traits of the parent plants. There have been many failures and many successes in this venture. Hybridization can stabilize growth factors, so there is a more-uniform harvest. Many vegetables have been hybridized to allow for long-term shipping and storage. Hybrids are very consistent from plant to plant from year to year. However, seeds are not true to the form of the parent or grandparent plant. If seed is collected and sown the following year, plants tend to be weak and unproductive. Hybrids have been scientifically proven to be safe for animal and human consumption. Hybridization is not to be mistaken with Genetically Modified Organisms (GMO). Hybridization uses low-tech, natural methods of breeding, whereas GMO methods alter the DNA in a plant gene to make the plant act in an unnatural way. Genetic modification is done in a sophisticated high-tech lab where the gene of a seed is sliced into and bacteria injected into it. The idea behind this is to create crops and other food items that will be more insect and disease resistant; the pest insect will consume a portion of the plant eating the injected bacteria and perish. In altering the DNA of a plant, it creates a longer-ripening process, so there is not as much spoilage in shipping the product. This process is making these modified plants more resistant to herbicides, so the weeds in the growing site can be sprayed to kill them, but the altered crops will not be affected by the chemical. It is also supposed to make these crops more resistant to harsh weather conditions. This all sounds well and good, not overly harmful, but the GMO process is so new that there has not been enough time or studies done to determine how these unnatural new organisms will react in the consumer over time. At the time of the writing of this book, in Canada there were five GMO crops grown commercially. These are 95% of the canola production, 80% of corn production, 60% of soy-bean production, 100% of sugar-beet production (an alternative to granulated white sugar) and alfalfa production for animal feed. GMO products allowed into Canada were squash from the U.S.A., papaya from Hawaii, cottonseed, Atlantic salmon (shipped from Panama in 2017), and milk ingredients and related products from the U.S.A. As of 2015, Canada had no mandatory labelling system for products made with or containing GMOs but are decidedly working on a more transparent system for these items that are grown for human consumption.

Drawing your garden on paper and writing a list of the fruits and vegetables that you want to grow is pretty important. You will use this as a guide for crop rotation in years to come. Gather some seed catalogues around you and go through them. (As previously noted, I use West Coast Seeds, Stokes Seeds, and Heritage Harvest Seed). Most seed catalogues list the crop as cool weather or hot weather loving. At this point, we will go through some of the more common garden vegetables and the spacing of them, assuming you are using the square-foot gardening method. Also noted are some of their more common uses. Following are lists of vegetables, herbs, and fruits suitable to be grown in a moderate climate.

Use this information as a guide for drawing out your planting scheme. You can sometimes have a cool weather crop in one area, harvest it and then plant a hot weather crop in the same location.

➤ Vegetables

Asparagus: (It is a distant cousin to the onion and has been consumed for over 2000 years. It is believed to have originated in the Mediterranean countries, but traces of the wild variety have been found in Africa. In ancient Greece, the plant was considered to be an aphrodisiac and was also appreciated as a side dish by the early Romans. It lost its appeal during the Middle Ages but regained popularity in the 16th and 17th centuries when it was served to British royalty.)

Planting: Plant asparagus crowns in early spring when they become available at plant nurseries. Because it is a perennial, the plant will come back year after year so only needs to be planted once. Asparagus does very well when planted in raised beds. Dig trenches 12 inches deep x 12 inches wide (30.48 x 30.48 cm.) and 12 inches (30.48 cm.) apart. Place a crown of asparagus on a mound of compost, being sure it is six inches (15.25 cm.) below the soil surface. Cover with garden soil that has been amended with rock phosphate, and water well. As the shoots appear, add more soil until the trench has been completely refilled. Mulch to keep the planting bed free of weeds. Do not allow the soil to dry out, keeping it evenly moist.

Varieties: A very old variety is Martha Washington, but there are now all male hybrids and so they put energy into producing lush spears instead of seed. These male hybrids also produce twice as many spears per plant and can be grown in 6–12 inches (15.25–30.48 cm.) of soil instead of 18 inches (45.7 cm.).

Description: Asparagus is a perennial vegetable grown for its young green shoots freshly emerging from the soil in early to late spring. Grown in the right conditions, the asparagus plant can live for 20 to 30 years.

Conditions: Asparagus is a great choice for growing in raised beds, but that being said, it takes this perennial plant a few years to start to produce its maximum crop. Asparagus does not like any competition and so the planting bed needs to be completely weed free. Do not allow the soil to dry out; try to keep it evenly moist at all times.

Spacing: Plant crowns 18 inches apart in rows 12 inches apart.

USES: Asparagus spears can be steamed, grilled, roasted, or boiled. They can be chopped and added to salads, omelets, pizzas, and pasta dishes. Cream of asparagus soup is one of my favorites. They also make a fine pickle for a Caesar cocktail. Asparagus is always best if it is not overcooked.

Nutritional Values: Asparagus is high in vitamins A, C, E, K, and B6. It is a good source of folate, iron, copper, calcium, protein, and dietary fiber.

Yield: 25 plants will feed a family of four.

Beans are all legumes: (The first bean plant is believed to have originated in the Andes and Mesoamerica. Other varieties originated in Peru/Ecuador from 2000 B.C.–1000 B.C.)

Planting: Direct sow seeds in the end of May or the beginning of June when the ground has warmed up. They do not like to be transplanted, and they do not like cold, wet soil.

Varieties: There are at least six varieties of green beans and many cultivars of each variety. For sake of ease, we are going to discuss the Phaseolus vulgaris or common bean variety. The common bean is broken into two categories, those being the Bush Bean and the Pole Bean.

Description: Both of these categories bear fruit that can be eaten fresh as an unripe pod fruit. These fruits can be flat or round, curved or straight, stringless or stringed, green, yellow, or purple. All of these fruits can be allowed to fully ripen on the vine in order to use the mature seeds in a dried form. Some of the more common dried seeds are the kidney bean, black, pinto, and navy bean, ranging in colors from white, blue, black, red, beige, and spotted. Bush beans are quick growing and don't require support; they can grow up to three feet (one m.) tall and produce their crop in a two–three-week span. The Pole varieties require the support of strings, wire, or poles and continue to grow and produce all summer long. They can grow to a height of 12 feet (3.6 m.) or more.

Conditions: All beans are a hot weather crop. They like warmer weather for good germination and good production, so plant in full sun. They like good drainage and soil not too heavy with nitrogen.

Spacing: Dwarf or bush beans can be planted nine plants per square foot or four inches (ten cm.) apart with two feet (.6 m.) between rows. Pole beans can be planted three–four inches (7.6–10 cm.) apart on both sides of an upright lattice or double rows planted one inch apart against a fence.

Uses: All can be eaten fresh from the vine in a tender stage, served in salads or as a cooked vegetable. They can be pressure canned or frozen and made into pickles to be served in a Caesar cocktail. Or they can be allowed to mature on the vine. The seeds are then removed from the pod and dried for winter storage and cooking. Once dried, these beans are soaked and cooked for several hours to soften them up before being used in soups, stews, and meat dishes.

Seed to Harvest: Seeding to harvest is about eight weeks.

Nutritional Values: They are high in the B group of vitamins and vitamin C. They are high in dietary fiber and protein, containing phosphorous, potassium, folate, iron, calcium, and magnesium.

My Picks: Bush: Gold Rush, Ferrari.
Pole: Purple Peacock, Blue Lake, Kentucky Wonder.

Yield: One bean seed produces one plant. 40 plants will produce about five pounds of unshelled fruit.

Beets: (Beets grew in the gardens of Babylon and throughout the eras were used primarily for the leafy greens. The root part of the beet was cultivated in Germany or Italy in 1542).

Planting: Soaking the seed in warm water helps with the germination process. Direct sow first crop on May 15 and second crop in mid-July for a winter harvest. They do not like to be transplanted.

Description: This root crop comes in round or elongated varieties; they come in red, pink, gold, yellow, and striped. Beets can also be grown for their nutritious leaf tops as well as for the healthy root.

Conditions: Beets are a cool weather crop but will grow throughout summer heat. They prefer a rich soil. Once they have emerged, be sure to thin out the weaker seedlings, leaving the strongest plant, as one seed will produce multiple seedlings. A little extra potassium will help the beet grow to its fullest, as it is a root crop.

Spacing: Place seeds 12 per square foot. Allowing three–four inches (7.6-10 cm.) between plants and 8–12 inches (20–30.5 cm.) between rows.

Uses: The greens from the beet can be eaten the same as chard or spinach. The beet can be picked at any growth stage as long as it is of an edible size. Beets are great pickled, boiled, or roasted, in a salad or in a big pot of Borscht.

Seed to Harvest: Seeding to harvest is about eight weeks for young, tender beets, but they can be left in the soil for later harvest, although if left too long, they can become woody.

Nutritional Values: Beets are high in dietary fiber, vitamins C and B6. They also contain folate, manganese, potassium, copper, magnesium, iron, and phosphorus.

My Picks: Lutz Winterkeeper, Detroit Red.

Yield: If thinned properly, one seed will produce one beet ranging in size from three–four inches (7.6–10 cm.) depending on the variety planted. You can expect about ten pounds (4.5 kg.) from 40 plants.

Broccoli (is native to Eastern Mediterranean and Asia Minor. It was cultivated in Italy by the ancient Romans and brought to England and the Americas in the 1700s).

Planting: Start seeds indoors in late February to early March and transplant outdoors in mid-May when the seedlings are about six inches tall. Be sure you harden them off for a week prior to planting in the garden. Or purchase seedlings and plant out when all danger of frost has passed.

Description: Broccoli is part of the very large family of Brassica which includes cauliflower, kale, Brussels sprouts, cabbage, and collards. Broccoli is grown for its edible flower buds and stalks; the leaves can also be eaten. More commonly it comes in green but also in shades of blue, purple, yellow, and white.

Conditions: Broccoli is considered a cool weather crop but will carry on growing during summer, just with lighter yields. It prefers full sun, but in warm climate areas, it is better planted in partial shade to help prevent bolting. It is a heavy feeder and likes to be fertilized monthly.

Spacing: Plant your seedlings 12 inches apart and your rows 24 inches apart. One plant per square foot.

Seed to Harvest: Seed to first harvest is about 16 weeks.

Uses: Broccoli can be eaten fresh with a dip, in salads, boiled, steamed, made into a soup, or frozen for winter use.

Nutritional Values: Broccoli contains large amounts of vitamins A, B6, C, E, and B1. It also contains pantothenic acid, manganese, phosphorus, choline, potassium, copper, magnesium, zinc, calcium, niacin, selenium, and iron. It is a source of dietary fiber and omega-3 fatty acid.

My Picks: Di Cicco.

Yield: One seed can give you up to two pounds (one kg.) of product.

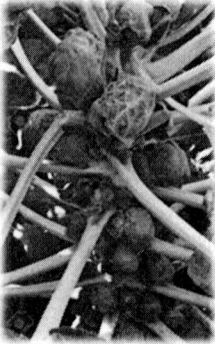

Brussels Sprouts: (Originated in Rome from as early as the 13th century and were cultivated in Belgium in 1587, hence the name 'Brussels').

Planting: Start seeds indoors in February for spring harvest and transplant outdoors in mid-May when the seedlings are about six inches (15–24 cm.) tall. Set them in the ground slightly deeper than they are growing in the pot. Be sure you harden them off for a week prior to planting in the garden. Direct sow seed mid-July to August for fall/winter harvest.

Description: This plant produces little mini cabbages along the stout center stem under the protection of the umbrella like foliage. It is the hardiest of all the cabbage family crops, survives freezing temperatures better than it does hot weather. Fall crops are often more successful.

Conditions: They are a cool weather crop and a heavy feeder, so they like to be fertilized monthly. Do not allow soil to dry; mulching helps to keep the soil moist.

Spacing: Plant your seedlings 12 inches (30–48 cm.) apart and your rows 24 inches (61 cm.) apart. One plant per square foot.

Uses: Use fried, steamed, boiled, or roasted with a little balsamic vinegar. They can be sliced up and added to salads. They freeze well for extended eating.

Nutritional Values: Brussels sprouts contain vitamins C, K, B6, and B1. Minerals in these sprouts are folate, manganese, choline, copper, potassium, and phosphorus. They are a source of dietary fiber and omega-3 fatty acids.

Seed to Harvest: Seed to harvest is 100 days.

My Picks: Long Island Improved, Igor.

Yield: One seed can produce up to one pound of product.

Cabbage: (Non-heading varieties were cultivated from as early as 3000 B.C. and were domesticated by the Celts in Central and Western Europe. Cabbage was a common food for the peoples of Egypt and was considered a luxury food in the early Roman days. The first round-headed cabbages came to England from as early as the 14th century, spreading to India around the 16th century and finally to Japan in the 18th century).

Planting: For summer harvest, start seeds indoors in early February and transplant outdoors in mid-May after hardening off for a week. A second crop for winter can be started in mid-July. Or purchase seedlings and plant out when all danger of frost has passed.

Description: Cabbage is part of the very large family of Brassica which includes cauliflower, kale, Brussels sprouts, broccoli, and collards. It grows a tight, large head with green, white, or purples leaves that are smooth or wrinkled.

Conditions: Cabbages are a cool weather crop. They like to be fertilized monthly. Do not allow soil to dry out; mulching helps to keep the soil moist. Although cabbage, broccoli, and cauliflower are closely related and require similar nutrients, it's best to not plant them together, as they are all heavy feeders, depleting the soil faster of required nutrients; plus, they will attract the same pests and diseases.

Spacing: Plant seedlings 12 inches (30.48 cm.) apart in rows 24 inches (61 cm.) apart. One plant per square foot.

Uses: Cabbages are used fresh in salads and coleslaws. They can be added to soups and stews, turned into sauerkraut, and be made into cabbage rolls.

<u>Seed to Harvest:</u> Seed to harvest is usually 16 weeks, depending on the variety.

<u>Nutritional Values:</u> Cabbage is a great source of vitamins K, C, B1, B2, and B6. It is also a very good source of manganese, dietary fiber, potassium, folate, copper, choline, phosphorus, magnesium, calcium, selenium, iron, pantothenic acid, protein, and niacin. Wow, for a humble vegetable, it holds a lot of nutrition!

<u>My Picks:</u> Summer harvest: Tiara, Early Jersey Wakefield, Super Red.

Winter harvest: January King, Danish Ballhead.

<u>Yield:</u> One seed will produce one cabbage head weighing between three lbs. to six lbs. depending on the variety.

<u>Carrots:</u> (Originated in Persia and Asia Minor from the tenth century and were primarily purple or white with a thin root. A mutant occurred with yellow pigmentation resulting in a new blend of orange colors. Diversification began in Central Asia and the carrot was soon domesticated in Afghanistan and regions of Russia, Iran, India, Pakistan, and Anatolia. It spread to the Mediterranean region and Western Europe in the 11-14th centuries and to China, India, and Japan in the 14–17th centuries and made its way to England in the 15th century).

<u>Planting:</u> Direct sow seed after all danger of frost is over. Work your soil very well to a depth of 12 inches, being sure to remove any rocks or debris to prevent the carrot root from forking. Water the soil well prior to planting. Does not transplant.

<u>Description:</u> Carrots are a root crop ranging in length from a couple of inches to 15 or so inches. They can be fat or skinny and come in colors of white, purple, black, red, and orange.

Conditions: Carrots require open, friable soil and do not like to be crowded. They are a warm weather crop. You can purchase seed tape which pretty much guarantees perfect spacing of the plants. Rotating carrot crops from year to year is a must. Keep soil evenly moist to prevent splitting. They like a little extra potassium, as they are a root crop.

Spacing: For years, one of my winter projects was to mix up some flour and water with a drop of food coloring. Dab this paste on a paper towel or a square foot of newspaper every three–four inches (7.6–10 cm.). Then drop a carrot seed on the paste and allow it to dry. Place the seeded paper in the garden in spring and cover with peat moss. 16 per square or three inches (7.6 cm.) apart.

USES: There are unlimited things to do with carrots. You can eat them fresh from the garden, put them in salads, soups, stews, or eat them slightly cooked with a bit of butter and some parsley. Carrots don't freeze well but can be pickled.

Seed to Harvest: Seed to harvest is ten weeks or when they are about half inch in diameter.

Nutritional Values: Carrots are a particularly good source of beta-carotene, fiber, vitamin K, potassium, and antioxidants.

My Picks: Scarlet Nantes, Rainbow Blend, Danvers.

Yield: One seed will give you one carrot weighing up to 1½ pounds (.68 kg.).

Notes: Carrots are prone to Carrot Rust Fly. The adult fly lays eggs at the base of the carrot plant, and once the larvae hatch, they begin feeding on the carrot root, leaving them riddled with scarring. To prevent this from happening, I build a cage out of half poly pipe and attach a shade cloth all around right after seeding. This prevention measure works very well.

Cauliflower: (Originated from the wild cabbage plant. The name cauliflower means cabbage flower, even though it is not actually the flower of the cabbage. The cauliflower plant was discovered in the first millennium around the Mediterranean and Asia Minor regions. It was written about by early scientists in the 12th and 13th centuries but didn't make its way to England until the 17th century. It was finally introduced to North America in the 1800–1900s).

Planting: Start seeds indoors in late February to early March. Plant out one month before your last frost for an early harvest. Seed outdoors in mid-June for a fall harvest. Cauliflower can be transplanted but can suffer setbacks if roots are disturbed.

Description: The more common cauliflower comes with a white, edible head of florets. It also comes in yellow, purple, and green.

Conditions: Cauliflower is a temperamental plant to grow. It is a heavy feeder so likes to be fertilized monthly. It requires steady moisture to produce large full heads. It is a cold weather crop, preferring temperatures between 60–75 degrees F. (15.5–23.8 degrees C.), so it will tolerate some shade.

Spacing: One plant per square foot or 12 inches (30.48 cm.) apart in rows two feet (61 cm.) apart.

Uses: Serve the florets fresh and raw with any type of salad dressing or dip. It is excellent chopped up in tossed salads. Cook by steaming, boiling, or in stir fries. Serve hot with cheese, melted butter, or just salt and pepper. It can be pickled or served in soups and stews. Mash it as you would mash potatoes.

Seed to Harvest: Seed to harvest is 14 weeks.

Nutritional Values: It is said that one serving of cauliflower contains 77 percent of the recommended daily value of vitamin C. It's also a good source of vitamin K, protein, thiamin, riboflavin, niacin, magnesium, phosphorus, fiber, vitamin B6, folate, pantothenic acid, potassium, and manganese.

My Picks: Early Snowball.

Yield: One seed produces one mature cauliflower head weighing in at one–two pounds (.45–.9 kg.).

Note: To prevent sunburn on the forming cauliflower heads, fold the inner leaves over top of the head and tuck them in on the opposite side or secure them with a rubber band or a length of string.

Chard: (Swiss chard is a native to Southern Europe and is much older than the beet. It was introduced into Europe during the Middle Ages. It was found in France in the 14th century and was brought to North America by the European settlers. It is unclear as to how it got the name Swiss chard, as it is not native to Switzerland.)

Planting: Chard transplants well, so seeds can be started indoors in mid-March to transplant out in mid-May, or direct sow seed from May through to August for successive harvest.

Description: Chard is grown for its edible leaves and juicy stems. The more common chard has white stems, but a rainbow mix is available with white, pink, red, and yellow stems, smooth or crinkled leaves.

Conditions: It prefers cool weather but will grow throughout summer if it is planted in some shade. It is very cold hardy. It is a very easy crop to grow and will tolerate most conditions. A must for every garden. It is a light feeder not requiring regular fertilizing.

Spacing: Four per square foot or six inches (15 cm.) apart in rows spaced two feet (61 cm.) apart.

Uses: Both the stems and leaves are like a milder version of spinach. Use as you would spinach.

Seed to Harvest: Seed to harvest is eight weeks.

Nutritional Values: Chard is a good source of thiamin, folate, and zinc, and a very good source of dietary fiber, vitamin A, C, E (Alpha Tocopherol), K, riboflavin, vitamin B6, calcium, iron, magnesium, phosphorus, potassium, copper, and manganese.

My Picks: Celebration, Five Color Silverbeet, Fordhook Giant.

Yield: One plant can produce up to one pound (.45 kg.) of uncooked product.

CORN: (Corn is said to have been developed from a wild grass called Teosinte in Central Mexico some 7000–10000 years ago and has been cultivated for over 4000 years. It is believed to be a human invention, as the actual corn plant does not exist naturally in the wild. The plant spread to the Southwestern United States and south down the coast to Peru. About 1000 years ago, it became a major part of the diet of the Indian people who called it Maize. It has since undergone much selective breeding, making the cobs larger with more rows of sweet, juicy kernels.)

Planting: Corn does not transplant well. Direct sow seed at least three weeks after the last frost when soil has had a chance to warm up to about 60 degrees F. (15.5 C.). For the home gardener, it is best to plant only one variety of corn, as it will cross-pollinate, causing starchy kernels.

Description: Sweet corn kernels are generally yellow but can be white, pink, and even red. Today's common varieties are a blend of yellow and white. Ornamental varieties are a blend of blue, yellow, brown, white, purple, and red that grow in regular size or miniature size. There is a flour corn, broom corn, and popcorn. The actual plant size ranges from three feet to six or seven feet (.91–1.8 or 2.1 m.).

Conditions: Corn is a warm weather crop and a heavy feeder needing to be fertilized monthly. Corn needs lots of sun and heat as well as a rich, moist soil. It takes up a fair bit of room in a garden, but there is nothing like going out and picking an ear of corn and cooking it immediately or just eating it fresh off the cob; it is the sweetest corn you will ever taste. It likes a long growing season, so you can only get one planting per growing season.

Spacing: Space your corn seeds one foot (30.48 cm.) apart in rows that are three feet (.91 m) apart or one plant per square foot.

Uses: Corn is best when used fresh as far as standard corn goes. On the cob, it doesn't really freeze well, but if you strip the kernels off, they will freeze and can quite well. (Canning corn requires a pressure canner.) The ornamental varieties need to dry for preservation, as does popcorn.

Seed to Harvest: Seed to harvest is 9–13 weeks depending on the variety.

Nutritional Values: Corn contains vitamins B and C as well as the two antioxidants, Zeaxanthin and Lutein.

My Picks: Golden Bantam, Peaches and Cream.

Yield: Generally, you will get two cobs per corn plant.

Notes: When you see the tassels emerging from the corn cob, give the plant a little shake every day. Each single tassel pollinates one corn kernel.

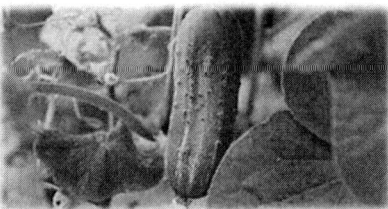

Cucumbers: (Originated in India and have been under cultivation for at least 3000 years. They spread to India and moved through Ancient Greece, Rome, Europe, the New World, and then

China. From there, they made their way to Greece, Turkey, Bulgaria, Africa, Serbia, and Italy. They didn't find their way to England until the 14th century, but the British didn't accept them as a part of their diet until the mid-17th century. They have since become the world's fourth largest cultivated crop.)

Planting: Direct sow presoaked seeds two–four weeks after the final frost when soil has warmed up. They can be started inside but don't like to have their roots disturbed when transplanting. If you do start them indoors, be sure to harden them off prior to outdoor planting.

Description: There are quite a few varieties of cucumbers. I break them down into three categories: Long English, slicing, and pickling. All of them have green skin and white flesh. Long English are a seedless variety and do best if greenhouse grown, although I have grown them outdoors successfully. The slicing varieties usually are smooth skinned and range in size from six inches to a foot (15.25–30.48 cm.) The pickling varieties are smaller and have bumpy skin. Two heirloom varieties are the Lemon Cucumber, with yellow skin and sweet flesh, and the Crystal Apple Cucumber.

Conditions: Cucumbers are a warm weather crop and heavy feeders, so fertilize monthly. Cucumbers also like the heat of the sun and enjoy a nutrient-rich, moist, well-drained soil. You can grow them on the ground in hills, but they also make an excellent trellis crop.

Spacing: I grow my cucumbers on a trellis and plant the seeds six inches (15.25 cm.) apart on both sides of the trellis. If planting in hills, place four seeds in each hill and hills three feet (one m.) apart from each other.

Uses: Slicing and Long English cucumbers are generally used in salads or as a garnish. A cucumber sandwich makes for a very refreshing summer treat. I have used both varieties for making Tzatziki sauce. Pickling cucumbers are used for bread-and-butter pickles, gherkins, dills, and relishes.

Seed to Harvest: Seed to harvest is nine weeks. Don't allow cucumbers to become overly large. Pick when young and tender. If you keep them picked, you will have cucumbers up until frost.

Nutritional Values: Cucumbers are an excellent source of vitamins K, C, and B1. They are also a very good source of pantothenic acid and molybdenum. They are also a good source of copper, potassium, manganese, phosphorus, magnesium, and biotin. They also contain the important, nail-health-promoting mineral, silica. The non-peeling varieties are more nutritious, as the skin contains large amounts of vitamins A and C along with a large number of minerals.

My Picks: Improved Long Green, Pioneer.

Yield: One seed can produce up to three pounds (1.3 kg.) of cucumbers. Allow three–four pickling cucumber plants for one quart of pickles.

Eggplant: (Was first cultivated in India 4000 years ago and migrated to Asia in the fourth century. It then made its way to Europe and China and finally came to the New World, being brought over by the early explorers.)

Planting: Start seeds indoors in February or purchase plants from a nursery to plant outdoors two–three weeks after the last frost. Try not to disturb the roots.

Description: All eggplants have white flesh, but the outer skin can be black, purple, white, rose, and some varieties even bear orange or green fruits. Most commonly is the tear-drop shape, but they can also be long and slim as well as oval.

Conditions: The eggplant is a warm weather crop, and because it requires such a long growing season, it needs to be grown in a warm, protected environment until the outdoor weather conditions are to its liking.

Spacing: Plant two–three feet (61 cm.–1 m.) apart in all directions.

Uses: The fruit of the eggplant is rather bland, but the flesh soaks up oils and flavors of other accompanying foods. Rich acidic foods such as tomato, onion, and garlic are a great accompaniment for this fruit. Eggplants can be stuffed, steamed, put into soups, stews, or used in vegetable and meat dishes. Do not store in the fridge.

Seed to Harvest: Seed to harvest is in five months.

Nutritional Values: Eggplant is a very good source of dietary fiber. It is a good source of vitamins B1, K, and vitamin B6, copper, manganese, niacin, potassium, and folate.

My Picks: I do not care for eggplant and so have never grown any, therefore, I don't have any picks.

Yield: Each plant will give you about one dozen fruits.

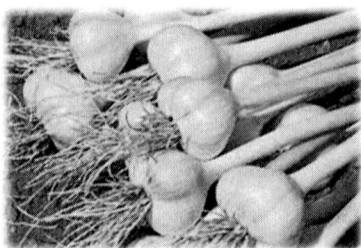

Garlic: (Garlic, which is really considered to be an herb, is believed to be a native of Central Asia, South Asia, Northeastern Iran, and Southwestern Siberia. Although there is some debate over the origin of this herb, garlic has been used as a food, medicine, an aphrodisiac, and as a magic potion for over 5000 years. It is one of the world's oldest cultivated crops and was used by the Egyptians as local currency to pay the slaves and workers that built the great pyramids. Other cultural religions banned the use of garlic, as they considered it to be an aphrodisiac, and church members underwent a breath test prior to temple entry. It then made its way to Spain, France, and Portugal who in turn introduced it to North America.)

Planting: Plant healthy cloves in mid-October for next summer's harvest. Do not use bulbs purchased from a grocery store, as they probably have been treated with an anti-sprouting chemical.

Description: There are numerous varieties of garlic. Some have a stronger flavor than others; some are soft neck varieties and some are hard neck varieties. I have planted both soft neck and hard neck and prefer the hard neck variety, as I have found it has bigger bulbs and a better taste.

Conditions: Garlic is easy to grow and does best in a well-drained, deep, rich soil with a little bone meal added to it. It prefers full sun but will still perform well in part shade. It likes good drainage and doesn't like to be crowded. I try to get my cloves into the soil by the end of October. They don't like to be too wet, preferring soil a little on the drier side.

Spacing: You can plant garlic in single or double rows. The rows should be eight inches (20 cm.) apart and the bulbs four–six inches (10–15.25 cm.) apart. The tighter the spacing, the smaller the bulbs, but you will get more of them. The larger the spacing, the larger your bulbs will be. For square-foot gardening, plant nine per square foot.

Uses: Garlic is very universal and can be used for making pickles and is added to meat dishes and vegetable dishes. It is used to flavor egg dishes, oils, and what would a pasta dish be without garlic? I personally can't imagine a kitchen without garlic in it. The flowers (garlic scapes) can be used in salads, soups, and made into garlic-scape pesto. They can also be dehydrated to make a great garlic salt.

Harvest: Harvest in late July or early August once the tops have died back.

Nutritional Values: Garlic is an excellent source of vitamin B6. It is also a very good source of manganese, selenium, and vitamin C. In addition, garlic is a good source of other minerals, including phosphorous, calcium, potassium, iron, and copper.

My Picks: Red Russian, Elephant.

Yield: One clove of garlic will yield one bulb with 6–12 cloves, depending on the variety.

Kale: (Until the end of the Middle Ages, Kale was the most common green vegetable that was grown in the gardens of Europe. There is a similar plant to kale that is native to Eastern Mediterranean and Asia Minor. However, kale has been under cultivation and shifted about by prehistoric traders and migrating tribes, so we are not certain of its origin. We do know that the Greeks and Romans grew it prior to the Christian era. It has been written about by European writers in the 1st, 3rd, 4th and 13th centuries. We have mention of kale being in America in 1669. The variety known as Red Russian was introduced to America via Siberia by the Russian traders in the 19th century.)

Planting: Direct sow seeds as soon as the soil can be worked in the spring. A later crop can be direct sown in August for a fall harvest.

Description: Kale is a hardy, leafy, green plant that is part of the cabbage family. It grows best in the spring and fall and can tolerate fall frosts. It is considered to be a primitive form of non-heading cabbage with green and purple leaves.

Conditions: Kale is a cool-season crop and will tolerate partial shade conditions. It likes a soil rich in nitrogen.

Spacing: Plant four seeds per square foot.

Uses: Kale can be used in salads, as a garnish, braised with balsamic vinegar, or just plain boiled or steamed. Cook as you would any other leafy vegetable, but remove the ribs prior to cooking, as they are tough.

Seed to Harvest: Seed to first harvest is about 70–80 days.

Nutritional Values: This leafy green plant is low in saturated fat and very low in cholesterol. It is also a good source of dietary fiber, protein, thiamin, riboflavin, folate, iron, magnesium, phosphorus, and a very good source of vitamin A, C, K, B6, calcium, potassium, copper, and manganese.

My Picks: Red Russian.

Yield: One kale plant can produce about two pounds (0.9 kg.) of uncooked product if picked on a regular basis.

Lettuce: (Romaine lettuce has been traced back to the Eastern Mediterranean, and leaf lettuce was first cultivated in ancient Egypt in 2680 B.C., not for the succulent leaves but for the oil-producing seeds. High status Romans ate salads with leaf lettuce from as early as 81–96 A.D.)

Planting: Direct sow your first crop seeds outdoors in mid-May and then successively ever two weeks for a continuous harvest. Seeds sprout very rapidly.

Description: Grown for their edible leaves, there is no end to the varieties of lettuce plants one can grow. I prefer the mixed lettuce seeds. In these mixed seed packages, you can get red and green leaf lettuce, endive, chicory, spinach, mustard greens, romaine, arugula, and radicchio, just to name a few.

Conditions: Lettuce is a cool weather crop and will bolt in the intense summer heat. Bolting happens when the ground temperature goes above a certain temperature. This flips a switch in the plant to produce flowers and seeds very rapidly and to abandon leaf growth almost completely. Lettuce likes to be fertilized with monthly applications of a high nitrogen product and grown in a nutrient-rich, organic, moist soil, with the addition of a little extra calcium. Lettuce does well in the vegetable garden but is a good choice for pot gardens too. Mixing it in the flower garden will give a different dimension to the florals.

Spacing: I plant a pinch of mixed lettuce seeds every six inches (15.25 cm.) apart. That way you get a good mix of greens all at once. Plant only four–six pinches at a time to keep a successive season worth of salads.

Uses: Lettuces are generally used in salads and garnishes and recently the leaves are used as a wrap.

Seed to Harvest: Seed to harvest is seven weeks.

Nutritional Values: Lettuce is a very good source of dietary fiber, manganese, potassium, biotin, vitamin B1, copper, iron, and vitamin C. It is also a good source of vitamin B2, omega-3 fatty acids, vitamin B6, phosphorus, chromium, magnesium, calcium, and pantothenic acid.

My Picks: Green Towers, Gourmet Salad Blend.

Yield: One seed will give you one lettuce plant and, depending on the size of your family, up to three salads.

Leeks: (The Leek is noted in the first ever written cookbook from the third century in Rome. The writer of this cookbook recorded that, "The best leeks came from Egypt, and they were best served in their own right, unlike onions and garlic that were considered as a seasoning." It is unknown as to how leeks made their way to Europe, but they are highly regarded in Britain. The Irish have adopted the leek as their own, and on St. David's Day, the Welsh wear a daffodil or leek stem in memory of the victory of King Caldwallader over the Saxons in 640 A.D. We do know they originated in Central Asia, having been consumed since ancient Egyptian and Roman times.)

Planting: Start leek seeds indoors in the beginning of March or purchase plants from a nursery after all danger of frost. Transplant them outside at the end of May. They should be about eight inches (20 cm.) tall at transplant stage. Dig holes six inches (15.25 cm.) deep and plant all but two inches (five cm.) of the stem in the soil.

Description: Leeks are the sweetest and most delicately flavored of all onions. The edible part of the plant is made up of a bundle of leaf sheaths that have grown underground. The green part that has grown above ground is a little tough in texture. They take a little time to mature but are fairly easy to grow.

Conditions: They are a heavy feeder liking to be fed monthly. They prefer to have a loose, crumbly, rich, loamy soil.

Spacing: Four plants per square foot, or six inches (15.25 cm.) apart in rows 1½ feet (30–40 cm.) apart.

Uses: Use in any recipe that calls for mild onion flavors, but they are used mainly in soups and stews, casseroles, and risottos. Leeks and beets are a good pairing. Be sure to thoroughly clean leeks, as the white portion that grows underground can become quite gritty.

Seed to Harvest: Seed to harvest is 70–110 days.

Nutritional Values: Leeks are an excellent source of vitamin K. They are a very good source of manganese, vitamin B6, copper, iron, folate, vitamin C, and are also a good source of vitamin A (in the form of carotenoids), dietary fiber, magnesium, vitamin E, calcium, and omega-3 fatty acids.

My Picks: Comanche.

Yield: One seed produces one leek plant approximately one inch (2.5 cm.) in diameter.

Melons: (Melon is a very broad term for many of the sweet, summer-ripening, succulent fruits that we know today. A wild melon similar to a watermelon originated in Africa. The melon has been under cultivation for over 4000 years).

Planting: Start seeds indoors in March for transplanting out in June or purchase seedlings at a nursery. Transplants should have no tendrils and no more than four leaves.

Description: Melon is a loose term referring to many varieties of the *Cucurbitaceae* plant family. All of them have a sweet, edible, juicy, fleshy fruit with a thick, protective skin. The three most popular types for commercial growing are the honeydew, cantaloupe, and watermelon.

Conditions: All melons like a fertile, well-drained soil dug deep, as their roots can grow down to three feet (one m.) in depth. They love composted manure from cows, horses, sheep, goats, or poultry. Plant melons in the sunniest, warmest place in your garden, giving them room to spread. All melons are heavy feeders and need a monthly feeding.

Spacing: All melons require a lot of growing space and prefer to be planted on six–eight inch (15.25–20 cm.) high, flat-topped mounds. Space these mounds three–four feet wide (1–1.25 m.) and five–six feet (1.8 m.) apart, and water well. Set out three seedlings for each hill.

Uses: Melons are a sweet fruit and are generally used for fresh desserts. They can however be pickled, made into salsa, jellies, jams, soups, and drinks.

Seed to Harvest: Seed to harvest varies, but generally they need a long growing season 90–120 days.

Nutritional Values: Melons are mostly made up of water, but even so, they are a great source of vitamin C, the B group of vitamins, vitamin K and vitamin

A, potassium, magnesium, and dietary fiber. There are even trace amounts of copper in some melon varieties.

My Picks: Given that melons need such a lot of room to grow, I have never grown them, although I am considering planting them in my corn patch this year.

Yield: There are many extenuating circumstances affecting the yield of one plant, but the average is around ten smaller melons per seedling. To have one large fruit, remove all other pollinated flowers.

Onions: (Researchers believe the onion has been under cultivation for 5000 years or more and were first grown in Iran and West Pakistan. Little is known about the origin of cultivating the onion plant, however, wild onions are found growing throughout North America and various other regions throughout the world. In ancient Egypt, onions were considered to be an object of worship, and they are written about in the Old Testament as being eaten by the Israelites. In ancient India and Greece, the onion was used for medicinal purposes. The Romans brought the onion to England and Germany, and from there the first pilgrims brought it with them on the Mayflower to North America).

Planting: Onions can be grown from seeds, sets (young, small, dormant bulbs grown the previous year), or transplants. Growing onions from seed can take as much as five months. Sets are easier to plant than seeds or transplants. Onion sets are readily available at garden centers and can be planted at the end of May. Direct sow-bunching onions (green onions) in succession plantings.

Description: The onion plant has a grouping of hollow, green, tall leaves, and the bulb at the base of the plant begins to grow as the days get longer. The bulbs are made up of fleshy layers that envelop a central bud at the tip of the stem. A few common varieties are bunching (green onions), Spanish, yellow, purple, and white onion. Some are better keepers than others, some are early varieties, and some are late-season types.

Conditions: Onions are light feeders and they like heat but will tolerate some shade. They don't like to get overly wet and will grow in most soil conditions.

Spacing: I plant my bunching onions from seed. Plant them 1–1½ inches (2.5–3.7 cm.) apart in rows one foot (30.25 cm.) apart or 144 per square foot. I use onion sets for the other bulb varieties. Place these four inches apart in rows one foot apart or 16 per square foot.

USES: Onions are used around the world and served cooked in soups, stews, and many other savory dishes. The green onion is usually served raw in salads and used as a garnish. Onions can also be pickled, made into chutneys and relishes.

Seed to Harvest: Seed to harvest is generally 20 weeks.

Nutritional Values: Onions are considered to be a very healthy food. They are a very good source of biotin. They are also a good source of manganese, vitamin B6, copper, vitamin C, dietary fiber, phosphorus, potassium, folate, and vitamin B1. It is thought that onions have the ability to help regulate proper blood-fat levels as well as blood levels of cholesterol.

My Picks: I use the onion sets that are labeled yellow onions and good keepers.

Yield: One seed or set will produce one bulb for most varieties. Multiplier onions and shallots will produce multiple bulbs.

Note: Onions are prone to the onion maggot. The eggs laid by a small fly resembling a tiny house fly, hatch into white larvae which start feeding on the forming onion bulbs. An early infestation can kill and stunt young plants, and a later infestation is often not revealed until after harvest when the bulbs start to rot. Insecticides are ineffective to the onion maggot, as the fly has built up a resistance to these control methods. You can try planting your onions out a little later after the insect's first generation is over. Floating row covers have been proven to be a very effective method of control as long as they are installed as soon as the crop is planted.

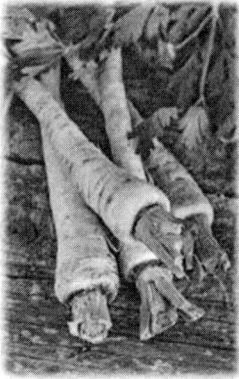

Parsnip: (Parsnips were popular with the ancient Greeks and Romans, but because they so closely resemble the carrot, some confusion exists in early literature writings. It is believed that they were cultivated during the early Roman times and a tastier and fleshier variety was developed during the Middle Ages. A plumper and sweeter variety was introduced to the British Isles and Northern Europe; it was then brought over to the new World with the first settlers).

Planting: Parsnips need a long growing season, so direct sow the seed as soon as the ground can be worked in the early spring. Pre-soaking the seed aids in quicker germination. They are a cool-season plant and taste best if harvested after a hard frost. Parsnips do not like to be transplanted.

Description: Parsnips are actually a biennial but are usually grown as an annual. Parsnips resemble a thick, white carrot. There are not many varieties of parsnip and it tends to be a favorite of old timers but is recently making a comeback as a gourmet vegetable.

Conditions: This vegetable is a cool weather crop that likes a sandy soil dug to a depth of 12–15 inches (30.48–50 cm.). Unlike other vegetables, the parsnip does not like a heavy, rich soil and will tolerate some dry conditions.

Spacing: Space the seed three inches (7.6 cm.) apart in ground. Or treat it as a carrot seed and dab some flour and water paste on a paper towel during winter to have them ready to plant in the spring. Plant two seeds per hole and then thin. Or 16 per square foot.

Uses: Parsnips are not only tasty in soups and stews but can also be enjoyed by themselves or cooked and mashed with carrots, turnips, and potatoes.

Seed to Harvest: Seed to harvest is 100–120 days.

Nutritional Values: They are a good source of vitamin C, folate, and manganese.

My Picks: Goliath.

Yield: One seed produces one large root weighing between four–six ounces (113–170 gr.).

PEAS: (Peas are believed to be the oldest crop cultivated by man, having originated in Middle Asia including Afghanistan and India in almost 10,000 B.C. Traces of a primitive pea were found in Switzerland and Hungary dating back to 3000 B.C. The Greeks and Romans cultivated the pea in 500 B.C. It reached China in 600 A.D. and made its way to England and Europe between 1100–1500 A.D.)

Planting: Peas do not transplant and should be direct sown right after the last frost with successive plantings every two weeks. Try planting another crop in the late summer for a fall harvest.

Description: Peas are a seed in a pod vegetable. There are edible pod varieties, shelled pod varieties, early, second early, main season, and late season varieties. Some are dwarf and only grow 15–16 inches (38–40 cm.) tall, and some are vines growing five–six feet (1.5–1.8 m.) tall. Peas are a legume, and so the roots will fix nitrogen in the soil, making it available for other plants.

Conditions: This is a cool weather crop that likes a well-drained, humus-rich soil without a lot of heavy fertilizer. Add a little wood ash for the potassium and some bone meal for phosphorous. Peas don't like to have wet feet, so avoid overwatering.

Spacing: I like to grow the taller varieties up chain-link fencing along the east-facing backside of my house. A lot of growing space is required for a large quantity if you were to process enough for winter. Pea seeds can be spaced two–three inches (5–7.6 cm.) apart in rows three feet (one m.) apart. Peas make an excellent trellis crop.

Uses: Peas are generally eaten as a cooked vegetable, side dish, or in a stir-fry. They can be added to soups, salads, stews, and pasta dishes.

Seed to Harvest: Seed to harvest is ten weeks.

Nutritional Values: Green peas are a very good source of vitamin K, manganese, dietary fiber, vitamin B1, copper, vitamin C, phosphorus, and folate. They are also a good source of vitamin B6, niacin, vitamin B2, molybdenum, zinc, protein, magnesium, iron, potassium, and choline.

My Picks: Lincoln.

Yield: Plant 25–60 plants per person, depending on the amount you want to store for winter use. Pole varieties produce five times more than the dwarf varieties.

Peppers: (There have been remains of peppers found in Peru where it is believed the Aztecs had them under cultivation over 5000 years ago. Peppers were used as a food in South America in 7500 B.C. and spread to Central America between 5200 B.C.–3400 B.C. Columbus was responsible for bringing the pepper to Europe in 1493, and from there the Portugal sailors and merchants brought them to Africa and Asia. Peppers have been used as a substitute for black pepper (not related to the capsicum of hot peppers) which was very expensive and actually used as a currency.)

Planting: Start seeds indoors in mid-March for transplanting outside two weeks after last frost, or purchase seedlings from a garden nursery. Be sure your soil has warmed up prior to planting your peppers outside. Peppers also make ideal plants for a pot garden.

Description: This is a very large family coming in colors of red, yellow, green, orange, purple, and black. Sweet bells, tapered bells, cherry, pimento, banana, and hot peppers, just to name a few. All peppers have a juicy outer flesh and a hollow inside with a membrane holding the seeds.

Conditions: Peppers are a hot weather crop and they need a long growing season. They are a heavy feeder and like a little extra shot of sulfur. I place an unlit matchstick at the base of each plant a couple of times throughout the growing season to give them their sulfur fix.

Spacing: Plant pepper plants 12 inches apart and keep well-watered. They do not like to be overcrowded. If planting in rows, space the rows two feet apart.

Uses: Peppers are a deliciously versatile vegetable. Sweet peppers can be eaten raw, grilled with meats, roasted, stuffed with a savory filling, baked, steamed, sautéed, or thrown into a simmering pot of soup. Add them to salads, sandwiches, and pastas. Other foods that complement chili peppers are cheeses such as mozzarella, parmesan, and goat. They can be dried, frozen, or pickled.

Seed to Harvest: Seed to harvest is 19 weeks.

Nutritional Values: Bell peppers are an excellent source of vitamin A (in the form of carotenoids), vitamin C, and vitamin B6. They are a very good source of folate, molybdenum, vitamin E, dietary fiber, vitamin B2, pantothenic acid, niacin, and potassium. As peppers change from green to yellow, orange, or red, both their vitamin content and flavor improve dramatically as does the intensity of hot peppers.

My Picks: California Wonder for bell peppers and Black Hungarian for the hot pepper.

<u>Yield:</u> You will generally get about eight peppers per bell-pepper plant and about 25–30 from a healthy hot-pepper plant.

<u>Notes:</u> Capsaicin is the oily compound that produces the heat in a hot pepper and is primarily concentrated in the veins, ribs, and seeds. If pepper juice gets in your eyes or nose, flush immediately with cold water. When the fire is in your mouth, drink milk or eat yogurt to counteract the burn. Burning hands means that capsaicin has penetrated skin or lodged under fingernails. Dipping hands into a five-to-one solution of water and bleach turns capsaicin into a salt that you can rinse away. Wash hands well after that with plenty of soap, rinse, and then dry.

- The heat value of peppers is measured by the Scoville Scale (SHUs). Here are a few of the more common varieties and their ratings.
- Pimento   100–500
- Jalapeno   2,500–8,000
- Black Hungarian   5,000–10,000
- Chipotle   15,000
- Cayenne   30,000–50,000
- Scotch Bonnet   100,000–350,000
- Habanero   100,000–350,000
- Ghost   855,000–1,041,427
- Pure Capsicum   15,000,000–16,000,000

<u>Potatoes:</u> (The Inca Indians of Peru were the first to cultivate the potato from as early as 8000 B.C. In 1536 A.D., the Spanish Conquistadors conquered Peru and

discovered this nutritious, new vegetable. They brought the potato back to Europe with them and started their own cultivation. Potatoes were introduced to Ireland in 1589, where they grew well and soon became the main staple crop of the working-class people. It wasn't until four decades later that the potato made its way to the rest of Europe. In 1840, a major outbreak of potato blight all but wiped out this main staple food crop in all of Europe, causing a major famine. During the course of this famine, almost one million people died and another million were forced to migrate to Canada and the United States).

Planting: Plant certified, disease-free seed potatoes, not ones purchased from a grocery store. Early potato varieties can be planted as soon as the ground can be worked. Successively plant mid and late-season varieties to have a continuous crop. When planting, cut up your seed potato to include at least two eyes per piece and allow them to sit for a couple of days prior to placing them in the ground.

Description: The humble potato is a staple vegetable crop worldwide. It is a starchy tuber that grows in the ground with the skins ranging in colors of brown, red, blue, and purple. There are literally thousands of varieties of potato.

Conditions: Potatoes do well in both cool weather and hot weather. They like sunshine and fertile, well-drained soil. They also like the soil to be a little on the acidic side. Potatoes prefer to be grown in hills; start hilling your potatoes when they are about six inches tall and continue to hill every couple of weeks until they flower. Hilling prevents them from becoming sunburned and turning green which can produce a chemical called solanine. Solanine makes the potato bitter and it can be mildly toxic to some people.

Spacing: In rows, plant the cut (two–three eyes per piece) six inches (15.25 cm.) apart in rows that are three feet (.91 m.) apart. Four pieces per square and then mulch as they begin to emerge.

Uses: Potatoes are always used in a cooked form; they can be boiled, mashed, and made into wedges, French fries and chips. They can be baked, roasted, scalloped, steamed, and stuffed. They are great in salads, soups, and stews.

Seed to Harvest: You can start harvesting those lovely little 'new' potatoes as soon as the plants start to flower.

Nutritional Values: They are an excellent source of vitamin C and potassium. A good source of vitamin B6, manganese, phosphorus, niacin, and pantothenic acid.

My Picks: Russet, Bintje.

Yield: Each potato plant can produce between six–ten pounds (2.7–4.5 kg.) of product.

Note: Potatoes are prone to potato scab, a condition that affects only the skin. Crop rotation and planting-resistant varieties helps to prevent this condition. Also, recent studies have found that by adding liberal amounts of Elemental Sulphur to the soil prior to planting brings the pH level to a lower level which helps to reduce potato scab.

Radish: (There are no archeological proofs of the domestication of the radish, but there are wild varieties growing in South East Asia, India, and Central China. Prior to the building of the great pyramids, the Egyptians write about the radish. Ancient Romans and Greeks have also written about them in very descriptive terms. It is believed the radish was one of the earliest vegetables to be brought to the Americas from Europe.)

Planting: The radish does not like to be transplanted. Direct sow seeds from last frost and every two weeks thereafter for successive harvests.

Description: These are an edible root crop usually consumed in the raw state. The most common radish is the red-skinned with white flesh, although there are pure, white radishes and ones with pink flesh as well as black-skinned varieties.

Conditions: Radishes tolerate cool and warm weather conditions but prefer cool weather. They are very easy to grow and do well anywhere in your garden as long as the soil stays moist. However, once the weather gets too hot for them, they become woody.

Spacing: 16 seeds per square or three–four inches (7.6–10 cm.) apart in rows that are two feet (61 cm.) apart.

Uses: They are used mostly in salads but can be cut and formed into cute garnishes. Daikon or Chinese white radish is used in a cooked form in Asian dishes but can be cooked and mashed with potatoes, carrots, and turnips.

Seed to Harvest: Seed to harvest is three–four weeks.

Nutritional Values: Radishes surprise us with their nutrient content of folate, riboflavin, and potassium, as well as good amounts of copper, vitamin B6, magnesium, and manganese. Radishes also contain fiber and are extremely low in calories.

My Picks: Rudolf.

Yield: One seed will produce one radish weighing about 1/3 of an ounce (nine gr.).

Spinach: (Little is known about the origin of spinach, but it is thought to have originated in ancient Prussia now known as Iran. It could have been bred from a wild, edible green found in Nepal. In 647 A.D., it was taken from Nepal to China, then to Northern Africa, and from there it made its way to Spain in the 11th century. By the Middle Ages, it was grown throughout all of Europe.)

Planting: It does not like to be transplanted. Seeds can be direct sown two weeks after the last frost and again in early fall.

Description: Spinach is grown for its edible leaf. The leaves can be either smooth or a crinkled form.

Conditions: Spinach is a cool weather crop and likes full sun in spring and fall but does not like the heat in summer, causing it to bolt. It does best in a well-drained, rich soil. It is a heavy feeder and likes to be feed monthly.

Spacing: Nine seeds per square foot or four inches (ten cm.) apart in rows that are two feet (61 cm.) apart.

Uses: Spinach goes well with any meal. It can be served raw in salads or wilted. Top with bacon bits and a hardboiled egg. Add to soups, pasta sauce, and stews just before serving. Feta cheese and mushrooms are a wonderful accompaniment.

Harvest: Seed to harvest is seven weeks.

Nutritional Values: Spinach is an excellent source of vitamin K, vitamin A, manganese, folate, magnesium, iron, copper, vitamin B2, vitamin B6, vitamin E, calcium, potassium, and vitamin C. It is a very good source of dietary fiber, phosphorus, vitamin B1, zinc, protein, and choline. When you eat spinach that has been heated, you will absorb higher levels of vitamins A and E, protein, fiber, zinc, thiamin, calcium, and iron.

My Picks: Bloomsdale Savoy, New Zealand (both heirloom varieties).

Yield: One seed will give you one spinach plant that will yield about 1½ pounds (.68 kg.) of uncooked product, if picked on a regular basis.

Squash: (The squash plant originated in Mexico and Central America some 10,000 years ago. Domestication was likely in part; the result of human selection for different traits related to edibility, as well as seed size and rind thickness. It has also been suggested that domestication may have been directed by the practicality of dried gourds as containers for fishing weights. By way of primitive trading, the squash plant was brought to the 'Old World' in 1492. In the 1800s, it became popular in the use of making pumpkin pie.)

Planting: Start seeds indoors two–four weeks before last frost and carefully transplant out two weeks later or direct sow when the soil has warmed up.

Description: As far as squash go, they can be broken down into two groups, Summer Squash (*Cucurbita pepo*) and Winter Squash *(Cucurbita maxima, moschata and pepo)*. Examples of Summer Squash are zucchini, and Winter Squash varieties include butternut, acorn, pumpkin, Turks Turban, and Hubbard. There is a color and shape of squash for everyone. There are round, flat, long, straight, and crookneck varieties all with their own particular flavors. There are bush types and vining types. All are easy to grow and are very productive.

Conditions: All squash are hot-weather crops requiring a lot of growing room and a sunny location. They all need plenty of water and a rich, well-draining soil. They are a hungry plant and like a good dose of fertilizer on a monthly basis.

Spacing: Vine types growing vertically can be planted one foot (30.48 cm.) apart against a fence or trellis. They will do well planted amongst corn, as they will use the corn stalks as climbing poles. Bush types need three square feet (one sq. m.) of space.

Uses: The fruits of the squash plant can be steamed, boiled, baked, or roasted. Bake the Winter Squash with butter, a bit of brown sugar or maple syrup, and a dash of balsamic vinegar. Cook Summer Squash lightly and serve with butter, cheese, and parsley or add to any vegetable combination. The grated flesh can be added to breads and even cakes. The flowers can be eaten as well. Pick the male flowers just as they open. Sauté in butter or stuff them and bake, or they can also be dipped in a batter and deep fried. The Winter Squash will make a delicious winter soup and even an amazing pie.

Seed to Harvest: Seed to harvest is eight weeks. Cut the fruits from the vine rather than breaking them off.

Nutritional Values: This food is a good source of protein, vitamin A, thiamin, niacin, phosphorus and copper, and a very good source of dietary fiber, vitamin C, vitamin K, riboflavin, vitamin B6, folate, magnesium, potassium, and manganese.

My Picks: Summer Squash-Zucchini, Winter Squash-Acorn, Turks Turban, Butternut.

Yield: One seed will give you one plant with a variable yield. Some squash will produce up to 80 pounds of fruit. The giant varieties can produce one fruit weighing in at over 2000 lbs.

Tomato: (The tomato originated in the Andes what is now known as Chile, Peru, Bolivia, and Ecuador, where it grew wild. It was then cultivated by the Aztecs and Incas as early as 700 A.D. After the Spanish Invasion in the 16th century, the tomato was taken to Europe. The wealthy Europeans considered it to be a poisonous fruit, as the rich people used plates made of pewter. The acid in tomatoes drew out the lead of the pewter, causing lead poisoning and consequently death. The poor people, however, used wooden plates and enjoyed the tomato all to themselves until the 1800s when pewter was no longer used as dishware. The pizza was also created in the 1800s where legend has it that baker, Raffaele Esposito of Naples, was enlisted to create a food to be served to the visiting Italian King Umberto I and Queen Margherita in 1889. His creation included sliced fresh tomatoes (red) on a flat bread, topped with basil leaves (green) and shredded mozzarella cheese (white), the color scheme representing the Italian flag in honor of the visiting royalty. Also, in the 1800s, there was a mass immigration to the Americas, but still the tomato was not regarded as a kitchen vegetable until the times preceding the Civil War period in the United States. From this point

forward, tomatoes have become a staple item in the kitchen throughout the world.)

Planting: Tomatoes transplant well, and because they need a long growing season, seeds should be started indoors in mid-March to transplant outdoors at the end of May or beginning of June. Be sure to harden off your transplants before permanently planting outside. Or purchase seedlings from a nursery, but don't be in too much of a hurry to plant them outside, as tomatoes are extremely cold sensitive. In many areas, the growing season is too short to direct sow seeds outdoors.

Description: Literally, there are thousands of tomato varieties. You can have early, midseason, or later varieties. They come in shades of red, orange, yellow, pink, green, and even black. The sizes range from marble-sized fruits to four-pound (1.8 kg.) fruits. There are varieties especially suited for juice, cooking, canning, or just plain raw-eating. There are bush varieties (determinate) and vining varieties (indeterminate). No matter the vastness of this fruit, they all have an edible skin which surrounds a rich, juicy flesh interspaced with multiple edible seeds.

Conditions: Tomatoes like heat and full sun with a soil that is deep, loose, and rich. Tomatoes are heavy feeders and like to be fertilized monthly. A little additional calcium will help prevent blossom end rot.

Spacing: Bush varieties can be planted two feet (61 cm.) apart, and vining varieties can be spaced one foot (30.48 cm.) apart against a trellis. All of your common tomato varieties, whether they are determinate or indeterminate, will have to be staked or grown in a tomato cage.

Uses: A whole book could be and probably has been written about all of the uses for tomatoes. They are used fresh in salads and sandwiches or just eaten fresh from the plant. They are used for juice, canning, sauces, pastes, soups, stews, and in any meat or vegetable dish you desire to put them in. They can be stuffed, dried, roasted, breaded, fried, and frozen.

Seed to Harvest: Seed to harvest is 17 weeks.

Nutritional Values: Tomatoes are sometimes considered to be one of the world's healthiest food. They are an excellent source of vitamin C, biotin, molybdenum, and vitamin K. They are also a very good source of copper, potassium, manganese, dietary fiber, vitamin A (in the form of beta-carotene), vitamin B6, folate, niacin, vitamin E, and phosphorus.

My Picks: Roma (for canning, sauces, and salsas.) Angelo's red for slicing. Zebra varieties for the unique appearance. Sweet 100 for the cherry variety.

Yield: Because of the tomatoes large range in size, it is difficult to provide a yield. I grow four–five Roma plants which give me 24 pints of stewed tomatoes, 12 pints of salsa, and about 20 pints of marinara sauce. Two cherry-tomato plants give me all the summer salads I, my friends, and nearby relatives can eat, and two slicing varieties provide many sandwiches, egg and tomato McMuffins, tuna melts, and BLTs.

Turnip: (This Brassica Root crop has been around for over 4000 years and was used by the early Romans to throw at unpopular people, giving it a bad reputation throughout the ages. The low esteem associated with this vegetable may have also been influenced by the fact that it was the primary food of poor country folks in ancient Greece and Rome. In the 1700s, this root vegetable made its way to Europe where it was used to fatten cattle. Prior to this discovery, farmers killed their livestock before winter because it was too expensive to grow and store hay for winter feed. From Europe, turnips were brought to North America by early European colonists and settlers and have been widely used ever since.)

Planting: Turnips don't like to be transplanted. Direct sow the seed in early spring as soon as the soil can be worked for summer greens and tender roots. For a fall crop, direct sow again in late summer for a sweeter root. Do not plant the seeds deeper than half inch.

Description: Turnips have a creamy-white skin with a purple top and pale-yellow flesh. Turnips are grown primarily for the three–four inch (7.6–10 cm.), oval, bulbous root, but the greens are also delicious.

Conditions: Turnips are a cool weather crop. They are a heavy feeder and prefer compost in the planting mix. They like a loose, deep, rich soil and like to be fertilized monthly.

Spacing: Plant seeds six inches (15.25 cm.) apart in rows 18 inches (45.7 cm.) apart or four per square foot.

USES: The roots can be diced or chopped, boiled, baked, or roasted, whereas the greens can be used in stews, soups, and salads. Baby turnips are quite delicious, tender, and sweet and can be added to salads or eaten raw. Try using turnips in place of potatoes or mash with cooked carrots.

Seed to Harvest: Seed to harvest for this root crop is six–ten weeks.

Nutritional Values: High in vitamin C and a good source of potassium, calcium, iron, vitamin B6, and magnesium. Also, it is a good source of dietary fiber.

My Picks: Purple Top White Globe.

Yield: One seed will produce one five-inch (12.7 cm.) diameter root.

➢ Herbs

I would never be without my culinary herbs. They are distinguished from vegetables in that, like spices, they are used in small amounts and provide flavor rather than substance to food. Although, in saying that, there are certain nutritional benefits to most herbs.

Herbs can be perennials such as thyme or lavender, biennials such as parsley, or annuals like basil. Perennial herbs can be shrubs such as rosemary and sage. Some plants are used as both herbs and spices, such as dill weed and dill seed or cilantro leaves and coriander seeds. Also, there are some herbs such as those in the mint family that are used for both culinary and medicinal purposes.

There are several methods to preserve herbs for winter use. Once your herbs have been harvested, wash them well. They can then be put in a dehydrator to dry the moisture out them. An oven on low temperatures can be used for the dehydration process and some gardeners use a microwave. Then place each type of herb in a food processor to finely chop them. You can then put the chopped herb in airtight jars or small baggies, label, and store them. You can also chop fresh herbs and place them in ice-cube trays filled with water and freeze them. They are just as tasty and green as if they were freshly picked.

There have been volumes written detailing all of the uses and benefits of the many herbs found throughout the world. Following is a list of the more common culinary and medicinal herbs with their unique characteristics.

Angelica (Culinary and Medicinal Herb)

The angelica plant has a long history dating back to pre-Christian times when it is said to bloom on May 8 in time for the feast day of St. Michael the Archangel, hence the name. It was believed to have mystical powers against disease and evil. It is a tall, biennial, and perennial herb growing three–ten feet in height (one–three meters). It is native to temperate and subarctic regions of the northern hemisphere, reaching as far north as Iceland, Lapland, and Greenland. Not only is Angelica used for medicinal and culinary purposes, it is a beautiful addition to your landscape as long as you have the space for it to stretch out. The leaves, root, seed, and fruit are all used.

Medicinally, Angelica is used to treat heartburn, intestinal gas, loss of appetite (anorexia), arthritis, circulation problems, 'runny nose' (inflammation of the mucous membranes in the airways), nervousness, plague, and trouble sleeping (insomnia). The oil of the root is added to bath water to aid in relaxation.

For culinary purposes Angelica is used to flavor gin, liqueurs, and sweet wines. The candied root is used to decorate cakes and desserts. The leaves can be added to salads, soups, stews or used as a garnish. The seeds can be used in sweet-yeast breads, quick breads, cakes, muffins, and cookies. The dried leaf makes a delightful afternoon tea.

Cultivation: Angelica is related to the carrot and parsley plant, and because it is considered to be a short-lived perennial or biennial, you should plant Angelica annually. It flowers after two years and then either dies or may hang on for another year or two. It is best to grow Angelica from seed, as division and propagation of side shoots doesn't work well. Once Angelica sets seed, it will die off. If its cycle is disrupted by cutting the flower heads off each year before the seeds form, the plant will sometimes continue to grow for many years.

Basil (Culinary and Medicinal Herb)

For centuries, basil was associated with love and romance. Women would place a basil plant on their window sill or door step, announcing that she was ready to receive her suitor. When a man gave a woman a sprig of basil, he believed she would fall in love with him. Basil was also thought to protect the dead from evil and that it would help them gain entry into paradise. In India, it was a sacred herb dedicated to the gods Vishnu and Krishna. Today, this fragrant herb is associated with fine dining and can be grown in pots, in the flower or vegetable garden, or on a sunny window ledge.

Medicinally, a cup of basil tea is recommended for an upset stomach and to help expel gas. It can also be used to stop vomiting and to aid in constipation. It has a slight, sedative action and can be used for nervous headaches and anxiety.

Culinary uses include it being used in traditional Italian, Mediterranean, and Thai cooking. Basil compliments most vegetable and meat dishes including veal, lamb, fish, poultry, dried beans, pasta, rice, cheese, and eggs. It blends particularly well with garlic and tomato and is well known as a pesto.

Cultivation: Basil is an annual plant that is very sensitive to cold weather. It is best to start seeds indoors around mid-March and transplant outside after hardening off when the soil temperature warms up to about 60 degrees F. (15.5 degrees C.). To encourage a bushy plant, prune the main stem out to promote side branches.

Borage (Culinary and Medicinal Herb)
Borage is believed to induce the user with a healthy dose of courage. The Ancient Celtic warriors drank a wine laced with borage prior to going into battle. (Maybe it was the wine that gave these warriors a false sense of bravery instead of the borage!)

Medicinally, borage is used in the treatment of depression. It is also considered to be a diuretic (increases the passing of urine) and is used as an emollient (skin-softening agent). Poultices made from the leaves are used to reduce inflammations and swellings; borage poultices are also used in the treatment of bronchitis.

Culinary uses include the vivid blue, star-shaped flowers to be used as a garnish. Borage has a cucumber-like flavor, and the flowers are used raw in salads or steamed and sautéed like spinach. In a candied form, the flowers make excellent decorations for pastries and other desserts. Try dropping a flower in your ice-cube trays to serve in a cooling summer drink.

Cultivation: Borage is best started from seeds and grown in an herb garden, as its habit is a little unruly for an ornamental garden. The bright blue flowers are a delight in the landscape and it is a wonderful bee attractant. Be aware, however, borage readily reseeds itself.

Chives (Culinary Herb)

Chives are a member of the onion family and in the raw form have been added to food dishes for 5,000 years. They originated in China and then made their way to Greece, Europe, and eventually America. This versatile herb was once thought to keep away evil influences and disease, so it was hung in bunches throughout the home.

Culinary uses are mostly limited to using chives as a garnish. Both the lush green stem and lavender/pink flowers are edible, having a very mild onion and/or garlic flavor enhancing the appearance and flavor of salads. They are a great compliment to potatoes, asparagus, cauliflower, corn, tomatoes, peas, carrots, spinach, poultry, fish, and shellfish. Add them to cream sauces, cheese, and egg dishes.

Cultivation: Chives are best grown from root division, and since they need to be divided every three years, it is always easy to find them at a farmer's market for sale or from a mutual gardening friend. You can start them from seed, but they germinate very slowly and require some tricky cultivating practices. Chives do very well as a container crop and love to be placed in a sunny window during the winter months.

Cilantro/Coriander (Culinary and Medicinal Herb)

Coriander has a fascinating history. It has been under cultivation for more than 3,000 years in ancient Egypt where the seeds have been found scattered among other funeral offerings in the ancient tombs. It was then brought to Greece and Rome and made into medicines by physicians including Hippocrates. The Chinese used it as far back as the Han dynasty (206 B.C.–220 A.D.), believing it had the power to make a person immortal. Today, this herb is an important ingredient in the spicy cuisine's worldwide. The leaves of this plant are called cilantro, the seeds have been labeled coriander.

Medicinally, the seeds are ground up and used in teas to aid digestion and to soothe upset stomachs.

Culinary: All parts of the plant are edible, but the fresh leaves and the dried seeds are the parts most traditionally used in cooking. It is used widely in the cuisine of Southeast Asia, China, Mexico, East India, South America, Spain, Central Africa, and Central America. The leaves have a sage-like flavor that combines well with mushrooms, tomatoes, beets, onions, sausage, clams, oysters, and potatoes. The seeds have a citrus flavor and add character to marinades, salad dressings, cheese, eggs, chili sauce, guacamole, and pickling brines. Both the seeds and leaves are used in curries, pilafs, and salsa sauce. The ground-up root is often added to salads and relishes. The leaves which are sometimes used as a garnish also go by the name 'Chinese Parsley.'

Cultivation: Cilantro is an annual herb that is easy to start by direct sowing the seeds as soon as the ground can be worked. It does not transplant well. For successive harvest, sow seeds every two weeks.

Dill (Culinary and Medicinal Herb)
Dill was commonly grown in the gardens of the ancient Athens and Romans. Traditionally, garlands were woven and worn by the returning warriors. Because of its fragrance and beauty, bunches of it were brought indoors, doubling its purpose to ward off the spells cast by witches. Today, this versatile herb with its rich green, feathery leaves, and the umbel-like flowers and seeds are grown in most gardens worldwide.

Medicinally, both the leaves and seeds, if taken internally, are believed to stimulate the appetite, relieve gas, settle an upset stomach, and relieve colic in babies. Dill contains an abundance of mineral salts and can be helpful for people of a low salt diet.

Culinary uses include the snipped leaves and flowers in the cooking of dishes of seafood, meats, cheese, cream, eggs, and every vegetable imaginable. Dill particularly goes well with tomatoes, cucumbers, feta cheese, pork, chicken, and salmon. Both the leaves and flowers are used in the making of pickles.

Cultivation: Once you have planted dill in the herb garden and allow some of the flower heads to go to seed, you won't have to plant it again. It will do well in any type of soil as long as it has a protected location to grow in, as the tall stalks are prone to breakage in strong winds. If you don't grow dill for its culinary uses, try adding the greenery to cut flower bouquets.

Horseradish (Culinary and Medicinal Herb)

Horseradish, aka Red Cole, is believed to be native to Eastern Europe, Western Asia, Russia, Poland, and Finland. It was used as a medicine until John Gerard, an Elizabethan herbalist, saw that the Germans mixed it with a little vinegar and ate it with fish and other meats. It was generally eaten by country people and hardworking men, as it was considered to be too strong for tender stomachs.

Medicinally, the fresh root is grated or chopped and, with a little water added, made into a compress to relieve stiffness and pain in the back of the neck. Internally, it is used to treat kidney conditions. It can also be made into a syrup and is used in the treatment of hoarseness.

Culinarily, the ground-up root with a little vinegar and white wine added is used traditionally as a spread to go over roast beef. Horseradish also goes well with fish, poultry, devilled eggs, beets, and potatoes. It is used in coleslaw dressings and other mayonnaise-based sauces. I like to put a couple of tablespoons full into a bowl of mashed potatoes, giving them a little added zing.

Cultivation: Horseradish is propagated by root cuttings, and unless you have a lot of growing area, it should be container grown. If even the tiniest bit of root is left in the ground, another plant will sprout, making it next to impossible to eradicate. A three-foot (one m.) diameter container at least two feet (61 cm.) deep makes the ideal home to grow horseradish in. Half of an old oak barrel works well if you can get your hands on one.

Lavender (Culinary and Medicinal Herb)

Lavender has a history of love and was considered to be an aphrodisiac way back in the Middle Ages. Traditionally, though, this old-fashioned, highly scented herb has been used in sachets and potpourris which are placed in dresser drawers to act as an insect repellant and linen freshener. The oils are used in soaps, creams, and perfumes. The flowers look lovely in dried flower arrangements and in wreaths.

Medicinally, the oils have been used as an antispasmodic, an antiseptic, and as a mild sedative. It has been used in the treatment of eczema and psoriasis and even in treatments for bruises and bug bites.

Culinary, uses are limited to using the mauve flowers and gray-green leaves in vinegars, jellies, salads, and teas.

Cultivation: Lavender is best propagated from cuttings or root division. It is a long-living, shrubby perennial that likes to grow in a sunny, dry, protected area. In cold climates, it should be mulched to protect it against frost damage. Given the beauty and longevity of lavender, it is a must in the landscape and herb garden.

Lemon Balm (Lemon Mint) (Culinary Herb)

The Greeks, Romans, and Arabs used this green, leafy member of the mint family for insect bites, rabies, heart disorders, an antidepressant, and pretty much everything in between. It was the sacred herb of the Greek Temple of Diana, otherwise known as the Temple of Artemis. Today, however, this humble, coarse-leaved, lemon-flavored plant is used primarily in the culinary world.

Culinary, uses include using the raw, chopped leaves in poultry dishes such as chicken salad and stuffing. It is great in marinades for fish, tossed salads, and steeped for a fine, lemon-tasting, relaxing cup of tea. The leaves can be dried and stored for winter use.

Cultivation: Lemon Balm can be started from seed, but it is faster and easier to start from root division. It likes a sunny location with a well-drained soil. It is a beneficial plant for the garden, as it is a bee attractant if allowed to go to flower.

Lovage (Culinary Herb)

Lovage has fallen out of the popularity it held in the Middle Ages where it was grown for its celery like flavor in both kitchen and physic herb gardens. The early Europeans used it as a cure for rheumatism, jaundice, malaria, sore throat, and kidney stones. Today, scientists say the roots can work as a diuretic but prefer the essential oil of angelica to treat this condition.

Culinarily: the stems, leaves, and seeds are all used. They have a taste like celery and can be used in dishes as a celery replacement. The fresh leaves are used in salads and as a garnish. Lovage goes particularly well with potatoes, tomatoes, and poultry. It can be used to flavor soups and savory pies.

Cultivation: Lovage is a strikingly beautiful, long-lasting plant suitable for the landscape and herb garden alike. It is an erect, herbaceous perennial growing up to eight feet (2.4 m.) in height. The flowers are produced in umbels at the top of the stems and should be clipped off prior to going to seed. The seeds are very viable and produce masses of tiny lovage plants.

Marjoram (Culinary Herb)

Marjoram in ancient times was used in wreaths and crowns for weddings and funerals alike. The Greeks called it 'Joy of the Mountains.' It is said to have been particularly precious to Aphrodite, the goddess of love, and was used as a symbol of love.

Culinary, uses are much the same as that of oregano, having a mild hint of balsam. The fresh flowers and leaves should be added to dishes at the end of the cooking process otherwise it will lose its delicate flavor. The cuisines of France, Italy, and Portugal use this herb in meat and fish dishes. It goes well with carrots, green vegetables, cauliflower, mushrooms, parsnips, potatoes, squash, and tomatoes. It is used in herb butters, spreads, marinades, dressings, soups, and stuffing. It is sometimes used in the making of sausages and for flavoring vinegars and oils.

Cultivation: Seeds are slow to germinate and should be started indoors in mid-March. Marjoram is an annual plant in our cooler climatic zone and likes a sunny location with a rich, well-drained soil.

Mint (Culinary and Medicinal Herb)

Mint is a rather loose term for a broad category of the Mentha family where it is estimated that 13 to 18 species exist, some of which are peppermint, spearmint, and pennyroyal. The Pharisees paid their tithes with mint and the Romans egotistically crowned themselves with this highly scented herb.

The Greeks, being more practical, used it in various herbal treatments believing it could clear the voice, cure hiccups, and counteract sea-serpent stings. Peppermint and spearmint came to the New World with the colonists where it was and still is used for medicinal purposes.

Medicinally, mint is used in the treatment of upset stomach, flatulence, colic, and menstrual cramps. The oils in mint stimulate the flow of bile to the stomach, which promotes digestion, making it a staple as a home remedy. It also acts as an antispasmodic by calming the action of muscles.

Culinarily, mint is used in jams, jellies, sauces, and hot or cold teas. The tender leaves can be dipped in melted chocolate or crystalized and used as decorations on cakes and other pastries. Mint is used commercially in the making of gum, candies, chocolates, cordials, and liqueurs such as Crème de menthe. It goes particularly well with peas, new potatoes, lamb, and carrots. What would a *Mint Julep* be without the *Mint?* Chop the leaves up and add them to cream cheese and cottage-cheese dishes. Mint is one of the main ingredients in Tzatziki Sauce and is used in other Greek, Arabic, North African, Middle Eastern, and Indian foods.

Cultivation: Mint is extremely easy to start by root division, and most gardeners are more than willing to give a root or two away to the nearest taker. It is a hardy perennial and a rampant plant. It should be container grown in a pot at least two feet (61 cm.) in diameter to keep the roots from spreading. It grows well in a shady, moist soil with very little in the way of fertilization. When container grown, the plants will need to be divided annually so it doesn't become root bound and choke itself out.

Oregano (Culinary and Medicinal Herb)

Oregano and marjoram are very similar and have often been confused with one another. The flavor is much the same, although oregano has a bit of a bolder taste. Its history is almost identical as well. The colonists brought this voracious, spreading perennial to the Americas where it escaped cultivation and is now listed as a wildflower. Oregano quickly became a staple in the medicine cabinet, as it was used for pain relief, to aid in male baldness, and to open the bronchial tubes during colds and asthma attacks. It wasn't until after World War II when the service men brought some of the traditional Italian recipes, that they had grown to love, home to their wives that it started making its way into our spaghetti sauce and onto our pizza pie in North America.

Medicinally, oregano is used in modern remedies for indigestion, coughs, headaches, toothaches, and to promote menstruation. Commercially, oregano is grown on a large scale, as it takes 200 pounds (91 kg.) of the plant to produce one pound (.45 kg.) of the potent oil.

Culinary uses include adding the peppery-flavored leaves to tomato sauce and egg dishes including frittatas, quiches, and omelets. Oregano goes well in yeast breads, with roasted bell peppers, onions, garlic, mushrooms, zucchini, bean dishes, and potatoes. It is used in stews and soups, with beef, pork, poultry, shellfish, and wild game.

CULTIVATION: Oregano is another herb that should be container grown and best started from a cutting or root division, as the flavor varies greatly when grown from seed. Try the trailing variety in decorative hanging baskets.

Parsley (Culinary and Medicinal Herb)

Unlike many other herbs, parsley had a humble beginning in history. Instead of being

associated with love, it was used in funeral ceremonies because the Greeks associated it with obliviation and death. By the Middle Ages, it had made an appearance as a medicinal herb and was used to treat conditions related to the kidneys, bladder, lungs, thyroid, and liver. It was also used against plague, asthma, dropsy, and jaundice as well as being used to aid in digestion. It has been used to treat chest and heart pain, fluid retention, indigestion, bed wetting, obesity, prostate disorders, and even for the elimination of head lice. Today, parsley is one of the most commonly used herbs and no kitchen garden should be without it.

Medicinally, parsley, unlike most other herbs, holds a wealth of vitamins. It contains vitamin A, several B vitamins, calcium, iron, and has more vitamin C per volume than an orange. Doctors prescribe parsley tea for female patients with bladder problems and the root has laxative properties. It has also been used to help reduce high blood pressure and to sweeten the breath.

Culinarily, this versatile herb is used in food dishes throughout the world. In the Middle East, it is used in tabbouleh (a vegetarian salad made of mostly finely chopped parsley with tomatoes, mint, onion, bulgur (cracked wheat), and seasoned with olive oil, lemon juice, salt, and pepper). In Belgium and Switzerland, it is deep fried. The Japanese also deep fry it in a tempura batter, and the Mexicans and Spaniards use it to make salsa Verde. In North America, it is used in soups, stews, garlic butter, seafood dishes, egg dishes, or simply as a decorative, leafy garnish. It has a gentle flavor and works at blending other flavors around it, acting much like salt does in creative cooking.

Cultivation: There are two varieties of this deep-rooted herb; the flat leaf variety (Italian Parsley) and the curly leaf variety. It is a biennial, meaning it only comes back after two gardening seasons. However, it readily seeds itself, so you should never be without this well-rounded plant. It prefers a sunny location and a well-drained soil but will enjoy a stay on a sunny window ledge during the winter months. It also makes a striking plant in the decorative landscape and adds a dimension to cut flower arrangements.

Rosemary (Culinary and Medicinal Herb)

Way back in the Middle Ages, rosemary was thought to possess the power to ward off evil spirits, and so sprigs were placed under the pillow as the potential victims slept. It was used as an air purifier in the form of incense and became a symbol of friendship, love, and remembrance as quoted in Shakespeare's Ophelia where Hamlet is petitioned with, *"There's rosemary, that's for remembrance, pray you love, remember."* Much later in time, it became an important medicinal herb in the treatment of rheumatism and arthritis.

Medicinally, Rosemary has long held a reputation for enhancing the memory. Our modern-day researchers have discovered that certain phytochemicals in the herb prevent the degradation of acetylcholine, an important brain chemical needed for normal neurotransmission. A deficiency of this chemical is commonly seen in Alzheimer's patients. It is commonly still used in the treatment of headaches, joint, and muscle pain. A main ingredient in rosemary is salicylic acid which is used for a variety of skin disorders including wart removal, calluses, acne, and dandruff. Rosemary is also being studied for its potential anti-cancer effects. This pine-scented herb may hold the key to some very important health cures in the future.

Culinary uses include it as a seasoning for many Mediterranean dishes, which is no surprise, as it is native to the Mediterranean, Portugal, and Spain. Its pine, mint, and ginger flavors enhance the taste of tomatoes, garlic, spinach, peas, mushrooms, squash, cheese, and egg dishes. It does well in marinades, soups, stews, bean dishes, salad dressings, poultry stuffing, and cream sauces. The spiky sprigs of rosemary make for an interesting garnish.

Cultivation: Rosemary is a perennial, evergreen shrub in temperate climates but should be treated as an annual in cooler climates. It is hardy in Zone 8-10 but won't handle temperatures below ten degrees F. (-12 C). It is best started from cuttings or by layering. It is an extremely slow-growing plant that likes a sunny location and a lot of room to stretch out its roots. It does not like to be container grown; however, I usually am able to keep one on my kitchen-window ledge throughout the winter months.

Sage (Culinary and Medicinal Herb)

In those ancient Arabian days, sage was associated with immortality and was trusted with the ability of increasing mental capacity. As quoted in the 10th century, "Why should a man die when he can go to his garden for sage?" Much later, the herb was used to counteract snake bites, and the North American Indians used it in a bear-grease salve to cure skin sores. In the 1800s, it was used as a cure for epilepsy, insomnia, measles, seasickness, and stomach worms. Today, it is used in Feng Shui by burning tightly tied-together stems. It is believed the scented, smoldering smoke clears away negative energy that is hanging in the air around your home.

Medicinally, the oils and tannins in sage are thought to dry perspiration and has been marketed as an anhidrotic (a dysfunction where a person cannot sweat when hot). The oils derived from sage have antiseptic, astringent, and irritant properties and are used in treating sore throats, mouth irritations, cuts, and bruises. It has also been proven to dry up breast milk and is sometimes used in the weaning process. It is also used to help lower blood sugar.

Culinarily, it has many uses including the popular poultry dressing. Since sage has a lemony, camphor-like flavor, it goes well in egg dishes, meat pies, yeast breads, and in the production of sausage meats. Sage goes particularly well with lamb, poultry, duck, goose, beef, and fish. It accents tomatoes, beans, potatoes, carrots, corn, garlic, onions, and cheese. Sage is compatible with rosemary, thyme, oregano, parsley, and bay.

Cultivation: Sage is best propagated from four-inch cuttings, as its seeds store poorly and may not be viable. Sage is a woody shrub and should be planted in a permanent, sunny location in your garden. There are several varieties of sage;

my favorite is Purple Sage, as it is very decorative with its purple/green leaves, lavender/blue flowers, and its 18-inch (45.7 cm.) height compact nature.

SUMMER SAVORY (Culinary Herb)

Unlike many other herbs, savory did not have as much of a history as a medicinal herb as it did as a culinary herb. The early Romans used it extensively in their cooking and often used it to flavor vinegars. It was believed to produce a pleasant-tasting honey when planted near beehives. Italians were some of the first to cultivate this peppery-tasting herb for their many well-known dishes. However, in the 17th century, medicinally it was claimed to dispel gas from the stomach and bowels and was used as a promoter of regular menstruation and as a tonic for the reproductive system.

Culinary uses include it being used with other flavors to bring them together. It is used in teas, herb butters, and to flavor vinegars. It goes well in bean and lentil dishes, soups, and stews. Summer savory is used to enhance the flavor of eggs, peas, turnip, carrots, parsnip, onions, cabbage, squash, Brussels sprouts, and, in particular, trout.

Cultivation: Summer Savory is easy to start from seeds and can be direct sown once the soil has warmed up. This savory plant is considered to be an annual in cooler climates and works well as a container plant.

Tarragon (Culinary Herb)

Unlike other herbs, this anise-like-tasting herb has little ancient history. It is believed to be native to Siberia and Mongolia and thought to have been brought to Italy around the tenth century by invading Mongols. It is believed to have been brought to France in the 14th century by St. Catherine, on a visit to Pope Clement VI. It then made its way to England around 1548. Tarragon has only been under cultivation for around 600 years.

Culinarily, this fine herb is associated with French cuisine where it is used primarily in vinegars and with fish. It is used in classic dishes such as remoulade sauce, tartar sauce, and béarnaise sauce as well as French salad dressing and veal Marengo. Tarragon can be somewhat overpowering and should be used sparingly. It can be used to enhance mushrooms, cauliflower, beets, peas, asparagus, and rice dishes. It is a good addition to feta cheese and tomato dishes.

Cultivation: Tarragon is fairly easy to start from seed. It is a hardy perennial to Zone 4 and grows in an unruly manner with a twisted root system. Tarragon can be brought inside in a pot and set on a sunny window ledge as long as the pot is large enough to hold the twisted root mass and good drainage is provided.

Thyme (Medicinal and Culinary Herb)
Thyme is native to the western Mediterranean region and is widely cultivated throughout the world. Over 400 varieties of thyme exist; some are cultivated for landscaping purposes, some for culinary purposes. All thyme plants are low growing, have scented as well as flavored leaves and sprigs of pretty little flowers that attract bees. We are going to concentrate on common thyme, the variety mostly used in cooking.

Medicinally, the early Greeks used thyme for nervous conditions and as an antiseptic and fumigator. It has been used as a treatment for flatulence, colic, stomach cramps, whooping cough, asthma, headache, and menstrual cramping. Inflammation and sores may be soothed by making a poultice from ground-up leaves.

Culinary uses are wide, including its use in many French and Italian dishes. It has a gentle clove-like taste that blends well with veal, lamb, beef, poultry, and fish. It is used as a seasoning in sausages, stews, soups, bean, and lentil dishes. It goes particularly well with potatoes, peas, tomatoes, onions, cucumbers, peppers, mushrooms, and corn. It can be added to herbed butters, herbed mayonnaise, vinegars, mustards, and creamed cheeses.

Cultivation: Thyme is a cute, little, woody shrub growing only about six inches (15.25 cm) tall. It likes to be planted in its forever home, bearing many tiny pink flowers that act as a bee attractant. You can start these plants from seed, but it is much faster to establish them from root division. Thyme is also a great addition to a rock garden.

➢ Common Garden Small Fruits

Growing small fruits in your garden is attractive because you have the choice of many cultivars that can't be purchased in stores. The varieties in stores are mass produced and are the best cultivars for shipping and storing, not taste. Another attractive thing about growing your own fruit is you can enjoy various fresh fruits from June right on up until fall. Most of these small shrub fruits don't do well in raised beds and require very little care. They need a spot that is in full sun with well-drained soil and a good water supply.

Blackberries: As a kid growing up on the west coast of British Columbia, there were masses of thorny blackberry bushes growing everywhere. I totally took these vigorous growing vines for granted. As I recall, three varieties of blackberry plants are native to the lower mainland. Each and every summer, a time was allotted for us to go blackberry picking. The little trailing variety didn't have as much of a harvest, but the flavor was delightful. There are actually 237 species of blackberry vines worldwide, including dozens native to North America. They have a hardiness of Zones 5–10, so be sure to plant the ones hardy to your climatic zone.

Growing: The best time to plant these spreading vines is in the spring. If you have chosen to plant an upright variety, you will have to place it against a fence or provide a trellis for it to cling to. The canes can grow to 12 feet (3.65 m.) in length unless they are controlled. The native varieties all have large, dangerous thorns, but many domestic varieties are thornless, making for a pain-free harvest. Blackberries are self-fertile (able to fertilize themselves), so you don't have to have pollinator plants.

Care: A blackberry vine can live indefinitely when cared for properly. The fruits bear on one and two-year-old woody canes, so all older canes should be pruned out. The bearing canes can be lopped off at five–six feet (1.5–1.8 m) in mid-July. This improves the productivity, makes the plant more manageable, and allows for an easier harvest. Allow 6–12 canes per plant.

Blueberries: Blueberries are a large species of fruiting shrubs that are native to North America, growing naturally in mountains and meadows. As a forestry worker, I was always thrilled to come across a patch of wild blueberry bushes in an old burned-out logging block. I would take a little extra time to pick a handful or two for a batch of blueberry pancakes for the next day's breakfast. Of all the blueberries, the wild ones are the sweetest and most flavorful, albeit a little smaller in size. There are three types of blueberry for the home gardener today. The Lowbush blueberry, the Highbush blueberry, and the Rabbiteye blueberry.

Growing: Blueberries like a very acidic soil, with a soil pH in the range of 4.0 to 4.5. Try to find bare root plants that are two–three years old or potted plants that are in three–five-gallon pots. Plants older than three years suffer more transplant shock and will take a few years to begin producing large harvests. Dig a hole twice the width and depth of the pot or root mass and amend the soil with peat moss, but be sure to keep the soil loose and well-draining. Plant blueberries so that the roots are spread out in the hole and completely covered in soil. If they were container grown, plant about one inch (2.5 cm.) deeper than they were in the pot. The best time to plant your blueberry bushes is in early spring. Blueberries are not self-pollinating and need another variety to allow for cross-pollination. Planting multiple varieties with different maturity dates also stretches out the harvest season. Space your plants four–five feet (1.2–1.5 m.) apart and in rows that are nine–ten feet (2.75–3 m.) apart.

Care: Mulch around the base of the plant to help keep the soil moist and water lightly at least every other day. Pinch back any blossoms to prevent fruiting on newly set plants for the first year or two. This allows more plant growth and root establishment. Apply a light fertilizer in the second year of growth. You should not have to prune your plants for the first four years, but from then on pruning is needed to stimulate growth of new shoots for fruit bearing the following season.

Currants: As a child growing up, there was a mini farm across the street from our house. We politely called the owners of this mini farm 'Grandma and Grandpa Towland.' They grew several currant bushes; some were red currants and some were black currants. There were always plenty to go around to everyone in the neighborhood, so we had currant jelly for our toast all year long. Available to us are plants that produce pink and white currants that are less acidic. Currant canes lack spines on their stems and produce their pea-sized fruit in clusters of 8 to 30 berries.

Growing: Currant bushes prefer a protected site with full sun, although will do well in partial shade. They like a well-drained soil with plenty of organic matter and a soil pH of between 5.5 and 7.0. Plant currant bushes slightly deeper than they grew in their nursery container, and space them four to five feet (1.2–1.5 m) apart. Currant bushes are hardy to Zones 3–5. Water currant shrubs regularly to keep the soil moist from the time they begin growing in spring until after harvest. Plants that don't get enough water during spring and summer may develop mildew. Currants are self-fertile, meaning one plant will set fruit without any other currant cultivar nearby.

Care: Plants tend to lose their leaves when temperatures exceed 85 degrees F. (29.5 degrees C.) for an extended period of time. If you live in a climate with warm summer temperatures, a four-inch (ten cm.) layer of mulch helps keep the soil moist and cool. Pruning out dead wood annually is helpful for the plant in both maintaining its form and inducing a bigger, healthier harvest each year.

Gooseberries: The same mini farm I spoke of earlier also had gooseberry bushes. When the fruits were ripe, they reminded me of little, round, hairy, jelly fish hanging along the branches. Only a child's imagination could conjure up a picture such as this, I suppose, since we lived on a saltwater inlet that housed many varieties of jellyfish! Gooseberries also come in a realm of colors. The more common is a green fruit, but there are red, pink, purple, yellow, white, and even black varieties. The currant and gooseberry bush are closely related. However, where the currant stems lack spines, the gooseberry is thickly set with sharp spines. Instead of growing in clusters, gooseberry fruits are usually set in pairs.

Growing: Although the gooseberry is tolerant of a wide range of soil conditions, they prefer moisture-retentive, well-drained soil. Avoid very shallow, dry soils, as this can cause problems with American gooseberry mildew. Gooseberries are a hardy fruit and do particularly well in cool areas. The fruit slowly ripens on the bush while its flavor develops and matures. Despite very early flowering, they are reasonably resilient to harsh frosts, although planting in a frost pocket can reduce yields. They can tolerate some shade. The gooseberry bush is a straggly plant that can grow to five feet (1.5 m.) in height. It will, however, do well growing against a fence or wall, making harvesting more manageable. A gooseberry bush can live for 30 years, so be sure to plant it in its forever home. Like currants, gooseberries are also self-fertile.

Care: Unlike most plants, gooseberries require little feeding, preferring only a dash of potassium in early spring. Avoid giving them nitrogen, as this will encourage weak growth. Gooseberry bushes are also fairly drought tolerant and will do well for an extended period of time without being watered. Fruit is born on two–three-year-old wood, so prune out branches older than four years old. Prune out branches close to the ground to avoid fungal disease, and prune out any cross branching to give the bush a nice vase shape.

Grapes: Grapes are broken into three main types. The American which is the hardiest, the European that is grown for wine rather than a table grape, and the North American

native, Muscabine, that is thick-skinned and more suitable to being grown in the south. Plant breeders have crossed and recrossed these main types of grapes to satisfy almost every taste and use imaginable. The grape was first cultivated and domesticated 6000–8000 years ago in Western Asia. Grape growing is a very large industry worldwide. In 2012, 29,292 sq. miles (75,866 sq. kilometers) of land was used for growing this vigorous versatile vine. 71% of grape production was used for wine making, 27% for fresh fruit, and only 2% used for dried fruit (raisins). It is estimated that an additional 2% of land per year goes into the growing of grapes. Grapes grow in clusters of 15–300 berries and come in colors ranging from crimson, black, dark blue, yellow, green, orange, and pink.

Growing: Prior to planting a grape vine, be sure to have a trellis for these vigorous vines to grow along. Grapes prefer to be planted in a sunny location with well-drained, loose soil. They also like to have good air circulation. They bear their fruit on new shoots, so annual pruning is very important. They don't like to have any vegetative competition, so weeding is equally important, as they like to have warm roots. Most but not all grapevines are self-fertile, so be sure to check this out when purchasing your plants.

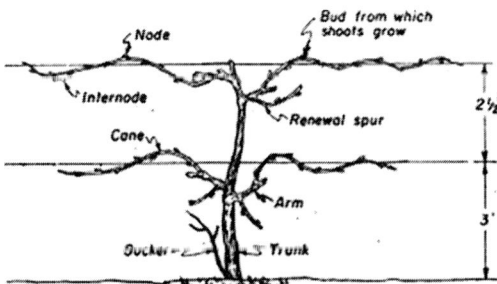

Care: The pruning of grapevines can be a little complicated, so instead of writing a descriptive entry on this topic, I have chosen to include a simple diagram. Proper pruning allows for a three-year training pattern. The first year, you can simply allow the vines to sprawl wherever they like, allowing them to build up strong roots. The second year, you can remove all but two shoots from the trunk. Tie the two chosen shoots to a training wire. In the third year, continue to prune off any shoots or suckers on the trunks, and cut the two chosen branches back to include about ten buds.

Raspberries: Raspberries are sometimes called brambles. There are two types of raspberry bushes; the summer-bearing variety which come in colors of red and yellow. They are the easiest to grow. The fall-bearing raspberry will produce fruits that are black, purple, red, and yellow. Blackberries and raspberries can often be confused, as they are similar in appearance, being made up of clusters of drupelets each containing a seed. The difference is in the cap. When the berry is picked, the raspberry has a hollow where the stem was, whereas the blackberry has a solid core.

Growing: Be it a bramble or a raspberry plant, support is required for these vigorous berry-producing canes. A simple hedgerow trellis system gives a good support and helps to reduce disease, molds, and mildews by allowing for better air circulation. A trellis makes for an easier harvest, easy pruning, and saves space in your backyard garden. These plants like a deep, sandy-loam, organic-rich soil in a sunny location.

Care: The two types of raspberries require different pruning methods. The fall-bearing variety like to simply be cut right to the ground after the leaves have fallen. Be sure to cut the canes off as close to the ground as possible. The summer-bearing variety are a little trickier. These berry plants produce fruit on second-year wood. Prune these two-year-old canes as close to the ground as possible after the harvest has finished. As you prune these canes out, remove any spindly canes at the same time. Look for two–four strong one-year-old canes per plant that have not yet produced. Tie these canes to the support wires on your trellis and cut them back to four–five feet (1.2–1.5 m.).

BUILDING a TRELLIS for BRAMBLES:

1. Set a sturdy eight-inch long 4'x4' cedar post at each end of your row to a maximum of 30 feet (nine m.).

2. Drill holes through the 4x4 post at three feet (.91 m.) and five feet (1.5 m.) intervals from ground level and insert a grapevine trellis anchor in each hole.

3. Cut two lengths of heavy wire slightly longer than the trellis and insert into the anchor.
4. Tie the new canes to the wires using zip ties, twist ties, or old, cut-up panty hose.

Rhubarb: Where I grew up in the '50s and '60s, there was a rhubarb plant in every backyard garden. Rhubarb is incredibly easy to grow, as it is a perennial, faithfully emerging from the cold soil every spring and dying back every winter. In those years, it was customary to have a dessert served every night at the family dinner table. Most commonly was stewed rhubarb with a custard sauce over top. Rhubarb pie was also a popular dessert, and because strawberries and rhubarb ripened at the same time, there was always a stock of strawberry/rhubarb jam preserved for the winter months.

Growing: Rhubarb prefers a sunny, well-drained soil in an out-of-the-way spot. It does not like to dry out even when it goes into dormancy. When the leaf stalks become thin, it is an indication that the plant needs to be divided so that each crown has only one–three buds.

Strawberries: Is there anything more fantastic than walking out to your backyard garden in June and picking the first, sweet, juicy strawberry and popping into your mouth? If you have never experienced this pleasure, growing strawberry plants is a must for you! Growing strawberries is incredibly easy, and they require very little space for the pleasure they give.

Growing: Strawberries are also broken into two categories; there is the June-bearing variety and the ever-bearing variety. The June-bearing variety produce a single large crop over three–four weeks in June and July. The ever-bearing produce a moderate crop in June and keep producing smaller crops through to the end of August and sometimes even into September. This variety also produce fewer runners than the June bearers and so are easier to control. Strawberries like a sandy loam soil with a little higher acid content but will thrive pretty much in any soil type as long as it has good drainage. Just be sure to plant them in a sunny location to maximize the sweet, juicy flavor.

Care: Strawberries don't like competition, so to reduce weed growth, apply a heavy layer of straw mulch on both sides of your planting row. This will also make pruning the runners or daughter plants off much easier. To build a healthy, strong root system, pick off the blossoms in the first year. Continue to prune the runners off. Strawberries produce the best in their second and third years. After the third year, they start to weaken. To continue with a strong harvest year after year, remove a row of older, weaker plants and replace them with the removed daughter plants.

➢ Companion Planting

The topic of **companion planting** was, for a long time, based on 'gardening folklore,' referring to observations among gardening peoples for eons and passed down from generation to generation. Much of these myths and legends was based on annual observation of the moon cycles and mixed with a lot of common sense. Even today, many farmers and gardeners do their planting based on the moon's cycle. These observant gardeners, from eons ago, also noted that some plants tended to grow and produce better when planted near others. So was born the realistic belief of **'Companion Planting.'** Even though this topic started out as Folklore, there is now scientific proof that not all is based on legends and myths. For instance, it has been found that by masking the odor of some plants with the stronger scent of marigolds, nasturtium, and mints, it will confuse and deter pests. Other crops are planted as a trap to draw pests away from the more-lucrative crops.

Last year, I experienced the result, or rather the negative result, of not abiding to a companion-planting list. Somehow or another, I had forgotten to start my Brussels-sprout seeds and so went to my local nursery and purchased a few seedling plants. I looked around my garden space and chose to plant these Brussels sprouts behind my Early Girl Tomato plant. I didn't even think to refer to a companion-plant list. After a week or so, I noticed the tomato plant was looking a little sickly. I thought maybe it needed a boost of fertilizer and so I watered it with diluted liquid seaweed. That poor tomato plant got sicker and sicker and eventually died. I wondered about it for the remainder of the summer. Well, as I was compiling the following companion-plant list, I noticed that tomatoes don't like Brussels sprouts. I can think of no other reason why that Early Girl Tomato plant died when all of my other tomato plants thrived and were not in the area of the Brussels sprouts.

Companion Plant List		
Plant	**Like**	**Dislike**
Basil	Tomato, Sweet Peppers	Rue, Anise
Beets	Beets, Broccoli, Cabbage, Carrots, Cauliflower, Celery, Corn, Cucumber, Eggplant, Marigold, Pea, Potato, Radish, Strawberry, Summer Savoury, Tomato	Onion, Garlic, Fennel, Pepper, Sunflower
Broccoli	Beet, Celery, Cucumber, Dill, Garlic, Lettuce, Mint, Nasturtium, Onion, Potato, Rosemary, Sage, Spinach, Chard	Tomato, Beans, Pea, Squash, Strawberry
Borage	Strawberry, Fruit Trees	
Cabbage	Beans, Celery, Cucumber, Dill, Kale, Lettuce, Onion, Potato, Sage, Spinach, Thyme	Broccoli, Cauliflower, Strawberry, Tomato
Carrot	Beans, Lettuce, Chives, Onion, Leek, Pea, Radish, Rosemary, Sage, Tomato	Anise, Dill, Parsley
Cauliflower	Beans, Celery, Onion	Peas, Strawberry, Tomato
Celery	Leek, Tomato, Bush Bean, Cauliflower, Cabbage	
Chard	Root Crops, Lettuce, Radish, Celery, Mint	
Chive	Carrot, Apple Trees	Peas, Beans
Cilantro	Anise, Carrot, Radish, Chard	Fennel
Corn	Beans, Cucumber, Lettuce, Pea, Potato, Pumpkin, Squash, Melons, Marigold, Sunflower	Tomato
Cucumber	Beans, Cabbage, Cauliflower, Corn, Lettuce, Pea, Radish, Sunflower	Potato, Aromatic Herbs

Eggplant	Beans, Marigolds, Peas Peppers, Spinach, Thyme	Fennel, Potato, Tomato
Garlic	Beets, Broccoli, Cauliflower, Cabbage, Brussels Sprouts, Celery, Lettuce, Potatoes Tomatoes, Strawberry	Peas, Beans
Kale	Cabbage, Dill, Potatoes, Rosemary, Sage	Strawberries, Tomatoes
Lettuce	Asparagus, Beets, Brussels Sprouts, Cabbage, Carrots, Corn, Cucumbers, Eggplant, Onions, Peas, Potatoes, Radishes, Spinach, Strawberries, Sunflowers, Tomatoes	Broccoli
Lettuce	Asparagus, Beets, Brussels Sprouts, Cabbage, Carrots, Corn, Cucumbers, Eggplant, Onions, Peas, Potatoes, Radishes, Spinach, Strawberries, Sunflowers, Tomatoes	Broccoli
Melons	Corn, Marigold, Nasturtiums, Peas, Pumpkin, Radish, Sunflowers, Tomatoes	Cucumbers, Potatoes
Onions	Beets, Broccoli, Cabbage, Carrot, Leek, Lettuce, Peppers, Potatoes, Spinach, Tomatoes	Beans, Peas, Sage
Parsnip	Onions, Radish, Peppers Beans, Peas	

*The West Coast Seed catalogue and website offer some interesting information on the topic of companion planting.

➤ Edible Flowers

Having edible flowers in our diet is nothing new. The Ancient Greeks and Romans grew flowers in their gardens specifically to add an elegant flair to their foods. Throughout history, flowers have been used in the Chinese, Middle Eastern, and Indian cuisine. This beautiful habit was lost but regained its popularity in the Victorian era. And then it once again became a lost art, but in our modern, exotic cuisine, it has been revived and has gained a novel popularity.

Edible flowers can be annuals (a plant that germinates, grows, flowers, sets seed, and dies in one growing season), biennials (a plant that completes its life cycle in two years), perennials (a plant that faithfully returns year after year), and shrubs (a plant with multiple woody stems).

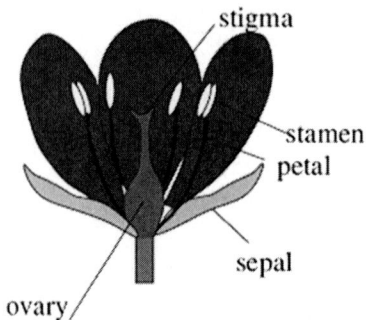

We have touched briefly on the topic of edible flowers when we talked about stuffed squash blossoms and the cooling cucumber taste of borage flowers. Edible flowers add a very tasty and beautiful twist to any type of salad. They also make a lovely garnish, but they are not limited to making a meal look beautiful. Edible flowers can be added to stir-fries and other dishes for their unique taste and colors too. A word of warning here though; some garden flowers have toxic qualities, so be sure you know what you are using in your meals. Flowers are best picked in the early morning, and be sure to give them a good swish in cool water to dislodge any insects that may be lurking. Then gently place them on a damp paper towel and place in an airtight container in the fridge until ready to use. To prepare them, remove the stamens and pistils which contain pollen prior to eating, as the pollen can cause allergies to sensitive people.

Don't use any flowers that have been sprayed with pesticides or herbicides either. You probably have some edibles in your flower garden right now, but it doesn't hurt to scatter some seed into your vegetable garden to grow some of these decorative flowers.

➢ List of Edible Flowers

Agastache (Licorice Mint)

Taste: Leaves and flowers tastes of a mild licorice flavor.

Description: Tall spikes of edible lavender-colored flowers growing to a height of four feet (1.2 m.). An attractant for butterflies, hummingbirds, and bees. Agastache is a perennial, returning year after year, and can be started from seed or root division.

Uses: Use in fruit or vegetable salads. The flowers and leaves can be crystalized for decorations on ice cream, cakes, or other dessert dishes. Makes a wonderful medicinal tea.

Bachelor Button (AKA Cornflower or Centaurea)

Taste: Flowers have a sweet taste.

Description: Centaurea is an annual plant that readily reseeds itself. The plant has medium-sized, fluffy but orderly aster-like flowers that come in shades of blue, pink, purple, and white. The stems are long and sparse with narrow gray/green leaves.

Uses: Use as a garnish for vegetable platters. Great in fruit salads. Can be crystalized and used as a decoration on desserts. It also makes a delightful cut flower.

Basil (Flowers and Leaves)

Taste: The flowers have a milder flavor than the leaves.

Description: Grown for its leaves, this annual is easy to start from seed. As the flowers form on the plants, the production of the leaves slows. The white and purple flowers can then be snipped off and used.

Uses: Sprinkle on salads of fresh fruit or green salads. Great garnish for pasta dishes, cheese and meat platters, and a pizza topping. They can also be used in pesto. Great for teas.

Bean (Flower)

Taste: A very mild bean flavor.

Description: An annual garden vegetable grown for the seedpods or the seeds within the pods. It grows in a bush form or vining form and is started easily from seed. Green and yellow beans have white flowers, purple beans have purple flowers, and many runner beans have orange flowers.

Uses: Use in meat dishes, a topping for pasta and pizza, and a colorful twist in vegetable salads.

Begonia (Tuberous and Wax Varieties)

Taste: These flowers have a tart taste with a succulent, juicy texture with an added slightly citrus flavor.

Description: Both the tuberous and the wax begonia are annuals. The wax variety can be started from seed, but the tuberous are best started from a tuber. The tuberous variety have very showy, large double and single flowers of peach, yellow, orange, pink, red, and creamy white. The wax variety have small, single flowers of pinks, reds, and whites with a large clump of yellow pistils in the center.

Uses: The flowers can either be cooked or eaten raw in stir-fries or salads. They pair beautifully with seafood. They look lovely in cocktails and make a fine finishing touch for desserts. They crystalize nicely for dessert decorations.

Borage (Flower Only)
Taste: A cool cucumber taste.

Description: The borage plant is an annual that readily reseeds itself. The whole plant is rather rough in nature with white prickles on the stems. Its flowers, however, are a lovely pale pink when they first open and later turn into an intense, bright sky-blue, five-petaled star shape. One of the few true-blue garden flowers. The borage flower is also an attractant to bees and butterflies.

Uses: Freeze in ice cubes to float in summer drinks. Great in fresh fruit salads or green salads. A great garnish for ice cream and other desserts. They can be crystalized for dessert decorations.

Broccoli (Flower)
Taste: A mild broccoli taste.

Description: Broccoli is an annual garden vegetable grown for the massive clumps of flower buds, but if your broccoli goes to flower, you don't have to throw it away. Use these perfect four-petaled, delicate, white blossoms with a bright yellow center.

Uses: Use in vegetable salads or as a garnish on vegetable, meat, and cheese platters.

Calendula (Petals Only)
Taste: Peppery citrus flavor with a mild tartness.

Description: This plant that grows to a height of about 24 inches (61 cm.) is a reseeding annual and, depending on your climatic zone, can be considered to be a biennial. It has masses of bright orange and yellow daisy-like flowers.

Uses: Remove the petals as a substitute for saffron. Use in pasta and rice dishes, soups, scrambled eggs, garnishes, and spreads.

Carnation (AKA Clove Pink) (Petals Only) A Member of the Dianthus Family Taste: A mild, sweet, nutmeg flavor with a crunchy texture.

Description: This carnation flower is made up of many petals which form a pompom. It is a long-lasting herbaceous perennial and can be started by direct sowing seed in spring. It comes in soft pinks, whites, reds, mauves, and purple shades.

Uses: Makes a beautiful garnish for desserts, salads, and aspics. Can be crystalized for cake and dessert decoration. Use in cheesecakes and Crème Brûlée.

Chamomile (Leaves and Flowers Can Be Used)
Taste: A sweet, mild, green-apple flavor with a hint of pineapple.

Description: This is a hardy, self-seeding annual with sweet, little, white, daisy flowers that have a yellow center.

Uses: The leaves and petals can be dried or used fresh in teas, salads, soups, or just as a garnish.

Chives (Flowers, Stems, and Leaves Can Be Used)
Taste: A delicate onion flavor.

Description: We all know the green stem of the chive is edible, but so are the pretty, little, puffball-like flower head. The flower is a cluster of florets that can be pulled apart. Each is its own individual flower.

Uses: Pull the flower apart and use in savory dishes and soups. Put in mashed potatoes or devilled eggs. You can even add them to biscuits or try them in cream sauces.

Chrysanthemum (Leaves and Flowers, Remove the Flower Base)

Taste: Tangy, peppery flavor with a mild cauliflower taste.

Description: This is a show-stopping fall-flowering perennial in colors of orange, yellow, pink, red, mauve, burgundy, white, and even green. Double flowers, single flowers, a shape and size for everyone. Best to start from cuttings in the spring for fall-blooming flowers.

Uses: Beautiful in fruit salads. Use in vinegars, adds interest to stir-fries, and makes a show-stopping garnish to cheese, egg, meat, and vegetable platters.

Cosmos (Flower)

Taste: A mild mango-like flavor.

Description: An annual that readily reseeds. The flowers are made up of eight petals and come in shades of pinks, purples, whites, some with frilly edges, some with smooth edges.

Uses: Use the whole flower or just the petals to add a flair to fruit salad. They can be crystalized to use on ice cream, cake decoration, and other dessert dishes. Place on fresh food platters as a stunning garnish.

Cucumber

Taste: A Fresh, Mild, Cucumber Flavor.

Description: Pretty, little, delicate, five-petaled, yellow flowers growing on an annual vine.

Uses: Use the male flowers, as it is the female flowers that bear the cucumber fruit. These dainty flowers look very pretty floating on summer drinks. They make a great little appetizer when gently stuffed, or simply place in fresh salads.

Dames Rocket (Leaves and Flowers)

Taste: Both flowers and leaves have a bitter taste so should be used sparingly.

Description: Pretty, little, sweet-smelling, four-petaled flowers come in shades of purple, violet, pink, and white. It can be invasive with its self-seeding quality.

Uses: Use in both fruit salads and green salads or as a garnish for fresh food platters.

Dandelion (Leaves and Flower Petals)

Taste: The flowers have a surprisingly sweet taste, much like honey, with a hint of lemon. No wonder bees like them so much.

Description: Not the type of plant that one would grow intentionally, but if you have any growing in the lawn that have not been subjected to chemical sprays, they can be used for a few purposes.

Uses: The dandelion flower can be turned into a bright yellow jelly for toast. It makes an excellent white wine and also a liqueur. The petals can be sprinkled on salads and the greens can be sautéed, added to soups and stews, or dried for a tea.

Daylily (Buds, Flowers, Young Shoots, and Tubers)

Taste: The buds taste slightly of radish and green bean. The tubers of sweet turnip. The shoots have a green bean/onion flavor and the flowers have a sweet, pungent taste.

Description: Stunning, large, vase-shaped flowers ranging in color from pink, yellow, orange, red, and purple, they come in solid colors and variegated patterns. Daylily is a tuberous perennial plant returning year after year as long it is divided every few years.

Uses: The buds can be sautéed and served as a side dish. The tubers can be treated as young fingerling potatoes. The new shoots add crunch to salads, stir fries, soups, stews, and casseroles. The decorative prize is the flower. Remove the green base before using in salads and soups. They can be battered and deep fried or stuffed with cottage cheese salad and cracker spreads. Or fill them with sweet cream fillings for a surprise dessert.

Flax (Flower)

Taste: A sweet cabbage-like flavor.

Description: Flax flowers are a perfect, five-petaled, pale, sky-blue color. We know of flax seed and flax-seed oil, but these delicate flowers are also edible. They readily reseed but are not invasive.

Uses: The seeds can be harvested and sprouted for use in salads, or the delicate flowers can be used as a garnish on egg, fruit, meat, and vegetable platters.

Fuchsia (Flowers and Berries)

Taste: The berries have a lemony tart flavor. The flowers have a crunchy texture with a juicy tang.

Description: This plant is considered to be a tender shrub, but it can also be trained to be an indoor ornamental tree. The shrub form is mostly grown for container gardening and hanging baskets. These stunning droplet flowers come in a range of pinks, rich purples, whites, and fuchsia colors. The emerging berries are a deep purple. Fuchsias are fairly easy to propagate by cuttings.

Uses: The beautiful petals can be frozen in ice cubes to float in summer drinks. They make an exotic garnish for cheese, meat. and vegetable platters.

Garlic (Buds and Flowers)

Taste: A mild garlic flavor.

Description: Long before the garlic bulbs are ready to be harvested, the hard neck variety of garlic plants bud and flower. The buds are called garlic scapes which can be used, or you can wait for the buds to flower and use the florets. By removing the buds and flowers, the plant will put its energy into the bulb, so by using the flowering part, it is beneficial all around.

Uses: Garlic scapes make a wonderful pesto. The flowers, once open, are a whitish-pink color and can be added to salads, stir-fries, baked breads and biscuits, or just as a garnish. You can also dehydrate them, grind them up, and add them to table salt.

Geranium (Pelargonium or Scented Geranium Only) (Flowers and Leaves)

Taste: Depending on the variety, flavors vary. Some have a citrus flavor, while others can taste of almond, mint, peach, and nutmeg.

Description: The scented geranium is grown for its fragrant leaves. The small, delicate flowers come in hues of pink, mauve, and purple. The plants can be started from seed or cuttings.

Uses: Use in jams, jellies, and syrups. The flowers and leaves can be used in vinegars. Try the flowers in sweet cream sauces or in baked goods.

Gladiolus

Taste: A vague lettuce-like flavor.

Description: If you want a rainbow of colors, grow gladiolus. They come in every color imaginable with masses of funnel-shaped flowers growing up a large, sturdy stalk. They are grown from tender bulbs planted in the spring. The bulbs need to be lifted prior to frost and stored in a cool, dry environment to preserve for next year's plantings.

Uses: What the flowers lack in taste is made up for in elegant color. Because of their shape, they make an excellent receptacle for cream and seafood spreads. They can be used in stir-fries and will brighten up fruit and vegetable salads.

Hibiscus (Rose of Sharon)
Taste: A light, nutty flavor.

Description: The Rose of Sharon is a deciduous shrub growing about 12 feet (3.6 m.) tall. Its late summer flowers come in colors of pink, white, burgundy, and blue.

Uses: These pastel flowers make a beautiful presentation dish for sweet and savory spreads. Use them for an eye-popping garnish, or chop them up and add them to salads and quiche. They crystalize nicely for cake and dessert decorations.

Hollyhock (Petals Only)
Taste: No flavor.

Description: This is an herbaceous biennial or short-lived perennial which will sometimes reseed. Beautiful, large, single or double flowers of yellow, white, pink, and purple grow on stems four–eight feet (1.2–2.5 m.) tall. Start seeds indoors in early spring.

Uses: Use as a garnish. Sprinkle the petals over fruit salads or over ice-cream desserts.

Honeysuckle (Flowers Only)

Taste: Sweet honey taste. I remember, as a child, picking these tubular flowers and sucking the sweetness out of them.

Description: Honeysuckle is either an upright woody shrub or a vining shrub. Its long, tubular flowers of oranges, yellows, and pastel pinks are an attractant to bees, butterflies, and hummingbirds. Honeysuckle can be started by cuttings.

Uses: Use to make jellies and syrups or simply as a sweet-tasting garnish.

Impatiens (Flowers Only)

Taste: Sweet sugary taste.

Description: Pretty, little, single and double flowers of pinks, orange, peach, white, and mauve commonly grown as a bedding or hanging basket plant. Impatiens is an annual and seeds should be started indoors in early spring.

Uses: Use to float in summer drinks. Toss in fruit salads or use as a garnish. Crystalize for use on cakes, ice cream, and other desserts.

Johnny Jump-Up (Viola Sp.)

Taste: Has a mild, wintergreen taste.

Description: This has got to be the happiest flower in the garden. It is a miniature smiling parsley of white, yellow, and purple that readily reseeds itself.

Uses: A happy addition to fruit salads. One of the best to crystalize for cake, ice cream, and dessert decoration. Float in summer drinks or spruce up fresh-food platters.

Lavender (Flowers and Stalks)
Taste: Has a sweet, mild, herb flavor and is very aromatic.

Description: Blue/lavender and pink flowers on long stems above bluey green leaves. Lavender is a perennial and can be started by seed or root division.

Uses: The whole stem with flowers attached can be crystalized for cake decoration. It is a great addition to fruit salads. Try a lavender lemonade. Sprinkle the flowers over ice cream for an added zing.

Lilac (Flowers)
Taste: The scent of the flowers does not compare to the taste which is a slight, pungent, lemony flavor.

DESCRIPTION: This deciduous, woody shrub produces a mass of small flowers on a panicle. They are highly scented and come in blue, mauve, purple, pink, and white.

USES: The flower crystalizes beautifully for cake and dessert decorations. It can be added to fruit salads, floated in summer drinks, or used as a garnish on fruit platters and for teas.

Marigold

Taste: The flowers have a tangy, citrus flavor.

Description: These single and double flowers are a long-lasting brightness of red, yellow, and orange. Marigold is an annual plant that readily reseeds itself and acts as an insect repellant.

Uses: Use them for a great zing to appetizers. They make an interesting garnish to meat, vegetable, and fruit trays. Adds a new dimension to fruit salad and green salads.

Monarda (Bee Balm) (Flowers and Leaves)

Taste: The flavor is like a mint.

Description: Bee Balm is a bee and hummingbird-attractant perennial growing three–four feet (1–1.2 m) in height. The flowers are made up of tubular petals coming in colors of pink, purple, and red.

Uses: Use the petals to decorate cakes and other fine desserts. Float them in fancy drinks and to add a flair to salads. The leaves can be dried.

Nasturtium (Leaves, Flowers, and Seeds)

Taste: The buds have a strong, peppery flavor, whereas the petals have a sweet, mild, peppery taste.

Description: These easy-to-grow annuals are best known for their bright colors of yellow, orange, and red. There are trailing varieties and compact-bush varieties. Direct sow in late spring.

Uses: Stuff the open flowers with mousse or spreads. Chop the leaves and petals to use in salads, stir-fries, and pasta dishes. The flowers make an exotic vinegar. Use the buds on a pizza. The seeds, when pickled, taste and look just like capers.

Pansy (Petals Only)
Taste: The blue flowers have a mild, wintergreen flavor. The others have a sweet, mild, grassy flavor.

Description: These cheerful, easy-to-grow annuals come in shades of yellow, blue, burgundy, white, and pink. They always have a smiling face and readily reseed themselves.

Uses: Remove the stamens and pistils prior to using as a garnish. Add them to fruit salads, soups, and green salads. They crystalize nicely for use as cake and other dessert decorations, or float them in summer drinks.

Pinks (Dianthus)
Taste: These have a colorful, sweet taste of mild clove.

Description: Pinks are basically a single or semi-double carnation. They have vibrant, unique, variegated patterns of white, pink, magenta, and red.

Uses: These flowers, once the bitter, white base has been removed, can be steeped in wine. They crystalize beautifully for cake decoration. Float them in summer citrus cocktail drinks or as a garnish for salads.

PEA (Shoots, Tendrils, and Flowers) (Edible Vegetable Pea Only. Decorative Sweet Peas Are Toxic)

Taste: A sweet, delicate, mild pea flavor with a crunchy texture.

Description: Flowers are white, growing on long stems covered by tendrils.

Uses: Use in salads. They are a great addition to fish dishes.

Peony (Petals Only)

Taste: These have an exotic, sweet taste.

Description: These spring-flowering perennials have large, double, pompom-like flowers in pink, soft white, and occasionally pale yellow.

Uses: Dry the petals for teas or sprinkle over fruit salads. Float them in summer drinks and crystalize them for cake and other pastry decorations.

Pepper (Flowers)

Taste: They have a mild, bell-pepper flavor.

Description: This heat-loving annual plant is grown mainly for the fruit it bears, but the flowers are also edible. Depending on the variety, the flowers come in dark purple, white, and even green. Seed should be started indoors in early spring.

Uses: Use these pretty little blossoms in summer cocktails, green salads, and as a garnish on cheese and meat platters.

Phlox (Perennial Variety Only, Not the Creeping Variety)

Taste: A pleasant, spicy, peppery taste.

Description: Flowers form on long-stemmed panicles and come in shades of pinks, mauves, whites, and blue. These perennial plants are best started by root division but can also be started by seed.

Uses: The blossoms are used mostly in fruit salads but also make a lovely garnish. Crystalize for use as cake decorations.

Primrose (Petals Only)

Taste: Sweet and bland.

Description: Primula or primrose are one of the first-blooming perennials of spring. They come in a wide range of variegated shades of soft white, yellow, pink, red, purple, and blue. You can use root division for propagation or start seeds indoors in early spring.

Uses: The buds can be steamed as a side dish or pickled. The petals can be added to salads and stir fries. They make a beautiful garnish and crystalize for dessert decoration.

Roses (Petals)

Taste: The taste is according to the flower color ranging from strawberry, green apple, fruits, and mint flavors.

Description: I think roses are the most popular flower worldwide, and no wonder. This woody shrub has single blossoms, double blossoms, miniature blossoms in every color under the sun. There are wee miniature varieties growing only a few inches in height, shrub varieties growing to four feet (1.2 m.) in height and climbing varieties. Roses are started by stem cuttings.

Uses: Use as a garnish for fancy desserts. Freeze in ice cubes, float in summer drinks. Make syrups, jellies, butters, and sweet spreads. Crystalize for cake and other pastry decorations.

Snapdragon
Taste: The taste is bland to bitter, depending on the color.

Description: This unusual dragon-faced flower comes in shades of yellow, pink, white, and mauve on long stems. It is an annual that can easily be started by seed and will readily reseed itself.

Uses: The flower is edible, but because of its unpleasant flavor, it is best used as a garnish to add a new dimension to cheese, egg, fruit, meat, and vegetable platters.

Squash (Use Male Flowers so as Not to Lose the Fruit from the Female Flowers.)
Taste: They have a sweet zucchini taste with a tender texture.

Description: Bright yellow, large, open, tubular flowers from pumpkin plants to zucchini plants.

Uses: Most commonly stuffed with cheese, seafood, meat, and herbs to use as an appetizer. Also, can be battered and deep fried. Try as a topping for pizza and pasta dishes.

Sunflower (Known Mostly for the Seeds)

Taste: They have a bitter artichoke flavor.

Description: Very large, open, daisy-like flowers on tall stalks. Can be started by seed outdoors in spring.

Uses: Pull a few petals from the large flowers to use in soups and salads.

Sweet William (Dianthus)

Taste: The flowers have a sweet clove like taste and are very aromatic.

Description: Dense clusters of flowers grow atop a long stem in colors of pink, white, red, and purple on this biennial plant. Many are in a variegated pattern. Sweet William readily seeds itself but not in an invasive manner.

Uses: Use these pretty little flowers as a garnish on fruit and cheese platters. They crystalize very well to be used on cake and ice-cream desserts. Or use uncrystallized to decorate cupcakes and other pastries.

Yucca

Taste: These flowers have an unexpected, mild, sweet taste with a crunchy texture.

Description: Large bell-shaped flowers in a creamy white color grow on large four–five-foot (1.2–1.5 m.) stems amongst sharp, sword-like leaves on this perennial plant.

Uses: Because of the bell shape, they act as a great receptacle for sweet cream desserts or appetizers. They give fruit salads a special crunch and work well for a garnish on cheese, egg, and fruit platters.

➢ Draw Your Garden

So, you should be armed with enough information now to start drawing your garden plan on your grid paper. Following are examples of the garden plan that I used in 2017 and the one I have done up for the 2018 gardening season as an example for you. (You don't have to get as detailed as me). As you can see, you can fit a lot of crop into a small garden area when using the square-foot gardening method. For example, my total backyard vegetable, herb, and fruit-growing area consists of 264 square feet. In that space I can grow:

2 Green Zebra Tomato Plants	8 Purple Peacock Pole Beans	7 Parsley
2 Black Krim Tomato Plants	3 Cabbage	3 Basil
4 Red Zebra Tomato Plants	12 Pickling Cucumber	5 Rosemary
4 Yellow Cherry Tomato	12 Bush Beans	6 Broccoli
4 Red Cherry Tomato	40 Swiss Chard	200 Onions
4 Roma Tomato	160 Carrots	3 Thyme
48 Green Onions	48 Beets	3 Oregano
27 Radishes	4 Brussels Sprouts	1 Mint
24 Lettuce	4 Acorn Squash	3 Horseradish
4 Cauliflower	12 Hot Peppers	3 Grapevines
2 Long English Cucumbers	8 Sweet Peppers	16 Potatoes
1 Sage	16 Corn	16 Scarlet Runner Beans
60 Garlic	16 Pea	

So, let's get started!

2017

Need: onion sets
    seed potatoes
    broccoli
    brussels sprouts
    cabbage
    cauliflower

grapes

grapes

purple
peacock
beans

onions & horseradish

peas

walk way

Seeds: Greenhouse
·cauliflower
·pickling cuc.
·seedless cuc.
·peppers
·tomatoes
·Basil
·Broccoli
·Brussels Sprouts
·Cabbage

Herb Beds

carrots

cabbage
Brussels sprouts

broccoli

walk way   move trellis

Seeds:
Straight sow:
·Beets
·Carrots on paper
·Corn
·Romaine
·Swiss Chard
·Peas
·Beans

peppers

Parsley   Rosemary
        Herbs
12 homemade   4 early
pickling cucs.   fortune cuc.
        Herbs
        Basil

walk way

Need to purchase:
Broccoli
Brussels Sprouts
Beet seeds
Swiss Chard seeds
Basil Seeds

thyme

4 Roma tomato   2 eating tomatoes   cherry tomatoes

133

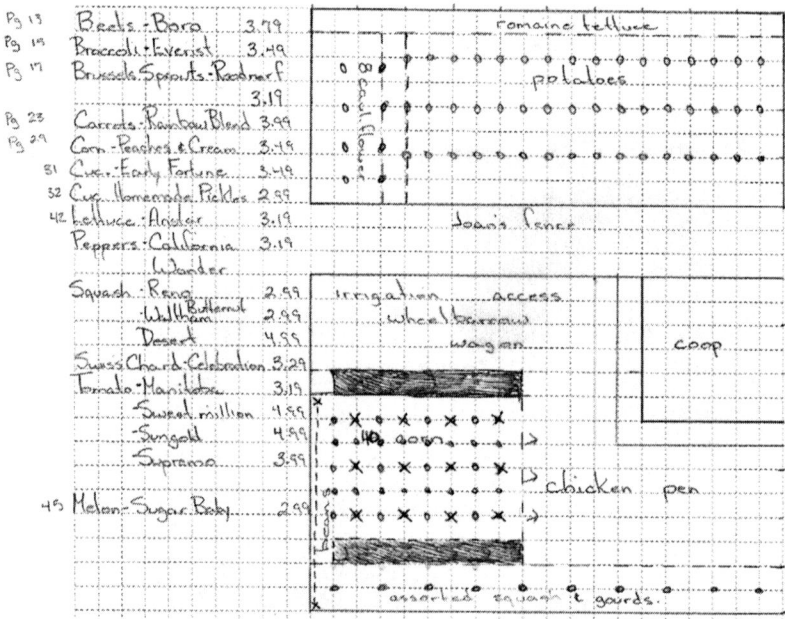

Pg 13   Beets - Boro   3.79
Pg 15   Broccoli - Everist   3.49
Pg 17   Brussels Sprouts - Roodner f
                    3.19
Pg 23   Carrots - Rainbow Blend   3.99
Pg 29   Corn - Peaches & Cream   3.49
   31   Cuc - Early Fortune   3.49
   32   Cuc - Homemade Pickles   2.99
   42   Lettuce - Anster   3.19
       Peppers - California   3.19
           Wonder
       Squash - Rang   2.59
           Waltham Butternut   2.99
           Desert   4.55
       Swiss Chard - Celebration   3.29
       Tomato - Manitoba   3.15
           Sweet million   4.55
           - Sungold   4.99
           - Suprema   3.59
   45   Melon - Sugar Baby   2.99

romaine lettuce

potatoes

Joan's fence

irrigation   access
wheelbarrow
wagon

coop

40 corn

chicken pen

assorted squash & gourds

Gourds   Stokes
     West Coast Seeds
D. Cicco   BR210   Broccoli   3.19   Pg 15
Igor   BS219   Brussels Sprts 4.99   Pg 17
Merlin   BT179   Beets   3.39   Pg 13
Fordhook   SW750   Chard   2.99   Pg 72
Royal Blend   FL3281   Sweet Pea   2.99   Pg 103
Sweet Basil   HR1034   2.99   Pg 82
Cilantro   HR1074   3.19   Pg 84
                 24.93

2011

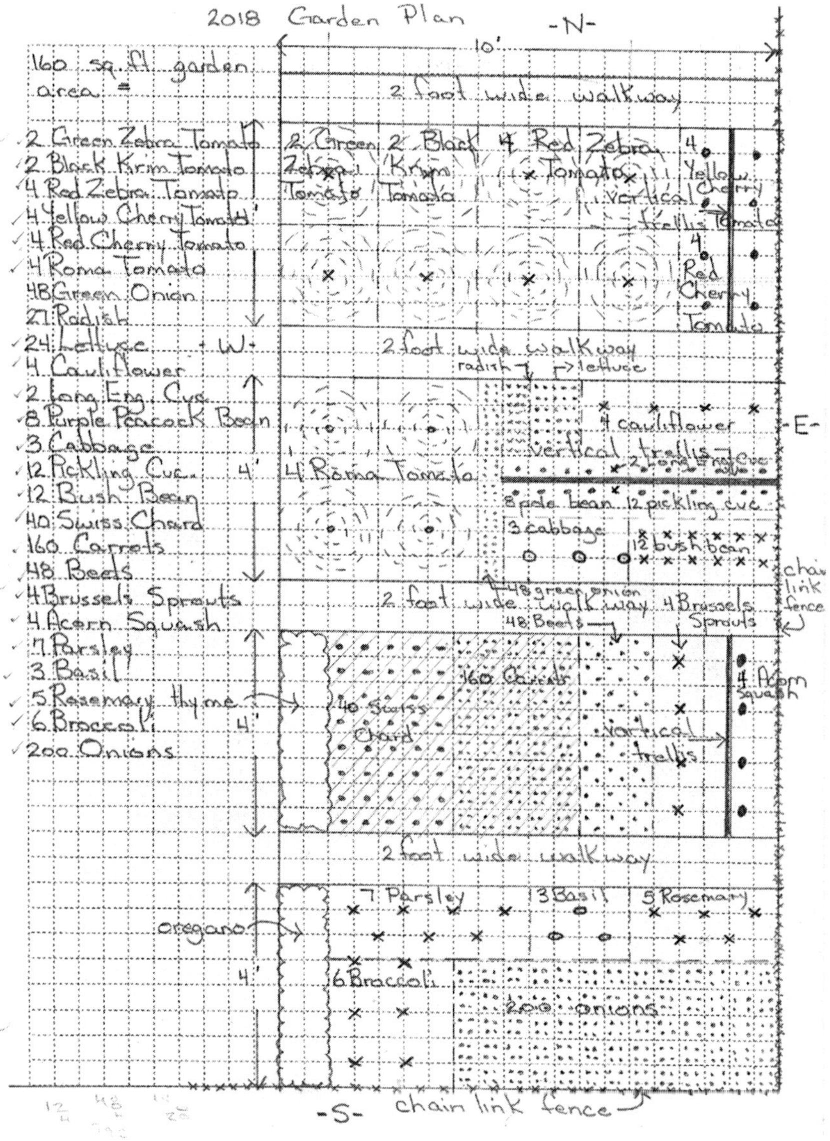

2018 Garden Plan   -N-

160 sq. ft. garden area =

- 2 Green Zebra Tomato
- 2 Black Krim Tomato
- 4 Red Zebra Tomato
- 4 Yellow Cherry Tomato
- 4 Red Cherry Tomato
- 4 Roma Tomato
- 48 Green Onion
- 21 Radish
- 24 Lettuce
- 4 Cauliflower
- 2 Long Eng. Cuc.
- 8 Purple Peacock Bean
- 3 Cabbage
- 12 Pickling Cuc.
- 12 Bush Bean
- 40 Swiss Chard
- 160 Carrots
- 48 Beets
- 4 Brussels Sprouts
- 4 Acorn Squash
- 7 Parsley
- 3 Basil
- 5 Rosemary thyme
- 6 Broccoli
- 200 Onions

-W-

10'

2 foot wide walkway

2 Green 2 Black 4 Red Zebra
Zebra Krim Tomato
Tomato Tomato

4
Yellow
Cherry
vertical trellis Tomato

4
Red
Cherry
Tomato

2 foot wide walkway
radish → ← lettuce

4 cauliflower

vertical trellis
8 pole bean 12 pickling cuc.
3 cabbage
12 bush bean

4 Roma Tomato

4'

2 foot wide walkway
48 green onion   4 Brussels Sprouts
48 Beets →

40 Swiss Chard

160 Carrots

4 Acorn Squash

vertical trellis →

4'

chain link fence

-E-

2 foot wide walkway

7 Parsley   3 Basil   5 Rosemary

oregano →

6 Broccoli

200 onions

4'

-S-   chain link fence

135

Chapter Five
Planting Your Garden

➤ Starting Seeds

For some of you planting your garden will start with starting seeds indoors on heat and under light, so let's start with that. Some good reasons for starting your own seeds is you have a bigger variety of plant material available to you than you do if you purchase seedlings at a garden center. It is more cost effective and you know that your plants have not been soaked in a mixture of chemicals.

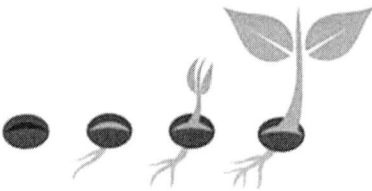

Seeds are a living and, yes, breathing container full of the genetic makeup of its particular species from generations long past. Most seeds are viable for one–three years if stored in a cool, dry area, although some are only good for one year and others can remain viable for 100s of years. In order to release the genetics from these amazing little containers, moisture and warmth is required. When a seed absorbs moisture is in a warm environment, it swells up and the outer coat ruptures. The growth hormones deep inside the seed go into action by encouraging growth of new tissue. Some seeds only require a few days for this process to take place, while others require a few weeks. Once this process has taken place, it is important to keep these newly sprouted gems happy. They like their home to be a porous-growing medium that is kept evenly moist at all times. They also need air movement to prevent what is called

'Damping off.' Damping off is a fungal disease that causes the new sprouts to rot off at soil level. Some seeds need light in order to germinate, and some require darkness, so it is important to read the back of your seed package to determine the likes and dislikes of each variety. It is also very important to keep the growing medium at a regulated temperature. Most seeds like to be in a cozy temperature of between 75–85 degrees F. (24–29 degrees C.).

You can make your own growing medium by mixing equal portions of peat moss, vermiculite, and perlite if you have the space to mix and store it, but I find it much easier to purchase a bag of seed starting mix at my local garden center. There are several types of soil-holding containers available on the market, some of which are peat pots, peat pellets, individual plastic containers of various shapes and sizes, and paper pots. The peat and paper containers are biodegradable, breaking down in the soil when planted out. My personal preference are the plastic containers, as they can be reused year after year as long as they are cleaned and sanitized and made ready for the next growing season.

You don't need a big, fancy greenhouse to germinate your own seeds. For years I used a shelf on my bookcase. I placed plastic, draining flats on solid plastic-boot trays on the shelf and hung a four-foot long, florescent light with blue spectrum light tubes over top of the flats full of growing medium. The light was mounted on a chain that I could raise up as the plants grew and I put it on a timer so the seedlings had the allocated amount of daily light for optimum growth. I didn't have a bottom heat source but kept my house at around 70 degrees F. (20 degrees C.) and never had much of a problem with the germination or growth process. I now have a better situation out in the backyard shed. I have a four-foot long heating mat on a long shelf with natural light from two, large windows. Once the germination has taken place, I put the sprouted seed in a mini five-shelved plastic greenhouse atop the heating mat, and each shelf is outfitted with a grow light on a timer. I place a small fan on the shelf to keep the air moving. This system works very well, giving me more space for transplanting. You can set up a small area in a basement, carport, or even in a closet space as long as you have an electrical source nearby.

Once your seeds have germinated, have started to get a good solid root structure, and are putting out the first true leaves (not just the first two cotyledon leaves), you will have to transplant them into a larger container. Also, by transplanting, you have the opportunity to choose the stronger plants and discard the weaker ones. There are enough nutrients in the seed cavity to feed your seedlings up until this stage. However, as they grow, you will have to start feeding these little guys now, as well as keeping them warm and moist. Feeding and watering is best done by using a fine mist sprayer with a liquid fertilizer. I prefer using liquid seaweed, as it doesn't have the same harsh smell as liquid fish fertilizer. Or you can purchase a nutrient-rich potting soil to eliminate the need of a liquid fertilizer. By using a fine mist sprayer, you will avoid the problem of displacing your seedlings by the force of a heavy gush of water. As the plants get larger, you can start watering them from the bottom by placing the containers in an undraining tray. Apply just enough tepid water for the soil to become moist and not turn into a pool of mud. Keep the air moving to strengthen the stems and to prevent rot.

You can start many seeds for the sheer pleasure and fun of it, but unless you plan on purchasing seedlings from a garden center in the spring, it is important to start your own for the long, growing, season plants such as tomatoes, peppers, and eggplant. The chart of vegetables in Chapter Four includes the seed to harvest ratio for each plant, but a rule of thumb is if a plant can be harvested in 12–14 weeks, you can start your seeds outdoors. Any that have a longer growing season than that should be started indoors in February or March.

Most bedding and hanging basket plants should be started inside in February or March as well, so they are in full flower after your last frost. It is important to transplant seedlings in the right-sized containers, and be sure to label them. I use popsicle sticks from the dollar store and mark them with a ball-point pen.

➢ Starting Cuttings

Many plants can be propagated by taking cuttings from a parent plant. By using this method, you are guaranteed to have a new plant that is identical to the parent plant. When taking cuttings, it is important to have all of your tools, soils, and pots sterilized to prevent diseases. These cuttings, like seeds, need light, moisture, and warmth in order to become the mature plant you are hoping for. Types of cuttings are:

- ➢ Softwood cuttings are taken from the succulent, new, tip growth of woody and herbaceous plants. These cuttings are taken in the spring from April to June. Start by filling a pot with peat moss, and water it well. With a sharp, sterile blade, cut a healthy four–five-inch (10–12.7 cm.) stem from a mature plant in the morning or on a cloudy, cool day. Remove all the leaves from the lower portion of the stem, leaving a couple of nodes. At this point, you can dip the stem in a rooting hormone if you choose. With a pencil or your finger, make a hole in the peat moss and insert the cutting in the pot, being sure the nodes will be covered with soil. Firm the soil around the stem and enclose the pot in a clear plastic bag or in a cold frame. Place the cutting in a warm place with indirect light and keep moistened, not wet. Roots should appear within two–four weeks.
- Hardwood cuttings are taken from woody plants such as vines and shrubs during their dormant period. Take these cuttings once the parent plant has lost its leaves in mid-autumn. Start by filling a pot with peat moss and water it well. Cut a stem from one-year-old wood, about five inches (12.7 cm.) long including the top terminal bud. With a sharp, sterile blade, make a straight cut at the top, a little above a bud, and another diagonal cut at the base a little below a bud. With a pencil or your finger, make a hole in the peat moss and insert the cutting in the pot, being sure the base of the cutting is in the soil. Place these cuttings outdoors under a thick layer of mulch. Transplant them once all danger of frost is over.
- Root-plant cuttings are started in water and is done by taking a cutting three–five inches (7.6–12.7 cm.) long including the tip, from the parent plant. Remove all the leaves from the lower portion of the stem and any flowers or buds that may be growing. Place the cutting in a water-filled jar so that the leafless portion of the stem is submerged and the remaining

leaves are out of the water or hanging over the lip of the jar. Place the jar in a place with indirect light. Add more water, as it evaporates and change the water on a weekly basis. Once the stem has rooted, insert it in a pot filled with moist, sterile potting mix.

➤ Starting by Root Division

Root division gives you an instant plant that guarantees a plant identical to the parent plant. This easy but brutal method consists of using a sharp spade or axe to cut through a large clump of overgrown perennial roots. This method is also sometimes used to separate suckers from shrubs. These pieces are then dug and immediately replanted in a compost-amended soil. Root division doesn't only give you a few more plants, it also gives the parent plant an extended life, as once plants start to wrap roots around each other, they choke themselves out.

Once your plants have been started and you have had to repot them, you are probably starting to run out of space in your greenhouse. I run into this problem every year. Having a cold frame is a great solution to this problem. A cold frame is a square or rectangular boxlike structure that is set up outside. It has an open bottom and a glass or plastic top that can be opened and closed or is removable. Most are slanted with the low end facing south in order to catch the sun's rays. A cold frame is a good thing to have for several reasons. It protects young plants from weather exposure and helps to harden them off. You can place an electrical heating cable in the bottom to keep the inside temperature above freezing if your season is particularly long and cold. On warm, sunny days, the glass or plastic lid can be raised or removed so the young plants don't cook.

➤ Building a Cold Frame

1. Start by finding an old window or glass door. This will dictate the size of the frame. If you can't locate an old door or window, you can purchase a sheet of corrugated plastic. I simply have a sheet of heavy gauge plastic stapled to the back of the frame.

2. For the frame, cut lengths of pressure-treated wood (your plants will not be exposed to the wood treatment) or cedar to match the dimensions of you lid. Make the back wall one board higher than the front wall. This allows the sun's rays to be maximized as well as shedding rainwater. Build the side wall the same height as the back wall and cut it in half diagonally, giving you two perfectly matched side walls. Screw four vertical corner posts that have been cut to match the height of each wall to all four walls. You have now created a square or rectangular cold frame.

3. You are now ready to mount your top. Screw some strong hinges to the back of the cold frame and to the window frame. You can also, at this point, add a handle for ease of lifting. If you are using heavy gauge plastic, staple a strip of lath to the back of the back wall at the top. Then staple the plastic that has been cut to fit to the lath. Lay the plastic over the cold frame and allow an overhang. Fold the plastic over another lath and staple. You can fold the plastic back for sun exposure and replace it for cold protection.

Following is a chart of how and where to start your plants and a suggestion as to what container to start these plants in. This alphabetized list includes all of the herbs and edible flowers we have talked about previously. Seed-starting information on vegetables is given in the vegetable section in Chapter Four.

Agastache: Start individual seeds indoors in two-inch (five cm.) cell packs mid-Feb. Press seeds into soil, but do not cover, as they need light for germination. Transplant into larger containers as needed. Transplant outdoors in mid-May, or direct sow seed outdoors in September or October for spring plants.

Angelica: Start seeds indoors in individual two-inch (five cm.) cell packs mid-Feb. Press three or four seeds into soil, but do not cover, as they need light for germination. Angelica has a low germination rate. Transplant into larger containers as needed. Transplant outdoors in mid-May.

Bachelor Button: Direct sow seeds outdoors after the last frost by sprinkling over prepared soil and scratching in with a hand cultivator to slightly cover with a thin layer of soil. Tamp down the soil to remove air pockets. Seeds will germinate in one–two weeks. Thin as needed.

Basil: Sprinkle seeds over seed-starting mix indoors in a four-inch (ten cm.) cell pack in March, and cover with a thin layer of soil. Seeds will germinate in about a week. Transplant into individual pots by pricking out clumps of five or so seedlings. Transplant outdoors after your last frost.

Begonia (Wax): Seeds are very small and dust like. Lightly sprinkle over moist, soil-starting mix indoors in March in four-inch (ten cm.) cell packs. Do not cover, as they need light for germination. Transplant into larger containers as needed. Transplant outdoors after your last frost.

Borage: Direct sow seeds outdoors after the last frost by sprinkling over prepared soil and scratching in with a hand cultivator to slightly cover with a thin layer of soil. Tamp down the soil to remove air pockets. Seeds will germinate in one–two weeks. Thin as needed.

Calendula: Direct sow seeds outdoors two–three weeks before the last frost by sprinkling over prepared soil and scratching in with a hand cultivator to slightly cover with a thin layer of soil. Tamp down the soil to remove air pockets. Cool temperatures produce stronger healthier plants.

Carnation: It is best to start the seeds indoors six–eight weeks before the last frost. Use two-inch (five cm.) individual pots and cover them with a thin layer of soil. Repot into larger containers as needed and transplant them outdoors when they are four–five inches (10–12.7 cm.) tall and after your last frost.

Chamomile: Direct sow seeds outdoors after the last frost by sprinkling over prepared soil and scratching in with a hand cultivator to slightly cover with a thin layer of soil. Tamp down the soil to remove air pockets. Thin as needed.

Chives: If you don't know someone with a chive plant that they are dividing, start seeds indoors in mid-February for transplanting outdoors in May. In individual four-inch (ten cm.) pots, cover the seeds with a thin layer of soil.

Chrysanthemum: Chrysanthemums are best started by softwood cuttings. In three–four weeks, check for root growth and transplant into a larger container as needed. Transplant outdoors after your last frost.

Cilantro: Direct sow seeds outdoors after the last frost and every two weeks for a continuous harvest. Sprinkle over prepared soil and scratch in with a hand cultivator to slightly cover with a thin layer of soil. Tamp down the soil to remove air pockets. Thin as needed.

Cosmos: Direct sow seeds outdoors after the last frost by sprinkling over prepared soil and scratching in with a hand cultivator to slightly cover with a thin layer of soil. Tamp down the soil to remove air pockets. Thin as needed.

Dames Rocket: Direct sow seeds outdoors after the last frost by sprinkling over prepared soil and scratching in with a hand cultivator to slightly cover with a thin layer of soil. Tamp down the soil to remove air pockets. Thin as needed.

Daylily: Daylily's can be started indoors by seed, however, if using this method, don't expect flowers for about three years. It is much easier to grow them from tubers. Tubers and young plants can be purchased from a garden center, but you will get a wider variety if you order the tubers from notable suppliers via catalogue. Or if you know someone with a daylily that you like, they may be willing to do a root division and give you a clump or two. Plant the tubers or root mass by digging a fairly large hole. Mix well-composted manure or compost into the soil that you have removed from the hole. Place the tuber in the hole with the crown about one inch (2.5 cm.) below the soil surface. Scoop the remaining soil mixture around the base of the plant and gently press into place to remove air pockets. Apply a good dose of water.

Flax: Direct sow seeds outdoors after the last frost by sprinkling over prepared soil and scratching in with a hand cultivator to slightly cover with a thin layer of soil. Tamp down the soil to remove air pockets. Thin as needed.

Fuchsia: Fuchsia can be started from seed indoors, but it is a long, sporadic process with a low germination rate. You are best to start plants by softwood cuttings. In three–four weeks, check for root growth and transplant into a larger container in needed.

Geranium: Geraniums can be started from seed, but it will take a while before you get flowers. The benefit of starting from seed is you will get a greater variety. Start the seeds in January by placing on a moist paper towel and placing in a plastic bag. They should germinate in about 24 hours. You can then place two or three sprouted seeds in individual four-inch (ten cm.) cell packs and cover lightly with a layer of peat moss. With the seeding method, you should get blooms in three–four months. It is much faster to start geraniums from softwood cuttings, so if you know someone with some plants that you like or if you have overwintered some from the previous season, take a cutting and treat it as you would a chrysanthemum cutting. Once the plants are growing strong, pinch out the tops to promote a denser and more compact plant.

Gladiolus: Gladiolus can be started from seed, but you need to be a dedicated and patient gladiola grower for this task, as it takes about three years before you get any flowers. The easiest and fastest way to grow gladiolus is by starting by a corm (bulb). After the last frost, plant the bulb by digging a fairly large hole. Mix well-composted manure or compost into the soil that you have removed from the hole. Place the bulb in the hole about four inches (ten cm.) deep. Cover with the remaining soil and gently press into place to remove air pockets. Apply a good dose of water.

Hibiscus: The Rose of Sharon is very easy to propagate. You can use the softwood-cutting method or the hardwood-cutting method. Transplant outdoors after your last frost.

Hollyhock: It is best to start the seeds indoors six–eight weeks before the last frost. Use two-inch (five cm.) individual pots and provide bright light. Repot into larger containers as needed and transplant them outdoors when they are four–five inches (10–12.7 cm.) tall and after your last frost.

Honeysuckle: Honeysuckle will root easily just by placing a four–five-inch (10–12.7 cm.) softwood cutting in water, just be sure to change the water on a weekly basis. Once it roots, it can be planted in a six-inch (15.25 cm.) pot until it can be planted outside after your last frost.

Horseradish: Horseradish is easily grown from a root. Dig a fairly large hole about 12 inches (30.48 cm.) deep. Mix well-composted manure or compost into the soil that you have removed from the hole. Scoop the amended soil in the hole to within two inches (five cm.) of the soil surface. Place the root in the hole and scoop the remaining soil over top; gently press into place to remove air pockets. Apply a good dose of water. (Horseradish can be invasive but can be contained if planted in a large pot.)

Impatiens: Impatiens take a while to germinate, up to three weeks, and they also take a while to mature, another six–eight weeks, so they need to be started in mid-February. Use individual six-pack cells. Take three–four seeds and place on the moist soil mixture. Gently press the seed into the soil, but don't cover, as the seed needs light to germinate. Transplant into larger pots as needed.

Johnny Jump-Up: Direct sow seeds outdoors after the last frost by sprinkling over prepared soil and scratching in with a hand cultivator to slightly cover with a thin layer of soil. Tamp down the soil to remove air pockets. Thin as needed.

Lavender: Lavender can be started from seed, but if you want flowering plants in the first year, it is best to start plants by softwood cuttings. Transplant outdoors after your last frost.

Lemon Balm: In March, start seeds in individual four-inch (ten cm.) pots. Cover the seeds with a very thin layer of soil. Transplant into larger pots as needed. Transplant outdoors after your last frost.

Lilac: Lilacs can be started by cuttings, but it is far easier to start them from suckers that the parent plant puts out. Simply take a shovel and dig out a couple of suckers that have roots attached and plant them in their new home of composted, amended soil. Water them in well.

Lovage: In March, start seeds in individual six-inch (15.25 cm.) pots. Cover the seeds with a quarter-inch (6.3 mm.) layer of soil. Transplant into larger pots as needed. Transplant outdoors after your last frost.

Marjoram: In March, start seeds in individual four-inch (ten cm.) pots. Cover the seeds with a quarter-inch (6.3 mm.) layer of soil. Transplant into larger pots as needed. Transplant outdoors after your last frost.

Mint: Mint can be started by taking cuttings, but it is far faster and easier to use root division. Place the root mass in the hole with the stems at the same level as they were previously planted. Scoop the remaining soil mixture around the base of the plant and gently press into place to remove air pockets. Apply a good dose of water.

Marigold: Direct sow seeds outdoors after the last frost by sprinkling over prepared soil and scratching in with a hand cultivator to slightly cover with a thin layer of soil. Tamp down the soil to remove air pockets. Thin as needed.

Monarda: Start seeds indoors six–eight weeks before the last frost. Use two-inch (five cm.) individual pots and cover seeds with a thin layer of peat moss. Repot into larger containers as needed and transplant them outdoors when they are four–five inches (10–12.7 cm.) tall after all danger of frost. Or you can take a softwood cutting. Transplant outdoors after your last frost.

Nasturtium: Direct sow seeds outdoors after the last frost by sprinkling over prepared soil and scratching in with a hand cultivator to cover with a quarter-inch (6.3 mm.) layer of soil. Tamp down the soil to remove air pockets. Thin as needed.

Oregano: If you know someone with an oregano plant, they may be willing to do a root division and give you a clump or two. Plant the root mass by digging a fairly large hole. Mix well-composted manure or compost into the soil that you have removed from the hole. Place the root mass in the hole with the stems at the same level as they were previously planted at. Scoop the remaining soil mixture around the base of the plant and gently press into place to remove air pockets. Apply a good dose of water.

Pansy: The pansy takes a while to mature, up to 10–12 weeks, so they need to be started in mid-February. Use individual six-pack cells and place a couple of seeds on the moist soil mixture. Gently press the seed into the soil and cover with a thin layer of peat moss. Transplant into larger pots as needed. Transplant outdoors after your last frost.

Parsley: Parsley takes a while to mature, up to 10–12 weeks, so they need to be started in mid-February. Use individual four-inch (ten cm.) pots and place a couple seeds on the moist soil mixture. Gently press the seed into the soil, and cover with a quarter-inch (6.3 mm.) layer of peat moss. Parsley doesn't like to be disturbed, so be sure you have used a pot large enough for it to grow in until you are ready to plant it outside.

Peony: Peony can be started indoors by seed. If using this method, don't expect flowers for about five years. It is much easier to grow them from tubers. Divide a mature plant in the fall once it has gone into dormancy but before your first frost. Dig a fairly large hole. Mix well-composted manure or compost into the soil that you have removed from the hole. Place the tuber in the hole with the crown about one inch (2.5 cm.) below the soil surface. Scoop the remaining soil mixture around the base of the plant and gently press into place to remove air pockets. Apply a good dose of water.

Phlox: Start seeds indoors six–eight weeks before the last frost. Use two-inch (five cm.) individual pots and cover with a thin layer of peat moss. Repot into larger containers as needed and transplant them outdoors after your last frost.

Pinks: It is best to start the seeds indoors six–eight weeks before the last frost. Use two-inch (five cm.) individual pots and cover them with a thin layer of soil. Repot into larger containers as needed and transplant them outdoors when they are four–five inches (10–12.25) tall after your last frost.

Primrose: Primrose can be started from seed, and you will get a greater variety by using this propagation method. However, they are difficult to start from seed. I cheat when it comes to primula, as I am starved for flowers after a long winter. I purchase several of these pretty bright plants in February and transplant them outside after the last frost. They are easily propagated by root division once they are well-established.

Rose: Roses can be started from seeds, but the process is very complicated and time consuming. You are best to start them from softwood cuttings. Transplant outdoors after your last frost.

Rosemary: Rosemary can be started from seeds, but the process takes a long time, so if you want rosemary during the summer, it is best to start them from softwood cuttings. Transplant outdoors after your last frost.

Sage: Sage can also be started from seeds, but the process takes a long time. If you want it during the summer, it is best to start it from softwood cuttings. Transplant outdoors after your last frost.

Snapdragon: It is best to start the seeds indoors eight–ten weeks before the last frost. Use two-inch (five cm.) individual pots and provide bright light to germinate. Repot into larger containers as needed and transplant them outdoors after your last frost.

Summer Savory: Direct sow seeds outdoors after your last frost. Plant the seeds three–five inches (7.6–12.25 cm.) apart and cover with 1/8 inch (three mm.) of soil.

Sunflower: Direct sow seeds outdoors after your last frost. Plant the seeds 6–12 inches (15.25–30.48 cm.) apart and cover with one inch (2.5 cm.) of soil.

Sweet William: Direct sow seeds outdoors after the last frost by sprinkling over prepared soil and scratching in with a hand cultivator to cover with a quarter-inch (6.3 mm.) layer of soil. Tamp down the soil to remove air pockets. Thin as needed.

Tarragon: Start seeds indoors in individual two-inch (five cm.) cell packs mid-March. Press three or four seeds into soil and cover with a thin layer of peat moss. Or take softwood cuttings. Transplant into larger containers as needed. Transplant outdoors in mid-May.

Thyme: Thyme can be started from seeds, but the process is very time consuming and unpredictable. You are best to started them from softwood cuttings, but the easiest method is using root division.

Yucca: Yucca can be started from seeds, but the process is very time consuming. You are best to started them from softwood cuttings, but the easiest method is using root division.

➤ Hardening Off Your Seedlings and Cuttings

Hardening off seedlings is an important thing for you to do whether you have started seeds indoors on your own, as well as if you have purchased seedlings from a garden center. Hardening off is the process of slowly introducing your seedling to the harsher elements of the outside world after being inside the cozy environment they have been raised them in. These tender little plants need some time to acclimatize to strong winds, pelting rain, cold nights, and bright, hot sun. Start holding back on the fertilizing process about a week prior to hardening off. There are several ways to harden your plants off.

- Start by bringing the seedlings outside during the day for an hour or two at a time. Increase the time they remain outside each day for a period of ten days to two weeks.
- If you have a cold frame (a bottomless wooden box with a transparent lid that can be opened and closed), place them in the cold frame, keeping it open during the day and closing it at night.
- Place the flats on your garden-bed surface and place a floating row cover over top. Open the cover to expose the seedlings for an hour or two at a time during the day and cover over at night. Open the cover for a little more time each day.

➤ Planting Preparation

If you have not already done so and once your soil has thawed, pick a nice sunny afternoon and loosen up your growing medium with a good spade. You can add your amendments at this time too. Dig in a good dose of bone meal where you will be planting your root crops. Make sure your verticals are secured and in good shape. Rake out your growing medium, making it ready for planting. You can place strings across the soil to mark off the square footage for the correct seed and seedling placement, or you can wait for the actual planting process and score the soil with a stick to mark off the square footage. Clean out your cold frame, making it ready for hardening off the seedlings. All the preparation you do now will give you ample time to get all of your planting done after your last frost.

➤ Transplanting Your Seedlings Outdoors

After your seedlings have been hardened off, it is time for the transplanting stage. This is best done in the cool of morning or on an overcast day.

- Dig a hole twice the size of the cell pack that holds the root mass of your seedling.
- Dig some well-composted manure or compost into the soil that you have removed from the hole. Place half of this mixture in the hole.

- Turn the pot, holding your seedling upside down, and then gently remove the seedling. If it is reluctant to leave the pot, slap the bottom of the pot with your trowel or your hand to dislodge it. Do not dislodge it by pulling on the stem as this will damage the plant.
- Gently place it in the hole and scoop the remaining soil mixture around the base of the plant. Gently press it into place to remove air pockets and tamp to form a well that will collect water.
- Slowly pour a good dose of water to each seedling.

Chapter Six
Maintaining Your Garden

Maintenance of your garden includes watering, fertilizing, cultivating, weeding, disease and pest identification. Thankfully, in our climate we don't have hundreds of weeds, diseases, or insects to learn to identify. Only a few of each to take control of and your garden will free of the detrimental influences.

➢ Watering Your Garden

Plants, just like us, need water to grow. And like us, when the weather is hot, they require more moisture. If your plants dry out, it can be detrimental to their growth, the harvest, and their life. It is best to be consistent in watering. It is also best to water deeply; this promotes deep root growth, so the roots can get away from the higher temperatures at the soil surface. Place a cup in the garden when you are watering. Once there is about an inch of water in the cup, you can rest assured your plants will be well watered for a while. Depending on your climate, watering once every two days is usually good enough, but when temperatures soar to 90 degrees F. (30 degrees C.) or more, it is probably wise to water once a day. You can also place a mulch of straw, leaves, or pine needles on the garden surface to help reduce evaporation. Don't use products like plastic for a mulch, as this won't allow the water to penetrate to the soil.

- Automatic Irrigation System: If you are on a timed, automatic irrigation system, you won't have to spend as much time with a hose in your hand. You should have your garden plot on a zone of its own. Be sure to set the timer to water your garden in the late evening or early morning when temperatures are cooler. Watering during these times prevents a lot of evaporation and also helps to prevent plant shock from extreme temperature differences. Automatic irrigation is a great way to conserve water, an important aspect in our changing climate and imposed water restrictions. All you will need to do is check the moisture level of your garden on a daily basis. Do this by digging down a few inches to test the moisture level and water accordingly.

- Drip irrigation uses flexible hoses with tiny holes spaced evenly along the tubing. This is a great method, as the drip hose can be wrapped around the base of the plants so the water leaches down to the root zone, keeping excess moisture from the leaves and fruit. The downside to using drip irrigation is often the little holes plug up with fine dirt, and if this goes unnoticed, your plants may start to dehydrate before the problem is identified. Drip irrigation requires a wee bit of maintenance because as your plants grow, you will have to increase the length of time the system remains on.

- Automatic Sprinkler irrigation gives wonderful coverage that imitates a rainfall, delivering a uniform amount of water. The fine mist is visible so you know when it is working properly. The downside is that there can be water waste due to overspray. With using sprinkler irrigation, it is a must to have it on during the hours the sun is down to prevent sun burn on foliage and fruit.

- Hose and Manual Sprinkler: If you are using this system, it will be imitating a rainfall and the water will be raining from overhead. It is very important to water in the coolness of the evening or early morning so the water will have had a chance to evaporate from the leaves and fruit prior to the sun coming out in the morning. If the water is sitting on the leaves during the hot sun, the water droplets will act as a magnifying glass and holes will be burnt into the leaves and/or fruits. Having dry foliage also helps to prevent fungal disease and slug damage. You can set up a timer on this system so it can be set to water in the cooler hours. The downside to using manual sprinklers is the amount of water that is wasted on areas that don't require irrigating.

- Hose and Watering Wand: This system allows you to be more selective when you water. You can water the larger plants that require more moisture more often than the ones that don't need as much water. It also allows you to be more direct with the flow of water, aiming at the base of the stem and root mass rather than wasting the water on the foliage. If you use this system, use the shower setting so the flow of water is gentle to avoid a huge gush that can cause soil erosion. The downside to hand watering is it is time consuming.

➢ Fertilizing Your Garden

As your plants grow, they are using up the nutrients in the soil. These nutrients need to be replaced to promote healthy growth and fruiting. In Chapter Three, we talked about the two types of fertilizer that can be used, chemical and natural, so I won't dwell on that topic. Most plants need to be fed on a monthly basis. Not only are there the two types of fertilizers, there are two forms of these fertilizers, the dry form and the liquid form.

- Dry Form: Both chemical and organic fertilizers come in a dry form. The most common way to apply a dry fertilizer is by broadcasting it and then gently raking it into the top three or four inches (7.6 or 10 cm.) of soil. A word of caution though. If you are using a dry chemical form, because of its makeup, it can burn the roots and kill your plants. Most organic dry forms are not destructive and will not cause burn damage to the young plants.

- Liquid Form: Both chemical and organic fertilizers come in a liquid form. Liquid fertilizers are easy to apply and can be applied to the root zone or used as a foliar spray, as plants can absorb nutrients through their leaf pores as well as their roots. Leaf crops do well with a fertilizer application of foliage spray every two weeks. Always follow the dilution rates on the label of your liquid solution to prevent damage to your plants. More is not better. The best time to apply liquid fertilizer is on a cloudy day or in the evening.

➢ Cultivating Your Garden

Cultivating is different from tilling. Tilling is churning the soil up to great depths. Cultivating is gently scratching the surface of the soil to allow oxygen down to the root zone and uncompacting the soil to allow for better water penetration. I like to get out with my three-prong hand cultivator every two weeks or so. I always notice a spurt of growth within the next couple of days after a gentle cultivation session. Guard against digging too deep though, as you don't want to disturb too many roots. Don't cultivate when your soil is very dry or very wet. The cultivator is also a great little tool for weeding your garden, which we will talk about next.

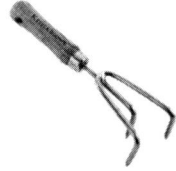

➢ Weeding

Well, just what is a weed? The definition of a weed basically is a common plant growing where it isn't wanted. Weeds are fast-growing, prolific plants that compete for moisture and nutrients causing stunted growth of the plants we are growing for a good harvest. Weeds are easiest to control by removing them prior to them going to seed. Some weeds such as chick weed can produce as many as 25,000 seeds, and many seeds can lay dormant for decades, just waiting for the right conditions to germinate. Many weed seeds arrive on the wind or from birds dropping them from overhead. Having a raised garden bed makes the weeding process much easier. Adding a layer of organic mulch not only aids in preventing soil evaporation but also helps prevent weed seeds from getting a root hold. Weeding is a disliked chore by many, usually because it seems to never be completely taken care of. To prevent weeds from overtaking your garden area, get out there with your hand cultivator and scratch the newly emerging weeds from the soil surface once a week. When you do go out to do

your weeding, make sure your soil is nicely moist. Moist soil will release the roots, whereas dry soil will hold the roots tightly.

- Hand pulling is simply extracting the weed by pulling the entire plant out of the soil with your hand. This method is effective when the weeds are still very young, haven't developed their massive root structure yet, and there are only a few to deal with. Once the weeds have matured or there is a thick patch of them, you will have to use tools for the removal process. Your dexterity and flexibility will determine your use of short-handled weeding tools or long-handled tools. Many short-handled tools are the same as long-handled tools but with a shorter handle allowing you to have a more 'hands on approach.' Some examples of hand-weeding tools are the three-prong cultivator, garden trowel, hand hoe, and the dandelion digger. All of these tools come in various shapes and sizes and are available at any garden center.
- An herbicide is a chemical that is used to kill plants or prevent them from growing. Sometimes, as a last resort, using a herbicide is the only way to get rid of a patch of pesky weeds. It is very important to carefully read the label on the container of herbicide and follow the directions completely. Herbicides are dangerous chemicals and should not be used around pets, children, or near any water bodies. Always wear protective gear when using chemical sprays and apply on a calm day. The two main types of herbicides are:

  o Selective which you can use to target individual weeds while leaving the surrounding plants alone.
  o Non-selective which will kill most plants in a given area, which makes it an easy way to clear weeds from a new unplanted garden patch.

• Identifying Common Garden Weeds

Field Bindweed (Convolvulus arvensis) A member of the Morning Glory Family)

Description: Bindweed is a fast-growing, spreading ground cover with pretty, little, white to pink trumpet-shaped flowers. Its twining habit chokes out cultivated plants. Each fruit it produces has two seeds that can remain viable for up to 20 years. It has deep extensive roots and new plants will sprout from tiny root fragments. Fortunately, it doesn't like growing in good, cultivated, moist soil, so if you are maintaining your garden on a regular basis, bindweed won't be a problem for you.

Control and Eradication: If you do have bindweed, the best way to remove it is lift to the stems up in your hand and, with a pair of scissors, snip them off at ground level. Mark the spot where it was growing and when it emerges again, repeat the snipping process. Continue with the snipping until the plant finally gives up. You can also pour boiling water over and around the plant, repeat as necessary. As a last resort, an herbicide can be used.

Burdock (Arctium minus)

Description: This plant is identifiable by the large heart-shaped leaves with wavy edges and hairy undersides. The rosette of leaves at the base of the plant can grow to a width of three feet (one m.). The stems are coarse with a reddish tinge and are heavily branched. The flowers are similar to thistle but are somewhat smaller. As the flower goes to seed, the pod dries, becoming a brittle burr which clings to animal fur and clothing. The root is a very deep taproot. The plant can grow up to six feet (two m.) in height. Even though this plant is detrimental to the cattle industry, it does have its benefits. The root is used for medicinal purposes and the dried burr was the inspiration for Velcro.

Control and Eradication: Up to a year-old, Burdock is fairly easy to eradicate, as the taproot hasn't gotten very deep yet. Simply loosen the soil around the base of the plant and lift it out before it has a chance to flower and seed. Once the plant is over a year old, it becomes very difficult to get rid of, as the taproot has extended deep into the soil. It may take three–four years to get rid of a mature plant. Just don't let it flower and go to seed. Dig down two–three inches (5–7.6 cm.) to expose the taproot, and with a pair of shears, snip it before it has a chance to flower. Continue the snipping process as it continues to emerge. As a last resort, an herbicide can be used, but for best results, application should be made in the spring. Fall applications are ineffective.

Creeping Buttercup (Ranunculus repens)

Description: Buttercup is quite a pretty plant when growing in its natural environment. It can be seen growing in damp areas, ditches, moist forest beds, and swamp land. It has five-petaled, yellow, shiny flowers with bright green three-lobed leaves. Buttercup is not a good seed producer, but new plants will sprout from the creeping stems and any root fragments left in the soil.

Control and Eradication: The best way to remove buttercup is to dig deep in order to remove all root masses. This may have to be repeated several times. When handling the plant, use gloves, as it has toxins that can cause skin irritation. As a last resort, an herbicide can be used.

Chickweed (Stellaria media)

Description: Chickweed is an herbaceous annual that prefers well cultivated moist fertile soil and so it habituates itself in urban landscapes. It has light green, tiny, oval leaves, hairy stems, and tiny, white, star-shaped flowers. Chickweed will take root wherever the branches touch the soil and each plant can produce 25,000 viable seeds in each season. However, if you are in short supply of a salad green, chickweed is edible and a very nutritious substitute.

Control and Eradication: Chickweed has a shallow root system and so manual hoeing can be used to dig the root system out. This will have to be repeated throughout the growing season. As a last resort, an herbicide can be used.

Clover (Trifolium repens)

Description: White clover is a perennial weed and is often used as a lawn substitute. It grows in a creeping manner and roots itself wherever its stems touch the soil. The teardrop-shaped green leaves grow in sets of three and often have a red stripe across them. The flowers are pom-pom clumps of spikes with a brownish/green center. The seeds from clover flowers can lay dormant for years.

Control and Eradication: Clover is not a lover of nitrogen and so it probably won't be growing in your leaf crops. The best way to control clover is to apply a thick layer of mulch. Hand weeding is also an effective method of keeping clover at bay. As a last resort, an herbicide can be used.

Dandelion (Taraxacum officinale)

Description: Dandelion flowers are cheerful yellow pom-poms that soon become a mass of wind-propelled seeds (Parachute seeds) that can float on the wind for miles. Because of this, dandelion weeding becomes an annual event. All parts of the dandelion are edible. The leaves are deeply toothed and grow in a rosette from the base of the plant. The stem, when broken, secretes a milky latex substance; it is hollow and suspends a single flower above the leaves. Dandelions can be found pretty well anywhere throughout North America and they are a great food source for bees.

Control and Eradication: It is virtually impossible to completely eradicate the dandelion. They have a deep taproot, and if the entire root isn't removed, the plant will grow back. Remove the plant prior to it going to flower and seeding. There are several tools on the market that are specifically designed just for dandelion removal. If the dandelion plant is not growing close to your crop plants, you can use pure white or apple cider vinegar on them. Pour the vinegar into a spray bottle and completely cover the plant in the heat of the day. Wilting should happen within the next couple of hours. If you are going with an herbicide for control, use it before the flowers emerge, as the plant is more resistant to chemicals after flowering.

Dock (Rumex) (Rumex crispus is curly dock and Rumex obtusifolius is broad-leaved dock)

Description: Dock emerges in the early spring and grows in basal rosettes of arrow-shaped foliage. In the summer, it produces tall flower stalks one–three feet

(30–100 cm.) tall covered in massive amounts of seeds. Dock has a taproot up to one foot (30 cm.) in length and so can be very drought tolerant but prefers to grow where there is plenty of moisture. The foliage of dock is edible and has a lemony flavor.

Control and Eradication: You will not be able to remove dock by hand pulling. The leaves pull away from the deep taproot very easily. When your soil is nicely moist, dig around the dock plant with a garden fork to loosen the soil around its deep taproot. You can then use your dandelion-removal tool and your hand to gradually pull the entire plant out of the ground. As a last resort, an herbicide can be used.

Hairy Bittercress (Cardamine hirsute)

Description: Hairy Bittercress is an annual weed, identifiable by the leafy rosettes at its

base with several long stems emerging from the base. The stems produce tiny white flowers at the tips which turn into explosive seedpods. When the pods explode, the seeds can be sent up to three feet (one m.) away on a still day and much farther if carried by the wind.

Control and Eradication: When the plant is young and before it flowers and sets seed, it can be hand weeded by digging around the base and lifting out. As it matures, the taproot becomes much deeper. Mulching helps to suppress this invasive weed, and as a last resort, an herbicide can be used.

Horsetail (Equisetum)

Description: Horsetail is one of the oldest plants on the planet. It is recognizable by its airy fern-like appearance. The green, hollow, segmented stems have whorls of needle-like branches surrounding it. Horsetail is considered to be an aquatic plant, but it will grow in any situation. Horsetail can be toxic to horses if eaten in large quantities. It spreads by tiny spores that float on the wind.

Control and Eradication: Horsetail is very difficult to control and eradicate. Pulling and digging is ineffective, as it has a massive rhizomic root system and the tiniest portion of root remaining in the soil will sprout another clump of weed. Most herbicides are also ineffective unless they are applied repeatedly. The best way to eradicate horsetail is to solarize the soil. This requires laying a heavy gauge plastic over the growing area for a full growing season to smother and burn this invasive plant out. DO NOT PUT ANY PORTION OF HORSETAIL IN YOUR COMPOST, as it will not compost down. No wonder it is one of the oldest plants on earth!

Lambs Quarters (Chenopodium album)

Description: Lamb's Quarters, also called pigweed, is an edible annual plant that frequents stream and riverbeds, moist forests, wastelands, and residential gardens. It is extremely hardy and is recognized by the white coating on the underside of its leaves, which allows water to bead and run off. The spike stems are covered by masses of tiny, green flowers which turn into seeds. One plant can produce up to 75,000 seeds that can remain viable for up to 20 years. The leaves can be picked and wilted like spinach, added to soups, stews, or chopped and added to salads.

Control and Eradication: If you have weeds in your garden, this is the one to have, as it is relatively easy to control and eradicate. It reproduces from the seed only and can be gently pulled by hand or removed with a hoe prior to setting seed. As a last resort, an herbicide can be used.

Nettle (Urtica divica procera)

Description: Stinging Nettle is so named by the hypodermic needle-like hairs on the stems and underside of the leaf that harbor toxins which cause a reddish, itchy rash lasting for a few hours when exposed to bare flesh. The plant is an unpleasant, erect, herbaceous perennial that reproduces by wind-blown seeds and creeping rhizome roots. Each plant can produce up to 20,000 seeds per season which remain viable for ten years. Even though this plant can act in an unpleasant manner, it is edible, and if picked with gloves while young and tender, once steamed, it tastes very much like spinach.

Control and Eradication: The best way to control Stinging Nettle is repeated hoeing which will eventually exhaust the massive root system. Of course, it is best to uproot the tiny plants before they can establish themselves. And here I must tell you my story concerning Stinging Nettle and Free-Range Cattle! One year, I had the brilliant idea to go up the mountain with a couple of garbage bags and collect dried cow patties to use as a fertilizer for my garden. BIG MISTAKE! The cow's digestive system doesn't get hot enough to kill the seeds of the nettle plant, and I didn't compost the manure, so every year from then on, I have young nettle plants to weed from my garden. Darn Free-Range Cows!

Plantain (Plantago major)

Description: Plantain has oval, egg-shaped leaves with insignificant flowers on leafless stems rising above the rosette of leaves. Plantain is an edible plant but is more commonly used as a healing herb. It can draw out toxins from insect stings and snakebites and can soothe rashes and sunburn. It spreads by way of windborne seeds.

Control and Eradication: Remove the plant prior to it setting seed by using a dandelion digger to loosen the soil around the fibrous root structure and then lifting the entire plant out. As a last resort, an herbicide can be used.

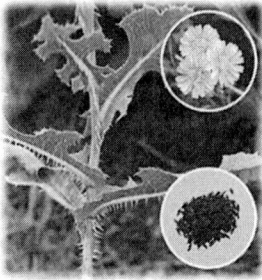

Prickly Lettuce (Lactuca serriola)

Prickly lettuce, otherwise known as Milk Thistle, is sometimes mistaken for dandelion. The leaves are similar with deep notches, and the stems secrete a milky latex sap much like the dandelion. The flowers are also similar, being yellow, daisy-like pom-poms, which turn into wind-propelled seeds. This weed prefers dry conditions but will germinate and grow in moist areas. One plant will produce 35–1,300 flowers which produce 20 seeds each. The seeds remain viable for one–three years.

Control and Eradication: It is best to remove Prickly Lettuce in its early stage prior to it going to seed. Use a dandelion digger to remove the deep tap root. As a last resort, an herbicide can be used.

Purslane (Portulaca oleracea)

Purslane is identifiable by its thick, reddish, succulent stems with small, fleshy, spoon-shaped leaves. It has tiny, yellow, five-petaled flowers that produce numerous seeds. The plant grows in a circle form close to the ground and has been recorded to produce 2,000,000 seeds per plant in one growing season. The plant has the ability to throw its seeds some distant from the parent plant. This invasive yet edible plant can reproduce through seeds and it can re-root from its stems, leaves, and any portion of root left in the soil.

Control and Eradication: As previously mentioned, purslane has the ability to reproduce from every part of itself. The seed will even continue to ripen once the plant is pulled out and placed in a weed heap. If you only have a few of these weeds, loosen the soil around it, being careful to keep the stems and leaves intact, and then lift the plant from the soil and immediately place it in a plastic bag. Once done, tie the plastic bag tightly and put it in your outdoor garbage. DO NOT PUT ANY PORTION OF PURSLANE IN YOUR COMPOST. If you have a bad infestation of purslane, solarize the soil by covering your entire growing area with black plastic for a season. Purslane seeds need light to germinate, and hopefully the heat of the sun will cook any stems, leaves, seeds, and roots to death. As a last resort, an herbicide can be used.

Quack Grass (Agropyron repens) Couch Grass (Elymus repens)

Quack grass, otherwise known as couch grass, has a rapid growth habit and reproduces by its creeping rhizomes and seeds. The leaves are flat and hairy; the stems are upright flower spikes. Each stem can produce 25–40 seeds, and any portion of rhizome left in the soil will develop a new plant. The rhizomes entangle themselves around the roots of desirable plants.

Control and Eradication: The best way to rid this grass from your garden area is to dig deep and sift the soil, removing all trace of the rhizome roots. As a last resort, an herbicide can be used.

Redshank (Persicaria macuosa)

Redshank is sometimes also called Spotted Knotweed because of the unusual burgundy markings in the center of narrow-pointed leaves and the knot that joins the leaves to the red stem. It is recognizable by the tiny pink flower balls that form on the upright spikey stem. Redshank is an annual and reproduces by seeds from May to September, which can remain viable for over 40 years. This weed is one of the first to emerge in the spring. Each plant produces between 200–6,000 seeds per season.

Control and Eradication: Hand pull it when it is still young and before the seeds form. It has a dense, shallow root system, so removal is easy in moist soil. As a last resort, an herbicide can be used.

Sticky Chickweed (Cerastim glomeratum)
Description: Sticky Chickweed has a similar appearance to common chickweed except for its more-upright straggly nature. The stems are hollow and brittle with mouse, ear-shaped leaves. The flowers form in clusters, are white, and five-petaled. The stems, leaves, and base of the flowers are finely haired and the hairs have a glandular secretion on them, making them sticky.

Control and Eradication: Diligent hand weeding or hoeing is the best control method for this weed. This will have to be repeated throughout the growing season. Mulching is also an effective control method.

Sorrel (Oxalis acetosella)
Description: Wood sorrel is identified by its three heart-shaped leaves forming a shamrock in shape. It has pretty little flowers, some have yellow flowers, some pink, and some white, each with five petals. Its seedpods bend sharply facing skyward. Wood sorrel has many relatives, but the yellow wood sorrel seems to be the common garden invader. It is an edible plant and has a sour taste that gives it its other name of Sour Grass. It is also a thirst quencher and naturally grows in moist, shady, wooded areas but also thrives in garden areas. It propagates from roots and seeds, each pod exploding to release up to 5,000 seeds and, with the right conditions, can throw them ten feet (three m.) away.

Control and Eradication: The root system of wood sorrel is extensive and spreading. The fragile roots easily break apart when the plant is hand pulled and will regenerate itself from every little broken root particle. The best way to remove wood sorrel is to carefully loosen the soil some distance away from the base of the plant. Lift as much of the root system as possible and sift the soil, discarding any bits of remaining roots. As a last resort, an herbicide can be used.

Thistle (Cardueae)

Description: The Canada Thistle, even though not native to Canada, is a spreading perennial weed with sharp prickles. The leaves, stems, and flowers all have painful prickles. The plant can grow up to three feet (one m.) in height with showy, pom-pom-shaped flowers in shades of pink to purple, each flower having a prickly base. The roots are made up of vertical and horizontal masses extending up to 20 feet (six m.) per plant. Even a small individual plant is usually connected to a massive, unseen, underground, root system. The plant also spreads by windborne seeds much like dandelion heads.

Control and Eradication: This one is a very difficult one to control because of its massive root structure. Pulling doesn't work because the root will split and two plants will grow back in the place of the one that was pulled. The thistle has a distaste for nutritious soils, so fertilize often to keep it at bay. Another method of control is to do the same as for bindweed. With a heavy pair of gardening gloves, locate the base of the plant, and with a pair of sharp scissors or pruning shears, snip it off at ground level. Mark the spot where it was growing and when it emerges again, repeat the snipping process. Continue with the snipping until the plant finally gives up. As a last resort, a herbicide can be used, but even with the chemical method weekly applications will have to be made.

Vetch (Vicia sativa)

Description: Vetch is a climbing annual that very quickly will cover over desirable plants. The stems are weak and trailing with pinnate leaves, each with three–nine leaflets growing opposite to each other. The older leaflets have tendrils giving them the ability to climb at a fast rate. The pea-like flowers come in pairs and range in color from purple, pink, and white. The flowers develop pods each holding 3–12 seeds. In the heat of the summer, as the pods dry, they pop open, expelling the seeds and making a clicking sound. The root system is deep and fibrous.

Control and Eradication: The best method of control is to hand pull the plant while it is still young, before it has had a chance to flower. Another method is to shear the plant off at the soil surface, as the remaining roots won't spread. As a last resort, an herbicide can be used.

➤ Disease

Plant diseases are caused by microorganisms such as fungi, bacteria, viruses, and pathogenic nematodes. Prevention is the best measure against having a disease problem. Practice the following, healthy, hygienic, methods to give your plants a natural resistance to disease:

- Clean all of your last seasons' residue up prior to planting this seasons garden.
- Have a healthy soil with a lot of rich humus material and keep it evenly moist.
- Use good quality seeds and healthy seedlings.
- Plant resistant varieties of the crop you are growing.
- Allow for airflow between your plants.
- Plant crops suitable to your climate.
- Use annual crop-rotation practices.

- Use companion planting, creating biodiversity in your garden area.
- Keep with a regular weeding program.
- Remove and discard dead and decaying leaves.
- Sanitize your gardening tools in a solution of one-part chlorine bleach to four parts water for 30 minutes after each use.

So, if you have maintained the organic practices of composting, improving the texture of your gardening soil, giving your plants good ventilation, and weeding regularly, you shouldn't have much problem with disease. However, if you do happen to end up with a disease, it is best to identify the problem and take the correct measures to control it.

Following is a list of common plant diseases, the plants that are most susceptible, and the control methods for each one.

- **Identifying Common Garden Diseases**

Blight

Cause: Blight is caused by a pathogenic organism or germ.

Identification: It starts as spots of yellow and rapidly becomes a browning of the leaves, branches, flowers, and fruits, resulting in the death of the plant. It is generally more prevalent in cool, moist conditions.

Affects: Tomato and potato, occasionally peppers, and small fruits.

Control: If you catch the problem early enough, remove and destroy all affected parts. If the problem is severe, remove and disposal of the entire plant. Do not compost. An alternative is to spray affected plants with a fungicide containing fixed copper as an active ingredient or use a copper-soap fungicide.

Blossom End Rot

Cause: The cause of this problem is more of an environmental one caused by uneven watering or a calcium deficiency in the soil. Other causes can be a high salt content in the soil or too much fertilizer high in nitrogen; both of these causes stem from mismanagement of chemical-fertilizer applications.

168

Identification: The water-soaked areas of a fruit become a wide, sunken, brown, leathery spot on the bottom end. It does not spread from plant to plant.

Affects: This affects both the ripe and unripe fruit of tomatoes, peppers, squash, cucumbers, melons, and eggplant.

Control: Once the fruit has become affected, pick it and discard it. To prevent this problem, use a foliar spray of liquid seaweed or liquid calcium. Applying bone meal or oyster shells to the area prior to planting helps to prevent the problem from occurring.

Club Root

Cause: Club root is caused by a soil-born fungus (Plasmodiophora brassicae) that infects the susceptible plant through the root hairs.

Identification: The roots become swollen, misshapen, and deformed so the plant can't absorb water and nutrients. The plants do poorly in the heat of the day and revive in the cool of the evening. Often the outer leaves become yellow, pink, or brown.

Affects: All of the cabbage family can be affected by club root including cabbage, broccoli, cauliflower, Brussels sprouts, and kale.

Control: This is a serious disease and very difficult to eradicate. Sterilization of the soil is one method that has been used to eradicate this disease. Do this by placing a heavy gauge plastic over the infected area for a year. The heat of the sun should destroy the fungus. If you do have club root, remove and destroy all brassicas and be sure to sanitize any equipment you use with a mild bleach solution. You can try raising the soil pH to an alkaline rate of 7.2, or you can import unaffected soil into an isolated garden space and use good crop-rotation methods.

Fusarium Wilt

Cause: This is a soil-born fungal disease (Fusariuj oxysporum) that enters the plant through the roots and interferes with the water uptake.

Identification: Because the water intake is affected, the older bottom leaves begin to wilt, yellow, and then turn brown. Younger plants will usually die. It often affects only one branch or one side of the plant.

Affects: Tomato, potato, eggplant, and peppers.

Control: Fusarium wilt can live in the soil for up to ten years. Don't plant susceptible plants in the affected area. Sterilization of the soil is one method that has been used to eradicate this fungal disease. Do this by placing a heavy gauge plastic over the infected area for a year. The heat of the sun should destroy the fungus. You can use a compatible fungicide and, as a last resort, replace the infected soil.

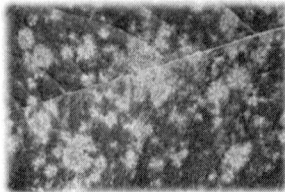

Mildew (Downy Mildew, Powdery Mildew, and Rust)

Cause: The cause of mildew is by a fungus-like organism that is spread from plant to plant in wet weather.

Identification: You will see discolored blotches on the upper sides of the leaves and white, gray, or even purple mold on the underside. The leaves turn yellow, then brown, and fall off the plant.

Affects: This is a common problem once the summer temperatures cool down. It affects vining crops such as grapes, cucumber, squash,

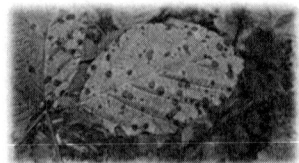

and melons. It can also affect brassicas, carrots, spinach, and parsnip.

Control: Try to avoid overhead watering. Pick off and destroy affected leaves. In a bad situation, remove and destroy the entire plant.

Mosaic Virus
Cause: This disease is caused by the transfer of the virus from chewing insects such as aphids, whitefly, leaf hoppers, and cucumber beetles. It can also be transferred through dirty gardening equipment.

Identification: The affected plant will develop leaves with yellow or green stripes or spots on them. The veins of the deformed leaves will become yellow.

Affects: Beans, tomatoes, potatoes, carrots, celery, cucumbers, squash, melon, lettuce, spinach, beets, and peppers can become affected by this virus.

Control: There is no cure for Mosaic Virus. The best control is a good garden cleanup of old debris at the end of the growing season, as the virus does not overwinter.

Potato Scab
Cause: This disease is caused by a bacterium-like organism (Streptomyces scabies) that overwinters in the soil and in fallen leaves. It transmits itself by way of infected tubers, wind, and water.

Identification: This disease disrupts the development of the cell walls causing dark-brown raised warts over the skin's surface of the tuber. This is an unsightly disease, but it is perfectly safe to eat the affected tuber. Just cut or peel the affected part away.

Affects: Not only does potato scab affect the potato but also beets, radish, turnip, carrot, and parsnip.

<u>Control</u>: Potato scab can live indefinitely in an alkaline soil but is rarely found in an acidic soil. If you have this problem, decrease your soil pH to 5.2 or lower. You can also add elemental sulfur to the soil and treat the seed potatoes with a sulfur fungicide prior to planting.

➢ Insects

The topic of insects is a vast one, as they are the most plentiful animal on earth. As a matter of fact, four out of every five animals are insects. Insects have strange and complicated lifecycles; some go through complete metamorphosis and others incomplete metamorphosis. Most insects lay their eggs when they sense the approach of autumn. Eggs can be laid in the soil, in organic debris, or in the cracks and crevices of shrubs and trees. Not all insects are destructive though; there are many beneficial insects, some of which war against the destructive ones. We will break this topic into two parts, Beneficial Insects and Destructive Insects.

- Beneficial Insects: Beneficial insects have a positive effect on the garden by aiding in pollination and acting as a natural pesticide. Some are predatory in nature, defending plants from harmful pests. Others, the pollinators are responsible for the majority of fruit production in our garden. There are a few simple things you can do to attract and keep these beneficial insects in your garden area:
  o Grow plants to attract these natural defenders and pollinators, such as sweet alyssum, lobelia, marigold, cosmos, yarrow, and lavender. Many herbs also act as attractants.
  o Provide drinking water for them by placing small water-filled dishes throughout the garden area.
  o Provide a natural environment for them by planting a few trees, shrubs, and perennials in the landscape.
  o Avoid using insecticides, even the 'soft' natural plant-based ones.
  o Avoid killing spiders, as they feed almost entirely on other insects.
  o You can also purchase many of these great bugs and Entomopathogenic nematodes from garden centers and biological

control facilities. Carefully introduce them to your garden and provide a natural environment for them by using a mulch layer on the soil surface.

- **Identifying Common Garden Beneficial Insects**

APHID MIDGE Predator
(Consumes about 60 species of aphid)
Description: The adult aphid midge is a flying insect that looks similar to a tiny 1/8th inch (four mm.) long mosquito with

long antennae that curls back from its head. The eggs are shiny and orange. The larvae are orange with a slug-like appearance.

Cycle: The adult midge feeds on the aphid secretion and then lays between 100–250 eggs on the undersides of leaves. The eggs hatch, becoming larvae. The larvae stage lasts from seven–ten days in which time each one can eat up to 65 aphids daily. The larvae then drop to the ground where they pupate and become adults.

Aphid Parasitic Wasp Predator
(The most effective aphid-controlling insect)

Description: These flying wasps don't sting. The female is identified by having a long-pointed structure at the end of her body called an ovipositor which resembles a stinger. This little wasp can control not only aphids but scale, whitefly, sawfly, ants, leaf miners, some types of caterpillars, tomato-horn worms, codling moth, cabbage loopers, and cabbage worms.

Cycle: The female parasitic wasp feeds on the secretion of aphids and uses her 'ovipositor' to pierce a pest insect and then deposits one egg into its body. She can deposit up to 300 eggs into 300 pests during her two–three-week lifespan. The eggs then hatch, becoming larvae which feed on the inside of the pest. The larvae then pierce a hole in its host and glues it to a leaf where it spins it into a tiny cocoon. It pupates within this cozy environment and emerges as an adult.

BEES Pollinator
(Bumblebees, Honeybees, and Mason bees)

Bees are the world's most important single species pollinator of many fruit-bearing plants. They do this by landing on a flower, picking up the pollen from the flower stamen (the male reproductive part of the plant), and placing it on the pistil (the female reproductive part of the plant). This is called fertilization, making it possible for the fruit to develop.

Bumblebees are large, ranging in size from ¾–1½ inches (19–31 mm.). They are a wild bee with about 46 species native to North America. They are fuzzy, having yellow and black stripes looking much like flying teddy bears. The female is twice the size of the male and is able to sting. Her stinger is smooth, so she is able to slip it out of her prey and reuse it. The male is not able to sting.

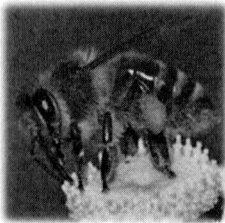

Honeybee There are almost 20,000 species of honey bee worldwide with about 4000 of them native to North America. We are primarily going to refer to the domesticated honeybee here. It is known that beekeeping was done over 10,000 years ago. The Egyptians built simple hives for honey production 4,500 years ago. So, beekeeping is nothing new. In North America today, there are numerous commercial and private apiaries (a collection of beehives) and almost each city and town have their own beekeeping association. These people recognize the importance that bees play in the food-chain cycle. Beehives are placed in orchards and on farms in the spring for guaranteed fruit production. Honey, beeswax, non-allergy-causing bee pollen, royal jelly, propolis, and beebread are all profitable and healthy byproducts that this wonderful little creature supplies us with. On a side note, honeybees can sting. They have a barbed stinger which rips out of their body and remains in its intended foe, causing a very painful symptom. Unfortunately, losing its stinger also kills the bee.

Mason Bees are a tiny, wild, gentle pollinator. They only collect pollen and so don't produce honey or beeswax. They are tiny enough to build their solitary homes in cracks and crevasses throughout the landscape using mud and other 'construction' materials. Since they aren't interested in the collection of nectar for honey production, they are three times better at pollination than the honeybee. Because of their gentle nature, their tiny housing units and their huge ability to pollinate flowers for fruiting, mason bees are being bred for sale to use in the home garden. For more information and sales of mason bees and their housing, go to the West Coast Seeds website.

BUTTERFLY Pollinator

Butterflies are not as good at pollinating as bees are, but they make up for it by their beauty. They have brightly colored patterned wings and gracefully flutter from flower to flower, feeding on the nectar and transferring pollen at the same time. There are close to 20,000 species of butterfly worldwide, 725 of those are native to the United States and 275 species are native to Canada. They reside in bogs, deserts, mountain meadows, ocean shorelines, grasslands, and forests. If you have children, try purchasing a butterfly kit so your children can watch the cycle and the day by transformation. For information and to order a kit go to, located in Langley, B.C.

Hoverfly Predator

(There are close to 6000 species of this mimicking fly worldwide.)

Description: The adult hoverfly body is usually shiny in bright colors and patterns of black and yellow, looking much like a wasp or hornet. Some species have a fuzzy body resembling a bee. However, none of the species sting, and unlike bees and wasps which have two sets of wings, the hoverfly is a true fly with only one set of wings. It also has a set of small stubs that act like a gyroscope, allowing it to quickly change direction and hover in midair. The body is stout and the antennae short. The eggs are an elongated whitish oval; the larvae have a maggot-like appearance.

Cycle: The adult feeds on nectar hovering above the flower, it particularly likes cosmos, and the female can lay up to 100 fertilized eggs on plant stems and leaves during her three–four-week lifespan. The eggs hatch in three days, becoming hungry larvae. These larvae can consume up to 1,200 aphids during this 10–15-day stage by capturing prey, holding it up in the air, and sucking it dry of juices. The larvae then fall to the ground and go through a two-week pupation period.

Ground Beetles Predator
(40,000 species worldwide and 2,500 in North America)

Description: The beetle is a shy, scary-looking insect but is very beneficial to your garden. The adults have a hard, shiny body usually black or brown in color, although some are metallic. Since there are so many species, they range in shape and size. However, the ones we are most familiar with range in size from about half–one inch (12.7–25.4 mm.) long. Even though beetles have wings, the wings are hardened and most species can't fly. The adult has six capable legs, but it can't climb well either, being reduced to ground level. The adult feeds at night and, if exposed during the day, runs for cover. These adult insects feed on caterpillars, root maggots, snails, cabbage worms, Colorado potato beetle, cut worms, and slugs. The eggs of the beetle start out being colorless, changing to yellow and then brown, and are football shaped. The larvae are usually the same length as the adult with chewing mouth parts, having long, slender, segmented bodies of a dark color. They resemble centipedes but have only six legs instead of anywhere between 15 to 100 pairs of legs. As they remain mostly in the soil during the larvae stage, this insect is not only a carnivore but consumes many weed seeds as well.

Cycle: After mating in late summer, the female lays eggs in a chamber she has made in the soil. The eggs hatch after about a week during the winter and remain in their chamber until spring at which time they emerge as larvae. The larvae go through three molts and continue to grow and feed for one–two years. They then cocoon themselves in the soil and pupate for a few weeks. The beetle can live for three–four years.

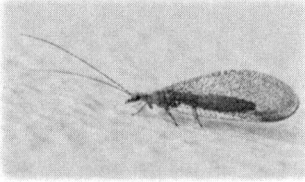

Lacewings Predator

Description: The adult is about ¾ inch (19 mm.) long with fine, mesh-like wings, a pale green body, and yellow eyes. The eggs are oval and pale green, changing to gray just before hatching. The larvae start out fairly small but grow to 3/8 inch (nine mm.) long and look like mini alligators with forceps-like mandibles (chewing mouth parts). They range in colors from gray to brown and feed on aphids, caterpillars, leaf hoppers, psyllids, whitefly, thrips, spiders, and mites.

Cycle: The female lays more than 800 eggs in its four-six-week lifespan on plant foliage atop hair-like filaments. The eggs hatch into larvae that then inject a paralyzing venom into the pest, they then suck out the contents of its body, killing it. They can devour 200 or more pests per week and live in this stage for two–three weeks. They then spin a cocoon and in five days' time emerge as adults.

LADY BUG	ASIAN LADY BEETLE
<ul><li>Black head with small white cheeks</li><li>Friendly and harmless</li><li>Good for the environment, lives outside</li></ul>	<ul><li>Large white cheeks with 'WM' marking its on head</li><li>Aggressive, bites, can be harmful to dogs</li><li>Invades homes in swarms</li><li>Has a foul odor and yellow staining</li><li>Can cause allergies</li></ul>

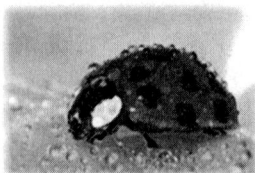

Ladybug Predator (Not to be mistaken for the Asian Beetle)

Description: These two insects are distantly related and have a similar

body which is a round, oval shape. Commonly, both have spots ranging in number from 2 to 24, although some species don't have any spots at all. Colors range from a tan to bright fire-engine red. Both are excellent fliers, having surprisingly long, transparent wings which fold up tightly under the hardened spotted elytron (forewing). Both consume garden-pest insects and both have the same lifecycle. The larvae are black and orange and look like mini alligators. In the pupae stage, they look like the adult but with a swollen body. The eggs are yellow and round, resembling golden nuggets.

Cycle: The female lays a cluster of about 20 tiny eggs on the undersides of leaves. The eggs hatch after about a week. The larvae emerge with ferocious appetites where they devour whitefly, scale, mites but mostly aphids; they can eat up to 5,000 aphids in their lifespan. The larvae stage lasts for about three weeks, they then pupate on plant leaves for a week and emerge as adults. The adult lives for about 12 weeks, feeding on aphids.

Minute Pirate Bug Predator

Description: The adult is a very small flying insect ranging in size from 1/8"–1/5" (3–6.3 mm.). The body is an oval to triangular shape with a soft flattened back with white and black patterns. They remain relatively obscure, feeding on aphids, thrips, spider mites, other insect eggs, and even flower pollen until late summer. They then reveal themselves by inflicting a harmless but irritating bite to humans with their short blunt beak. As a true bug, the minute pirate has two pairs of wings, one pair being a protective elytron and other set being lacy and transparent which it uses to take flight with. The larvae are orange and have the same short, blunt beak that the adults have. They use this to inject their prey with a digestive enzyme and proceed to sucking it dry of all juices. Both the adult and larvae can digest 20–30 spider mites per day.

Cycle: The female lays between 80–100 eggs by injecting them individually into plant tissue; the eggs hatch in three–five days, becoming larvae. The larvae go through five stages of growth, becoming larger with each stage, which takes 20 days. The lifespan of the adult is 35 days.

Nematodes Predator

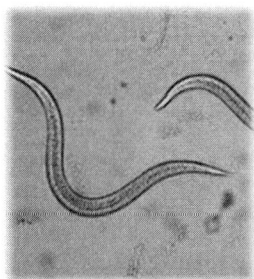

Description: There are good nematodes and bad nematodes. Here, we are going to refer to the beneficial variety that feed on pest insects. These creatures are microscopic worms invisible to the naked eye, but if you have them in your soil, one small handful will contain thousands of them. These Entomopathogenic nematodes rarely attack beneficial insect larvae, focusing on the hosts of destructive ones. They seek out the detrimental insect larvae, enter the body, and inject a bacterium which kills the host in one–two days.

Cycle: The nematode has a complicated reproductive cycle, but basically once they have entered the host body and have killed it, they then reproduce in its dead body, producing several hundred thousand offspring. They have a very short lifespan and reproduce best in moist soil temperatures ranging from 55–65 degrees F. (12.7-18.3 degrees C.).

Praying Mantis Predator

Description: The Mantis religiosa was accidentally introduced to the east coast of the United States from Europe in 1899 and spread to Eastern Canada. It was then intentionally introduced to the prairie grasslands to help control grasshopper infestations. The Litaneutria minor or ground mantis is native to Canada and lives in the Okanagan Valley of British Columbia. Of this species, only the male can fly, but the female can get around very well, often running at a good pace. When frightened, they display aggressive postures. They are masters of camouflage, often mimicking twigs, leaves, and even flowers. Mantis' have a flat, triangular head with bulging eyes on a long, flexible neck which has the ability to rotate 180 degrees in order to scan for their next meal. The body, when fully mature, can reach up to two inches (five cm.). It is elongated with large, thick forelegs with pointy spikes that it uses to catch and hold onto its prey. Being a true insect, it has two sets of wings and six legs. The mantis doesn't pupate. When the young hatch, they look like a smaller version of the adult and are the size of a small ant. The eggs are not visible but are enclosed in a hard capsule. The mantis only consumes living insects; the young prey on aphids, leafhoppers, mosquitos, and small caterpillars. The adults will go after larger prey such as beetles, grasshoppers, and crickets.

Cycle: In the fall, the female will lay between 100–200 eggs in a white frothy mass that turns into a hard capsule, protecting the eggs from the winter cold. In the spring, the eggs hatch into miniature-looking adults. Mantis do not pupate. The immature mantis goes through six–nine molts where they shed the rigid outer skin, allowing it to grow a little more with each molt. The lifespan of the mantis is one year.

- **Destructive Garden Insects**: Destructive insects are the ones that cause damage to landscape vegetation and the food crops we are growing.

• Identifying Common Destructive Garden Insects

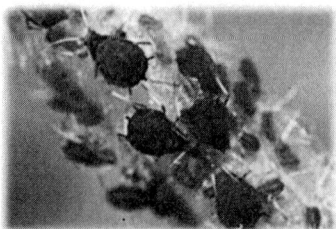

APHIDS:

Description: Aphids are tiny, almost-invisible, pear-shaped insects ranging in colors from white, black, brown, gray, yellow, light green,

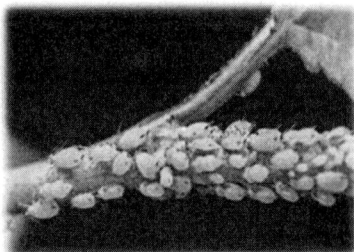

and even sometimes pink. They have two long antennae pointing rearward over their backs. They are always in large masses in plant foliage, on stems, and flowers. They are a sucking insect feeding on plant juices and then secreting a sticky honeydew substance, revealing their presence. Once they have decimated a crop, they can develop wings and fly to more feeding grounds.

Control: The best biological solution is to use beneficial insects to control these nasty little bugs. If you have a mild infestation, try blasting them with cold water to dislodge them. You can try mixing a teaspoon of liquid dish detergent in a quart of water with a pinch of cayenne pepper added and spray them. Don't use this spray in the heat of the day though. Insecticidal soaps can be purchased from garden centers to help control aphid infestations. Keep in mind that by using any of these sprays, you can be damaging beneficial insect populations too.

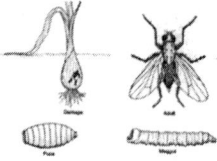

Cabbage Maggot:

Description: The adult cabbage maggot is a small, quarter-inch (6.3 mm.) gray fly that has overwintered in the soil in a cozy cocoon. She starts laying her eggs, anywhere between 50–200 of them,

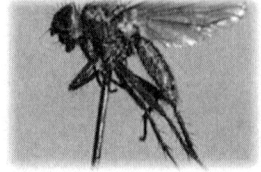

at the base of her favorite targets which are any and all of the brassicas. She carefully hides the eggs just under the soil surface. The eggs then hatch into small, white, legless maggots. They wiggle their way down through the soil, feeding on small roots and hairs as they go. They then tunnel into the plants taproot, causing the plant to wither and die.

Control: The best control measures for this damaging maggot is to have plenty of beneficial insects present to devour them. After you have set your transplants out, place sticky traps out periodically around your brassica plants to monitor these insects. If you find an infestation, gently dig the host plant out and hose the offenders away, then gently replace the plant. You can try placing a landscape fabric around the host plants so she can't lay her eggs in the soil, but the timing for this procedure is always a little tricky.

Carrot Rust Fly:

Description: These innocent-looking flies actually don't do any damage to crops, it is the larvae that will completely destroy carrot, turnip, celery, parsley, and other members of the

carrot family. The adult with her small, shiny, black body, reddish head, and yellow legs, is attracted to the scent of

the host plant. She lays her eggs at the base of the plant where they stay for only a few days. As the larvae hatch, they immediately start burrowing down into the soil and feed on the roots, causing tunneling throughout. Because we aren't accustomed to eating the parsley root, it is still able to produce the leaves we use. It is the edible root crops that are so badly affected by this insect.

Control: The only thing I have found to be affective in the control of the carrot rust fly is to plant my crop under a fully enclosed shade cloth. This keeps the fly from laying her eggs at the base of my carrots.

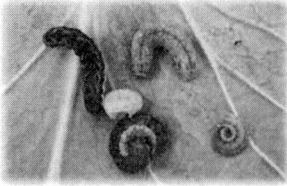

Caterpillars:
Description: Caterpillar bodies are soft and worm-like; some are smooth bodied and some are hairy.

Some even have stingers. Some have multiple legs; some don't have legs at all. Unfortunately, the beneficial butterfly that we attract to our gardens for pollination purposes started out as a caterpillar. Depending on the species, the

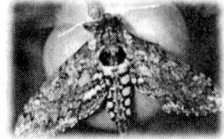

damage a caterpillar can cause takes different forms. Some eat entire leaves; some just chew holes in the leaves. Some scrape away the top layer of the leaf, and some fold the leaf up with a silk thread and hide inside the leaf. Cutworms are also under this category. They are active at night, chewing through stems at ground level.

Control: If you see caterpillars in your vegetable garden and you aren't sure about the species, it is best to look it up. I have found that the ones I see in my garden are usually the cabbage moth (picture to the left) or the tomato hornworm (picture to the right). For the best control, besides having beneficial insects in the garden is to simply handpick them off the plants and drop them into a container filled with soapy water. I have found that some birds will keep the number of caterpillars at bay as well, so having a couple of bird houses to attract small bird species in the yard can be very beneficial.

Colorado Potato Beetle:

Description: The eggs are yellow ovals and are laid in upright clusters of 10 to 30 on the undersides of leaves. After about two weeks, the eggs hatch and the larvae start to move throughout the host plant, eating the leaves as they go. The larvae are humpbacked, shiny, and orange, with black spots on the sides. They stay in this stage for about ten days, drop to the ground, pupate, and become adult beetles which continue to feed on the leaves. The adults are orange in color with ten distinctive black stripes on the wing covers. The damage they cause drastically reduces crop yields and the defoliation will kill young plants.

Control: If you start to notice chewing on the leaves of your potato plants, you probably have a few Colorado potato beetles roaming about. The best control method is to handpick the eggs, larvae, and adults off and drop them into a container filled with soapy water.

Onion Maggot:

Description: Once again, we have an innocent-looking fly that in itself is not responsible for any damage. This little multi-generational, quarter-inch (6.3 mm.) long, gray fly, resembling the common housefly, lays her eggs in the soil at the base of onions, garlic, shallots, and leeks. The eggs hatch into 1/3 inch (8.3 mm.) long, white larvae which start feeding on the forming bulbs. An early infestation can kill and stunt young plants and a later infestation is often not revealed until after harvest when the bulbs start to rot.

Control: Insecticides are ineffective to the onion maggot, as the fly has built up a resistance to these methods, as is often the case with chemical means. For early prevention, plant your onions out a little later after the insects first generation is over. You will get smaller bulbs but free of rot. You can set out sticky traps to catch the female fly. Floating row covers have been proven to be a very effective method of control as long as they are installed as soon as the crop is planted. The row cover can be removed by late June. Another proven effective control method is the use of Entomopathogenic nematodes. As a last resort, try growing onions in containers or raised beds with fresh, new, untainted soil.

- **OTHER CREEPIES AND CRAWLIES IN THE GARDEN**

MOLLUSC: (Slugs and snails) Destructive

Description:

You probably don't need a description of these critters, but in any case, they are the slow-moving,

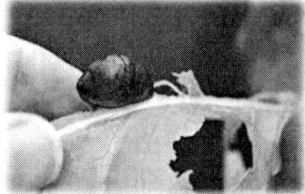

slimy creatures with a soft, long, legless body. A snail is a slug with a hard shell to house itself in, protecting it from predators. Both secrete a slimy mucus as they slide along surfaces. And both feed on plant material, consuming several times their body weight daily. Slugs and snails prefer moist, cool, shady spaces to live. They have both female and male body parts and so can reproduce all by themselves in their one–two-year lifespan.

Control: Slugs generally return to their 'nesting' sites after a night of heavy feeding. If you can locate the site, sprinkle the slug with salt. This will withdraw their moisture, causing dehydration and death. As kids, salting slugs was one of our evening chores before bedtime. You can also handpick, wearing gloves of course, and drop them into a container of salty water. Slugs are attracted to the smell of beer, so you can set up beer traps by digging a container into the soil and filling

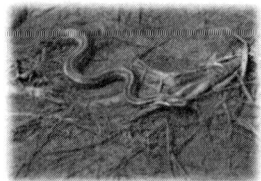

it with beer. The slug will fall in and drown. Or pour a little beer in plastic drinking bottles and lay them on their sides for slug collection. (I can think of better things to do with beer!) Be sure to keep beer traps away from where pets can get into them. Slugs don't like copper, so if you have raised garden beds, you can run copper tape around the perimeter to keep the slugs and snails out. Another natural deterrent is to spread a width of crushed oyster or clam shells around the perimeter of your garden or around the base of the garden plants. These mollusks don't like crawling over the shards of shell. Or, if you are not like me, being terrified by them, attract garter snakes to the garden. Give them some water and a small pile of rocks to curl up in. They love to dine on slugs and other small, chewing rodents.

Spiders (Probably the most abundant predators in the landscape)

Description: Many debate the pros and cons of having spiders in the garden, as many people have a fear and a dislike of these eight-legged arachnids. There are literally thousands of spider species worldwide and many of them have an irritating and harmful bite. Most of our gardens will have a dozen or more various types. Because of the voracious appetite of the spider, it not only consumes pest insects but will also eat the beneficial ones. My way of thinking is, if they are there in not too many numbers, let them stay. The garden variety usually don't spin webs, rather live in shallow underground burrows or on plant foliage. They pounce on their prey of aphids, leaf hoppers, spider mites, and thrips. One common type, the Wolf Spider, is identifiable by having a hairy, brown body with dark stripes. The female is very maternal. She carries her egg sac around with her, and if she drops it, she goes back to look for it. Once the eggs hatch, she carries the young on her back for weeks until they are old enough to look after themselves.

Chapter Seven
Harvesting Your Garden

We have finally reached our ultimate goal of harvesting the crops we lovingly started, planted, weeded, watered, and tended. To get the most flavor and nutritional value, harvest your crops at their peak of freshness. There is no perfect way of telling when that is, but doing a taste test is a good way to start. In Chapter Four, I included information on the seed to harvest ratio for vegetable crops, so by using that information as well as tasting, that will give you a pretty good idea of their maturity peak. Harvesting in the morning just after the dew has dried is always the best time. This also gives you a full day to do any processing of the crops you have harvested. Following is a little more detailed information on harvesting your garden crops, as well as a bit of information on storing and preserving. Chapter Eight will give details of the various preservation methods.

Angelica: In these plants' first year, harvest only the leaves in late spring to early summer. In its second year, the tender stalks can be harvested for candying in mid to late summer, and in the second fall, the roots can be harvested.

Storing and Preserving: The leaves can be dried for medicinal teas. The stems can be candied. The roots can be dried and used for medicinal remedies. *Recipe for candying angelica follows in Chapter Eight.

Asparagus: In the first year, pick only a few spears in the first two weeks of production, allowing the others to go into stem form which will feed the root system. Harvest for three weeks in the second year and for four–six weeks in the following years. Always allow a few spears to become ferny stems to feed the roots. Harvest when the spears are seven–nine inches (15.25–5 cm.) high and the tips are still tight. Cut or snap just above the soil level.

Storing and Preserving: Asparagus will freeze, but the texture is altered, making it a bit mushy. It can however be cut into pieces and frozen for use in soups, omelets, and frittatas. Asparagus will also make a fine pickle. *Recipe for pickles Asparagus follows in Chapter Eight.

Basil: For small harvests, pick the leaves off as needed and be sure to keep the buds picked out. For a larger harvest for freezing or dehydrating, snip the stems back, up to 1/3 of the length at a leaf junction. This will also promote thicker, bushier growth for future harvests. Basil is a tender annual, so just before your first frost, pull the entire plant out of the ground and strip off all the leaves.

Storing and Preserving: The leaves can be dried, but basil is best blanched and frozen to retaining the best color and flavor. Basil also makes a wonderful pesto.

Beans: Pole beans will give you a continuous crop throughout the season and produce twice as much as bush beans without taking up a lot of garden space. Bush beans give one large crop in a two–three-week span, which is more convenient for preserving. Harvest your crop often to encourage production of the fresh pods. For the edible pods, pick before you see the seeds bulging and when the pod is about as thick as a pencil. They should make a nice crisp snap when bent. Beans become overripe and tough quickly, so check them often. They will need almost daily harvesting to promote continuous production. Use a pair of small sharp scissors to cut the pod from the vine, so the stem doesn't tear, ruining future harvests. If you can't process them right away, store them in airtight freezer bags in the crisper unit of your fridge for up to four days.

Storing and Preserving: Fresh beans in the pod can be frozen; they can be pressure canned and pickled. You can make your own 'Pickled Bean Clamato Juice,' by pouring some of the pickled bean brine into regular Clamato juice, and there you have it. They can also be dried in a unique way called 'Leather Britches.'

For seed harvest, leave the full pods on the vine to dry for about a month. When they are ready for picking, the pods will be brown and the seeds inside will rattle when shaken. Lay the pods out in a single layer on old newspapers or paper towels out of the weather for a couple of weeks. Once you have shelled them, store the seeds in well-labeled airtight containers. They store best at temperatures between 32–41 degrees F. (0–5 degrees C.) *recipe for Leather Britches and Hot Pickled beans follows in Chapter Eight.

Beets: Beets can be pulled at any stage of growth once the shoulders have protruded the soil surface that will take place around the end of July if you planted them in mid-May. You can also eat the flavorful greens by cutting up to 1/3 of the outer leaves and leaving the inner ones to feed the root part of the crop. Pull the beetroot by grasping the leaf stems at the base and gently give a slight twist as you pull. Hose the soil residue off before bringing inside. Beets do tend to go woody if left in the ground for too long though, so harvest no later than September.

Storing and Preserving: You can preserve beets almost any way you want. They can be kept in cold storage, dried, or pickled. They can also be pressure canned and frozen. *Recipe for pickled beets follows in Chapter Eight.

Blackberries: Blackberries are ripe when they have turned from red to a deep black, usually in late August to early September. This transition takes from two-three days. It is always more painful and difficult to pick berries from vines that have thorns on them. The best way to do this is to bend down and look up into the mass of leaves and stems. Once you spot a clump of berries, carefully reach in and pluck as many as your hand will hold and gently withdraw your arm. Try to keep your picked berries as cool as you can. Don't leave the fruit on the vine for too long because many birds love the sweet-tasting berries. Don't wash the fruit until you are ready to use it. A well-trained vine can produce up to 20 pounds of berries in its third year and every year thereafter.

Storing and Preserving: So much can be done to preserve these tasty berries. Most commonly is to make jam or jelly. You can make an outstanding blackberry wine; I am so envious of you folks at the coastal regions that have this free crop in abundance everywhere. They make an excellent juice, syrup, and fruit leather. They also freeze beautifully, so in the winter months you can bring a little taste of summer back in the form of pies, cobblers, and crisps. It is a little time consuming, but you can also dehydrate blackberries.

Blueberries: Blueberries will be ready for picking in late July to mid-August, depending on the variety. Don't pull the berries from the stem but give them a gentle twist. If they don't come off easily, they aren't ready for picking yet. Birds love blueberries, so it is best to drape netting over top of the ripening fruits. Allow the berries to hang on the bush for a couple of days after they turn blue to sweeten them up. If you plant two-year-old blueberry plants, they should start to bear within a year or two. The maximum production of five–seven pints (three–four lt.) per plant is reached after six years.

Storing and Preserving: Blueberries are a versatile fruit and are most commonly frozen for winter use. However, you can also dehydrate them. They make an excellent jam, jelly, or syrup. If you have enough of them, you can turn these yummy little berries into juice, fruit leather, and wine. If you don't have room in your freezer, they can even be canned. They also make an excellent vinegar. *Recipe for blueberry vinegar follows in Chapter Eight.

Borage: Harvest only the top tender leaves as needed. The flowers will appear in late June through to September.

Storing and Preserving: Borage leaves can be dried for teas. The pretty blue flowers can be crystalized and they retain their color when frozen in ice cubes. You can even make a borage vinegar for dressing a salad.

Broccoli: If you started your broccoli inside in March, your seedlings would be close to eight weeks old when you transplanted them outside in May. Once they have established themselves outside, you should notice a thick stem with a large flower head forming. Cut the stem and the entire flower head when the buds are still green. If you see any sign of white or yellow flowers emerging from the buds, remove the flower head right away. This will be your main crop. You will then get numerous side-shoots emerging from the main stem at the branch junctions. This extended part of the crop will continue right up until frost if you are consistent in the picking process.

Storing and Preserving: Broccoli tends to lose its color and it goes to mush when canned, so the most common way of preserving broccoli is to freeze it. It can also be pickled, either in vinegar or in mustard, and when done this way, it is usually combined with other vegetables such as cauliflower, carrots, onions, and peppers.

Brussels Sprouts: Wait until after your first frost to begin the Brussels sprout harvest. This 'frosting' improves the flavor and sweetness. To harvest the small, tender, mini cabbages, simply twist the sprouts off the stem from the bottom of the stalk upward, gathering only as many as you need at one time. The remaining sprouts will keep on the plants through part of the winter. You can even pick Brussels sprouts when there's snow on the ground. You can extend your harvest before the deep, long, cold spell by pulling the plant out of the ground and hanging it upside down in a cool storage place.

Storing and Preserving: Brussels sprouts are most commonly frozen; they do however make an awesome pickle to wow your friends and family with, as you will probably never see any for sale on the shelf of a grocery store. They keep relatively well in cold storage.

Cabbage: Harvest when the heads reach the desired size and are firm, usually when they are about 16 weeks old. Most early varieties will produce one–three-pound (45–136 gr.) heads. Cut each cabbage head at its base with a sharp knife. After harvesting, bring the head inside or put it in the shade immediately. To get two crops from early cabbage plants, cut the cabbage head out of the plant, leaving the bottom outer leaves and root in the garden. The plant will send up new heads; pinch them off until only four or so smaller heads remain. When these grow to tennis-ball size, they'll be perfect for salad. If you leave cabbages in the ground for too long, they continue to grow and will split open but are still good to be used for sauerkraut.

Storing and Preserving: You can store cabbages in a root cellar or other cold storage place and even in your fridge if you have the room. You can preserve cabbage by freezing it; this alters the texture, so it is only suitable to be used in soups and stews. And, of course, it can be fermented and turned into sauerkraut.

Carrots: I usually keep my eye on the carrot tops to determine when the roots are ready for harvest. The tops should be tall and ferny. I then run my finger around the base of the stem to see the thickness of the root. Anything over half-inch (12.7 mm.) diameter is ready for harvest. If the width of the root is good, the length generally is too. Slide a small garden fork or trowel into the soil at the base of the carrot and pull the handle gently toward you to loosen the little rootlets, then grasp the leaf stems at the base and give a little pull. The carrot should come out of the soil without breaking. Carrots can be left in the soil, harvesting as needed, allowing them to continue to grow.

Storing and Preserving: You can leave intact mature carrots in the soil for storage if the ground doesn't freeze or mulch heavily to prevent freezing. Carrots keep in cold storage at temperatures just above freezing for months. Carrots can also be pickled, dried, and pressure canned. They can be frozen too, but the texture is altered, making them watery and limp.

Cauliflower: Harvest the heads when they are compact, white, and firm. Ideally, the heads will grow six–eight inches (15.24–20.32 cm.) in diameter. Cut the heads off the plant with a large, sharp knife, leaving some of the bottom leaves around the head to keep it protected. If you leave cauliflower in the garden for too long, it will become brown and have a mealy texture.

Storing and Preserving: If you have any cauliflower left in the garden just before frost, you can pull the plant up by the roots and hang it upside down in a cool storage place. Cauliflower freezes well and it can also be pickled either in vinegar or in mustard, and when done this way, it is usually combined with other vegetables such as broccoli, carrots, onions, and peppers.

Chard: Cut off the outer stems at the plant base to allow the smaller inner leaves to continue to grow and you will be harvesting chard right up to the first frost.

Storing and Preserving: Once the weather gets cold, chard starts to shut down. This is a good time to pick any remaining leaves and freeze them for winter use.

Chives: You can generally start to harvest the tubular leaves 30 days after you have transplanted your seedlings. To harvest, cut the stem down to the base of the plant. In its first year, only do three to four harvests. In subsequent years, you can harvest as often and as much as needed.

Storing and Preserving: If you don't have a bright window to keep a living plant in for winter use, it is best to freeze the leaves and flowers, as dehydrated chives lose their flavor.

Cilantro/Coriander: Harvest the cilantro leaves as needed and continue to prune out the stalk if you don't want it to bolt and go to seed. If you are growing the plant for the coriander seed, allow it to flower and go to seed. Once the plant turns brown, cut it right off at soil level and place it upside down in a paper bag to collect the seeds. Store them, once dried, in an airtight container.

Storing and Preserving: The leaves can be dried, but cilantro is best blanched and frozen in order to retain the best color and flavor. The leaves also make a wonderful pesto.

Corn: Three weeks after the corn silks appear, check the ears for ripeness by gently pulling back part of the husk and piercing a kernel with a fingernail. If the milk spurts out, it is ready to be picked. Grasp the ear tightly, give a little twist, and pull it downward. It should break away from the stem nicely. Harvest only what you need, as picked corn will become starchy as it sits. The bottom ear usually ripens first, the others should be ripe a few days later.

Storing and Preserving: Corn keeps its flavor, texture, and color when pressure canned. It also freezes well; you can either remove the kernels or freeze the entire cob. The removed and blanched kernels can also be dried.

Cucumbers: Cucumbers need to be picked almost daily to maintain a continuous harvest of up to six weeks. You can pick them at any size as long as they are not over mature. Once they are over mature, the plant will shut down and stop producing. Gherkins are harvested when they are only a couple of inches long, some dills when they are about six inches (15.24 cm.) long, and other slicing and serpent-shaped varieties much longer. Gently twist or clip the fruit from the vine to avoid stem damage and ruining future harvests.

Storing and Preserving: Cucumbers do not store in their fresh state, but they make wonderful relishes, sweet pickles, and dill pickles. *Recipe for dill pickles and bread and butter pickles follows in Chapter Eight.

Currants: When the fruit has become shiny, it is usually ready to be picked. The fruits of the early cultivars generally start to ripen in mid-June, later varieties ripen into September. To pick the fruit, pull the entire fruit cluster off rather than each individual berry. Once you are ready to use the fruit, remove the individual berries by running a fork down the mid-stem cluster. Currant bushes can live for 12–15 years, and a mature shrub can produce up to four quarts (3.78 lt.) of fruit annually.

Storing and Preserving: Well, what can't you do with currants? I'll start with the liquid processing; juicing and turning them into wine. They make a delightful jelly or syrup. They freeze very well, they can be made into fruit leather, and they can also be dried to be used in baked goods.

Dill: To harvest the leaves and the flower heads, be sure to use sharp scissors or pruning shears. The ferny foliage is called 'dill weed' and is milder in flavor. To get the best flavor when making pickles, pick the flower head right before the buds open. To harvest the seeds, allow the flower heads to go into full bloom, and when the plant starts to die down, cut it right off at soil level and place it upside down in a paper bag to collect the seeds.

Storing and Preserving: If you haven't used all of your dill up in making pickles, you can preserve the remainder by either drying it or freezing it in ice cubes.

Eggplant: Eggplant is ready for picking when the skin takes on a high gloss and when the indentation of a finger doesn't spring back. If left too long, the seeds turn brown and the flesh becomes pithy. Cut the fruit from the stem with a sharp knife or pruning shears rather than hand pulling it off.

Storing and Preserving: Pretty well, the only way to preserve eggplant is to freeze it.

Garlic: Hard neck garlic will send up flower stalks that should be picked to promote larger bulbs. Harvest when foliage browns and falls over. If you lift them too soon, the bulbs will be a little bit smaller. Once you have lifted the bulbs, the leaves can be braided and the roots trimmed off. Cure the bulbs by hanging these braids in a warm, dry area with good circulation for a few weeks.

Storing and Preserving: Garlic stores really well in a cool, dark, dry environment with good air circulation. Garlic also dehydrates well and can be made into a salt. For you hardened garlic lovers, they make a fine pickle.

Gooseberries: Gooseberries are usually ready for harvest in late June or early July in a series of two to three pickings. Some varieties don't ripen until mid-August. A test for ripeness can be done by a gentle squeeze to a berry. If it is hard, it isn't ready for picking. If it has a little give to it, it is ripe. Because gooseberry bushes have thorns, it is a good idea to wear thick gloves for this harvest. Gently give each berry a little tug to coax it from the stem. A mature plant of five years or more can produce 6–12 pounds (2.7–5.4 kg.) of fruit per year.

Storing and Preserving: Gooseberries make a delightful jam, jelly, or syrup. They freeze well, they can be made into fruit leather, and they can also be dried. But more commonly, gooseberries are turned into wine.

Grapes: Grapevines bear by their third or fourth growing season. Depending on the variety you have chosen, harvesting can take place from mid-June through to mid-October. To pick the ripe fruits, support the cluster with one hand and cut its stem with pruning shears. To avoid bruising, handle the clusters gently and lay them in a basket. The best time to harvest grapes in is the early morning while the temperatures are still cool. Move the clusters to a cool place as soon as you have completed your harvest.

Storing and Preserving: Anybody that drinks wine automatically thinks grapes! Grapes also make an excellent juice and jelly. Dried, they become raisins.

Horseradish: You can pick some of the tender new leaves for salads as they emerge. Harvest your horseradish roots in the fall, late September, and even into November before the ground freezes. The best way to dig this root out is to use a gardening fork rather than a shovel. Loosen the soil in a wide circle around the base of the plant. Then feel for the root to see which direction it is traveling. Continue to loosen the soil along the length of the root until you can remove the entire mass. Wash it, pat it dry, and place it in an airtight container in the fridge until you are ready to process it.

Storing and Preserving: The whole unwashed roots can be stored in moist sand or sawdust and placed in cold storage. The peeled and sliced or grated roots can be dried or frozen. More commonly, the peeled and grated root can be infused with vinegar and canned for winter use. *Recipe for Horseradish sauce follows in Chapter Eight.

Kale: You can harvest kale from spring right on through until the ground freezes and even longer if the plants are protected with a layer of mulch and a row cover. Use a sharp pair of scissors to pick the outer leaves when they are about six inches (15.25 cm.) long, allowing the tender inner leaves to grow for your next harvest.

Storing and Preserving: It is best to freeze kale, but it can also be dehydrated.

Lavender: The best time to harvest lavender is when the buds are formed but not yet opened. It will retain its color and scent better than if the flowers are in full bloom. Use a sharp pair of pruners and grasp a handful of stems to make a good clean cut, being sure to leave at least two sets of leaves on the green part of the stem. A brown stem will not regrow. When you've got a good-sized handful, secure it with twine, elastic, or zip ties. When you have finished your harvest, hang the bunches upside down in a warm, dry area out of the weather. They should be dry in two–four weeks.

<u>Storing and Preserving:</u> For the home gardener, pretty well the best way to preserve this aromatic herb is to dry it as mentioned above. However, lavender also makes a nice, flavored vinegar.

<u>Leeks:</u> You can start your leek harvest once the stalk is about an inch (2.5 cm.) in diameter. However, the flavor of the leek is much better after a light frost. Leeks aren't super cold hardy, but you can extend the harvest once the extreme cold sets in by hilling soil around the plants and applying a heavy layer of straw mulch. To get the leeks out of the soil without damaging them, dig lightly around the shaft with a garden fork before pulling it out of the ground.

<u>Storing and Preserving:</u> If you have mulched your leeks in the garden, you will want to lift them before the deep cold hits. Leeks do not freeze well, but they dehydrate relatively well. You can also try placing them in cold storage.

<u>Lemon Balm:</u> Lemon balm can be harvested on an as-needed basis by cutting a few sprigs at a time or removing a few leaves for salads. To do a big harvest, cut the whole plant back to about three inches (7.6 cm.) above ground level before it goes to flower. This will not kill the plant, but instead it encourages nice, new, fresh growth.

<u>Storing and Preserving:</u> Lemon balm leaves dry very well but can also be frozen either in freezer bags or in ice. The leaves can also be crystalized.

<u>Lettuce:</u> The best time to harvest lettuce is in the cool of the morning. To harvest your loose-leaf lettuce plants, don't pull the entire plant out. Just pick as many leaves as you require and let the plant continue to grow until it starts to form a flower stalk. Once this happens, the leaves turn bitter. For the head varieties, cut it off at soil level with a sharp knife or pull the entire plant out of the ground.

<u>Storing and Preserving:</u> You can extend the storage life of lettuce plants by wrapping the roots in damp paper towel and placing in an airtight container in the fridge. Check periodically and remoisten or replace the paper towel as needed. Lettuce leaves can be frozen, but they do not retain their crunchy texture.

Lovage: The nice, new, lighter green lovage leaves are best to harvest on an as-needed basis. The older darker green ones become tough. The leaves will lose a lot of their flavor if washed, so just give them a little shake. For a larger, final harvest, pick the leaves, tie them in bunches, and hang them upside down in dark, well-ventilated area.

Storing and Preserving: Lovage dries beautifully. You can also make a lovely flavored vinegar with it.

Marjoram: With a sharp pair of scissors, pick these flavorful leaves on an as-needed basis. For a full harvest in order to dry for winter storage, cut up to 1/3 of the leaves off just before the buds flower.

Storing and Preserving: This herb dries very well and is one that does not lose its flavor after drying. As with most herbs, it can be used to make a flavored vinegar.

Melons: It can sometimes be a little difficult to determine when melons are perfect for picking. Once the fruit has a full, sweet smell, look at the stem instead of the actual fruit to determine its ripeness. If the stem is brown, and the fruit separates from it easily without tugging or cutting, this usually means the fruit is ready. You can also determine the ripeness by looking to see if the stem has a crack in it where it attaches to the fruit.

Storing and Preserving: Melons can be dried for tasty snacks. Watermelon rinds can also be pickled. Freezing is also a good way to preserve these fruits.

Mint: Mint can be harvested on an as-needed basis by cutting a few sprigs at a time or removing a few leaves for salads. To do a big harvest, cut the whole plant back to about three inches (7.6 cm.) above ground level before it goes to flower. This will not kill the plant, but instead it encourages nice, new, fresh growth.

Storing and Preserving: As with lemon balm, mint leaves dry very well but can also be frozen either in freezer bags or in ice. The leaves can also be crystalized.

Onions: Once you notice the tops turning yellow, bend them over to stop the flow of sap. This allows the plant's energy to mature the bulb. Leave them like this until the tops turn brown. On a warm, sunny day, dig the bulbs out of the soil and lay them out to dry for a bit. Once you have lifted all the bulbs, the leaves can be braided. Cure the bulbs by hanging these braids in a warm, dry area with good circulation for a few weeks.

Storing and Preserving: Onions store really well in a cool, dark, dry environment with good air circulation. They also dehydrate well and can be made into a salt. If you have grown shallots or silver skins, they make a great pickle.

Oregano: Oregano can be harvested on an as-needed basis by cutting a few sprigs at a time or removing a few leaves for salads. To do a big harvest, cut the whole plant back to about three inches (7.6 cm.) above ground level before it goes to flower. This will not kill the plant, but instead it encourages nice new fresh growth.

Storing and Preserving: You can hang clumps of stems in a well-ventilated area to dry. Or trim the leaves from the stems and freeze either in freezer bags or in ice.

Parsley: Parsley can be harvested on an as-needed basis by cutting a few sprigs at a time or removing a few leaves for salads. To do a big harvest, cut the whole plant back to about three inches (7.6 cm.) above ground level before it goes to flower.

Storing and Preserving: You can hang clumps of stems in a well-ventilated area to dry. Or trim the leaves from the stems and freeze either in freezer bags or in ice.

Parsnip: For the best flavor, harvest after your first frost. Slide a small garden fork or hand trowel into the soil at the base of the plant and pull it gently toward you to loosen the little rootlets, then grasp the leaf stems at the base and give a little pull. The parsnip should come out of the soil without breaking.

Storing and Preserving: You can leave intact, mature parsnips in the soil for storage if the ground will not freeze or mulch heavily to prevent freezing. Parsnips keep in cold storage at temperatures just above freezing for months. Parsnips can also be dried and pressure canned. Surprisingly, they also freeze quite well.

PEA: About three weeks after the plants start to flower, you should keep an eye on the forming pods. For the shelled pod variety, wait for the pods to be nice and plump and a bright green color. The edible pod varieties should be about three inches (7.6 cm.) long and flat, barely showing the developing seeds. Keep your peas well picked to encourage more pods to develop. They are crispiest when picked in the morning after the dew has dried. Always use two hands when you pick peas. Secure the vine with one hand and pull the peas off with your other hand. Or use a shape pair of scissors to cut them from the vines.

Storing and Preserving: Shelled peas can be dried, pressure canned, or frozen. Canning peas alters their color and texture but are still useful in soups and for making mushy peas. The best way to preserve these sweet, little seeds is to freeze them.

Pepper: Sweet pepper varieties can be harvested when they are green and full sized. If they are left on the plant, they will continue to ripen, becoming sweeter as they change from green to yellow to orange and red. Use pruning shears or a sharp knife to cut peppers from the plants, leaving a stem stub on the fruit instead of pulling them off, as the stems are extremely fragile. When harvesting hot pepper varieties, use gloves, as the capsicum oil (heat) will stay on your hands, causing burns.

Storing and Preserving: Surprisingly, peppers freeze quite well; they don't retain all of their crunch, but they do retain their flavor. Peppers also dry very well and they can be canned in the form of salsas, sauces, and relishes. You can also pickle peppers.

Potatoes: You can start harvesting those lovely, little, 'new' potatoes as soon as the plants start to flower. Gently dig around the base of the plant and pull off only what you need. You can continue to harvest on an as-needed basis by feeling around in the soil and pulling off only the tubers you need for your nightly dinner. When the plants completely die back, it is time to complete the harvest. Dig them up carefully with a spading fork on an overcast day and give them a good rinse without damaging the tender skins. They will then need to be cured for winter storage. Curing them will harden up their skins. This is done by layering them in a dark place at temperatures between 45–60 degrees F. (7.2–15.5 C.) for a couple of weeks. They are then ready for winter storage.

Storing and Preserving: To keep potatoes in their fresh form, it is best to store them in cold storage. Potatoes can also be frozen and dehydrated, but they need to be cooked to an al dente stage first. You can also pressure can some of those nice, little, new potatoes.

Radish: You can start harvesting radish as soon as they mature to about half inch (1.25 cm.) in diameter. If they are left in the ground for too long, they will split and become woody. Simply grasp the cluster of stems, give a little yank and your radish will pop right out of the ground.

Storing and Preserving: You can store radishes with the stems and leaves removed in the fridge in a jar filled with water for up to a month. Replace the water often. Radishes also can be kept in cold storage but don't last as long as carrots or potatoes.

Raspberry: Red raspberries are usually the first to ripen, followed by blacks. These berries do not continue to ripen after they have been picked, so wait until they are fully ripe before harvesting. Try to harvest in the early morning while it is still cool. Handle them gently and refrigerate right away for use that day. Because raspberries have perennial roots and biennial canes, you will have these plants indefinitely. With proper care, you can get between one–two quarts (1.1–2.3 lt.) per plant.

Storing and Preserving: So much can be done to preserve these tasty berries. Most commonly is to make jam or jelly. You can make a great raspberry red wine. They also make an excellent juice, syrup, and fruit leather. They freeze beautifully, and they can also be dehydrated.

Rhubarb: Allow the plant to grow without any disturbance for the first year. In the early spring of the second year, when the leaves are fully developed, twist and pull the stalks from the crowns. You can harvest the rhubarb stalks for one–two months, but be sure to not eat any of the leaves, as they are toxic.

Storing and Preserving: Because rhubarb and strawberries are ready to be harvested at the same time, combined they make a tasty jam. It can also be stewed and then canned. But the best way to preserve rhubarb is to freeze it. *Recipe for Rhubarb Custard Pie follows in Chapter Eight.

Rosemary: With a sharp pair of scissors, snip off the tender new stems on an as-needed basis. This helps to create full bushy plants. For a big harvest to dry for winter use, prune all of the green stems off just before the plant starts to flower.

Storing and Preserving: Rosemary makes a fantastic flavored vinegar and oil. It freezes very well and retains most of its flavor. It also is a good herb to dry by hanging bunches upside down in a warm, dry, ventilated area out of the weather. They should be dry in two–four weeks.

Sage: You can pinch out the tender top part of a stem or just a few leaves at a time on an as-needed basis. For a big harvest to dry for winter use, prune the entire plant down to 1/3 in July or August, giving the plant enough time to recover before winter sets in.

Storing and Preserving: Sage is a hardy shrub and can be picked almost year-round, but if you have an abundance of it, hang some of the stems upside down in a warm, dry, ventilated area. Sage is also a great herb to freeze and make a flavored vinegar with.

Spinach: Spinach leaves are ready to harvest as soon as they are big enough to eat. Harvest by removing only the outer leaves and allowing the center leaves to grow larger; this will allow the plant to keep producing. Picking the outer leaves also gives the advantage of briefly delaying bolting. When the weather warms up in the spring, and you see the plants are about to bolt, pull the entire plant at once to enjoy the leaves before they become bitter.

Storing and Preserving: Spinach gives a bountiful harvest while the weather remains on the cool side, but it shuts down when the weather warms up. You will generally get more than you can use while it is producing, but spinach freezes very well for winter use.

Squash: Summer squash, such as zucchini, can be picked as soon as they are about six inches (15.25 cm.) long. If you leave them on the vine too long, the plant will shut down and stop producing flowers, so to have these summer squash until frost, pick the fruits often. Use a sharp pair of pruning shears to cut the stem from the vine.

Winter squash such as acorn, butternut, and pumpkin, need to be left on the vine until the outer shell is hard. This is best done by leaving them alone until the vine turns brown and dies. If they are left out after frost, the flavor improves but in turn can shorten their storage life. Use sharp pruning shears to cut the fruit from the vine, leaving a two–three-inch (5–7.6 cm.) stem attached to the fruit. Harvest in dry weather and don't wash the fruit, as this can promote rot.

Storing and Preserving: Summer squash don't store in their fresh state very well, however, they freeze and can also be pickled. On the other hand, most varieties of winter squash keep well in cold storage. Winter squash can also be pressure canned and dehydrated.

Strawberry: The berries are ready to be picked four–six weeks after flowering and when they are a bright, shiny, red color. Harvest berries by pinching or cutting through the stem instead of pulling on the berry, as this can cause bruising. Avoid picking your berries when they are wet to reduce mold. You can expect your yield to be between ¼–½ pound (113–226 gm.) from each ever-bearing plant and between ½–1 (226–453 gm.) pound per June-bearing plant.

Storing and Preserving: Strawberries are one of the first fruits to harvest in the garden, so it is always an exciting time. So much can be done to preserve these tasty, bright berries. Most commonly is to make jam or jelly. You can make a great strawberry wine as Deana Carter sings about. They also make an excellent syrup and fruit leather. They freeze beautifully and they can also be dehydrated.

Summer Savory: You can start picking summer savory when it is about six inches (15.25 cm.) tall on an as-needed basis. For a big harvest to dry for winter use, prune all of the green stems off.

Storing and Preserving: Summer Savory makes a fantastic flavored vinegar. It freezes very well and retains most of its flavor. It also is a good herb to dry by hanging bunches upside down in a warm, dry, ventilated area out of the weather. They should be dry in two–four weeks.

Tarragon: You can start harvesting the new green shoots using a pair of sharp scissors on an as-needed basis. To do a big harvest for winter storage, cut the plant back to 1/3 no later than mid-September. This will give the plant enough time to recover before winter sets in.

Storing and Preserving: Tarragon starts to lose its flavor as it sits, so dry or freeze it and store right away. It also makes a pretty vinegar.

Thyme: You can start picking thyme as soon as you can get out to the garden and once the snow has melted on as-needed basis. For a big harvest to dry for winter use, prune all of the green stems off before the plant flowers. Once you've got a good-sized handful, secure it with twine, elastic, or zip ties. Then hang the bunches upside down in a warm, dry, ventilated area out of the weather. They should be dry in two–four weeks.

Storing and Preserving: Thyme is similar to rosemary and makes a fantastic flavored vinegar. It freezes very well and retains most of its flavor. It also is a good herb to dry by hanging bunches upside down in a warm, dry, ventilated area out of the weather. They should be dry in two–four weeks.

Tomato: Tomatoes are ready for harvest when their color changes from a dull green to a rich, vibrant color and when they have a little give when gently squeezed in the palm of your hand. Once you have started your tomato harvest, you will have to check your plants on a daily basis in order to catch them at their peak of ripeness. Try to avoid pulling the fruit from the plant, as this can bruise the fruit and damage the plant. Use a pair of scissors to snip it off or give it a gentle twist while supporting the vine.

Storing and Preserving: Tomatoes store quite well in a dark, dry, storage area, especially the green ones you have picked prior to your first frost. The methods to preserve tomatoes are almost endless. They can be canned, frozen, dehydrated, made into a jam, and preserved in oil (sundried tomatoes). They can be made into ketchup, salsa, relish, sauce, and paste. You can juice them, pickle them, and make a tomato leather from them. *Recipes for salsa, sauce, and relishes follow in Chapter Eight.

Turnip: You can start to harvest up to 1/3 of the turnip greens once they are about six inches (15–25 cm.) tall. When your turnips have grown one–three inches (2.5–7.6 cm.) in diameter, they are young and tender and ready for harvest. For larger, mature crops, slide a small garden fork into the soil at the base and pull it gently toward you to loosen the little rootlets, then grasp the leaf stems and give a little pull. You can also leave mature turnips in the soil for storage if the ground will not freeze or mulch heavily to prevent freezing.

Storing and Preserving: Turnips keep in cold storage at temperatures just above freezing, for months if they are left unwashed (remove the leaves and stems) and stored in containers filled with moist sand or sawdust. Turnips can also be dried, and, surprisingly, they also freeze quite well.

Chapter Eight
Storing and Preserving Your Harvest

➤ Preserving

From the moment food is harvested, the spoilage process begins. Different foods have different windows of spoilage with heat, light, humidity, and microscopic organisms playing a large role in the rotting process. Eventually, all foods will spoil unless there is the intervention of preservation.

Preservation is nothing new to mankind. In early times, the people that lived in cold climates used ice to preserve their bounty, and the people living in warm, tropical areas used the wind and sun to preserve their foods. The people living in the Middle Ages built fires for heat in order to dry food when the sun lost its strength. By using this method, they soon discovered that the smoke from the fire acted as a preservation method as well. The natural process of fermentation was discovered and was used to preserve fruits and vegetables. From a spoiled batch of fermentation, pickling was discovered, as the spoiled batch had turned to vinegar. From as far back as the Roman days, honey was used to preserve fruits, and many peoples used salt to cure their meat and fish. As man evolved, so did the methods of food preservation.

In the early 19th century, a man by the name of Nicolas Appert made a major breakthrough in food preservation by discovering that by heating food and sealing it in a container, the food was preserved until the seal was broken. This method of canning has been improved upon throughout history.

It was long recognized that by keeping food cold, the spoilage process was delayed, and that by freezing it, the process was eliminated altogether. Iceboxes were introduced for home use in the early 19th century, and by the late 19th century, with the advent of residential electricity, fridges and freezers became common place.

So, now that you have a spectacular garden and have harvested your bounty, you will be preserving and storing some of your produce, even if it is only drying those aromatic herbs for winter use. Following are our modern-day preservation methods and attached are a few recipes to complete the garden-harvesting process.

➢ Methods of Preserving

- **Candying**: The candying method is used primarily for angelica stems.

Ingredients:

One cup (250 ml.) sugar
One cup (250 ml.) water
Half lb. (226 gr.) thick angelica stems cut in three–eight-inch (7.6–20 cm.) lengths

Directions:

Day 1:

1. Bring sugar and water to a boil. Remove from heat when the sugar is dissolved.
2. In a large pot, boil water; add stems. Cook on medium heat four–six minutes until tender. Drain, rinse in cold water, and drain again. Remove the outer skin.
3. Place peeled stems in a glass bowl and pour syrup from step 1 over them. Weigh them down so they stay submerged overnight.

Day 2:

1. Drain syrup into a sauce pan, boil until thickened or 225 degrees F. (107 C.) on a candy thermometer and pour it over the stems. Allow to sit overnight.

Day 3 and 4:

1. Repeat step 4 two more times. Stems should start to look translucent.
2. On day 4, pour syrup off once again and boil until thicken or 230 degrees F. (110 C.) on a candy thermometer.
3. Drain in a colander and place on racks in a dehydrator set on low temperature until they are dry to the touch. Sprinkle with fine sugar and store in an airtight container.

- **Canning:** There are two canning methods that are safe to use for today's foods. There is the water bath canning method and the pressure canning method. (It is not recommended to use the open kettle method, the oven method, or canning in a microwave.) I will start with the water bath canning method. Items needed for water bath canning are glass jars that have been manufactured for this specific purpose, sealing lids and jar screw rings, a canner, lifting tongs, regular kitchen tongs, a canning funnel, ladle, magnetic lid lifter, a bubble remover, and lots of kitchen towels.

- Water bath canning is used for fruits and vegetables with a high acid content. The acid in these foods will kill any lurking harmful bacteria. Suitable foods for water bath canning are: fruits and fruit juices, jams and jellies, salsa, relishes and pickles, as well as acidic tomatoes. There are also two methods to use when water bath canning, the cold pack method and the hot pack method. The cold pack method means packing raw fruits and vegetables into jars, adding hot liquid, and processing in a boiling water bath. The hot pack method means a short precooking of the fruits or vegetables, packing them into jars, adding hot liquid, and processing in a boiling water bath. The steps are the same for both of these methods.

- Prepare the jars by examining the top to make sure there are no nicks, cracks, or sharp edges. Discard any damaged jars in the appropriate manner.
- Wash jars and screw lids in hot, soapy water and rinse. Sterilize thoroughly either in a boiling water bath for 15 minutes or in the oven at 225 degrees F. (107 C.) for ten minutes. Keep warm until ready to use.
- Place the sealing lids in a pan of hot water to soften the rubber sealing ring. (Do not allow to boil.)
- Bring the water in your canner to a boil and keep it simmering until ready to use.
- Select fresh, firm, newly picked produce. Wash and prepare according to your recipe.
- Pack produce into hot jars to within one inch (2.5 cm.) of the top and add the hot liquid to cover the produce.
- Run the sterilized bubble remover around the inside of the jar to remove bubbles that have formed between the layers of produce.
- Wipe the top of the jar with a clean, damp, paper towel to remove any seeds or pulp.
- Place the hot sealing lid, rubber side down, on the rim of the jar and screw on the band until it is finger tight. Do not use too much force.
- Place jars in the simmering canner and return to a boil, being sure one–two inches (2.5–5 cm.) of water is covering the jars.
- Process according the following chart.
- Remove jars from the canner. Do not tighten the lids or press down on the sealing lid. Place jars on a dry thickness of cloth two–three inches (5–7.6 cm.) apart from each other out of a draft. Do not cover them. As they seal, you will hear a clicking sound.
- Once the jars are cool, test for a seal by tapping the lid with a spoon. A clear ringing sound means a seal. The sealing lid will also be concaved when a seal has been achieved.
- At this point, if you have not achieved a seal, remove the lids, wipe down the rim of the jar, replace the lids, and process in canner again.

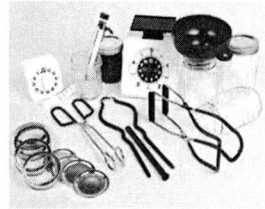

- Pressure canning is recommended for processing foods with a low acid content, as it gives a greater degree of safety. A pressure canner must be fitted with a rack in the bottom, steam-tight cover, petcock, safety valve, and an accurate pressure gauge. The jars of food processed in a pressure canner reach temperatures many degrees above the boiling point of water and are under pressure.

- Prepare the jars by examining the top to make sure there are no nicks, cracks or sharp edges. Discard any damaged jars in the appropriate manner.
- Wash jars and screw lids in hot, soapy water and rinse. Sterilize thoroughly either in a boiling water bath for 15 minutes or in the oven at 225 degrees F. (107 C.) for ten minutes. Keep warm until ready to use.
- Place the sealing lids in a pan of hot water to soften the rubber-sealing unit. Do not allow them to boil.
- Place the canner on low heat with the rack in the bottom and add enough water to a depth of one–two inches (2.5–5 cm.).
- Select fresh, firm, newly picked produce. Wash and prepare according to your recipe.
- Pack produce into hot jars to within one inch (2.5 cm.) of the top and add the hot liquid to cover the produce.
- Run the sterilized bubble remover around the inside of the jar to remove bubbles that have formed between the layers of produce.
- Wipe the top of the jar with a clean paper towel to remove any seeds or pulp.
- Place the hot sealing lid, rubber side down, on the rim of the jar and screw on the band until it is finger tight. Do not use too much force.
- As each jar is filled, it can be placed on the rack in the canner, but do not allow the jars to touch each other.
- When the canner is full, adjust the cover and fasten securely, leaving the petcock open to exhaust the canner for about ten minutes.
- After exhausting the canner, close the petcock and allow the canner to build up to the required pressure for the suitable processing time. Adjust the heat accordingly.

- Once the processing time is up, gently remove the canner from the heat and allow the pressure to reduce gradually; this prevents jar breakage.
- When the pressure gauge is back to zero, you can remove the lid and take the jars out of the canner. Do not tighten the lids or press down on the sealing lid. Place jars on a dry thickness of cloth two–three inches (5–7.6 cm.) apart from each other out of a draft. Do not cover them.
- Once the jars are cool, test for a seal by tapping the lid with a spoon. A clear ringing sound means a seal. The sealing lid will also be concaved when a seal has been achieved.

TIME TABLE FOR WATER BATH AND PRESSURE CANNING

PRODUCT	PREPARATION	WATER BATH TIME PINT	WATER BATH TIME QUART	PRESSURE CANNER TIME PINT AND QUART	POUNDS OF PRESSURE
Beans (snap)	Wash, string if necessary, cut if desired. Pack into hot sterilized jars and cover with boiling water, allowing one inch of head space. Add a bit of salt. Finger tighten lids.	N/A	N/A	Pint 20 min. Quart 25 min.	Ten pounds
Beets	Wash leaving root and two inches of stem. Cook about 15 minutes, dip in cold water, and remove skins. Leave whole, slice, or dice. Pack into hot sterilized jars, cover with boiling water, allowing one inch of head space. Add a bit of salt. Finger tighten lids.	N/A	N/A	Pint 30 min. Quart 35 min.	Ten pounds
Berries	Wash, stem, pack into hot sterilized jars. Add hot syrup, allowing one inch of head space. Finger tighten lids.	25 min.	30 min.	Pint eight min. Quart eight min.	Five pounds

Item	Instructions				
Carrots	Wash and cook for ten minutes, dip in cold water and remove skins. Leave whole or slice. Pack into hot sterilized jars, cover with boiling water, allowing one inch of head space. Add a bit of salt. Finger tighten lids.	N/A	N/A	Pint 25 min. Quart 30 min	Ten pounds
Chutney	Ladle your hot cooked product into hot sterilized jars, allowing one inch of head space. Finger tighten lids.	Ten min.	15 min.	Pints ten min. Quarts 15 min.	Ten pounds
Corn (whole kernel)	Shuck, cut from cob. Pack into hot sterilized jars loosely. Cover with boiling water, allowing one inch of head space. Add a bit of sugar and salt.	N/A	N/A	Pint 55 min. Quart 85 min.	Ten pounds
Fruit Juice	Heat your extracted and sweetened juice to just below the boiling point. Add lemon juice to increase the acid content for low acidic produce. Pour into hot sterilized jars, allowing one inch of head space. Finger tighten lids.	Five min.	Ten min.		
Horseradish	Wash, peel, and grate horseradish root. Add vinegar, salt, ascorbic acid and a wee bit of sugar. Bring to a boil. Pack in	Ten min.			

	hot sterilized jars, allowing one-inch head space. Finger tighten lids.				
Jams, Jellies & Syrups	Pour your hot cooked product into hot sterilized jars, allowing one inch of head space. Finger tighten lids.	Ten min.			
Peas	Bring young tender-shelled peas to a boil, pack loosely with the cooking liquid into hot sterilized jars, allowing one inch of head space. Add a bit of salt and sugar if desired. Finger tighten lids.	N/A	N/A	Pints 30 min. Quarts 35 min.	Ten pounds
Pickles	Pack your prepared product into hot sterilized jars. Pour in hot vinegar solution, allowing one inch of head space. Finger tighten lids.	Ten min.	15 min.		
Potatoes	Scrape or peel young potatoes. Boil for ten minutes and drain, discard water. Pack into hot sterilized jars. Cover with fresh boiling water, allowing one inch of head space. Add a bit of salt. Finger tighten lids.	N/A	N/A	Pints 35 min. Quarts 40 min.	Ten pounds
Pumpkin	Peel and cut into uniform pieces. Boil, bake, or steam until tender. Mash or put	N/A	N/A	Pints 65 min. Quarts 80 min.	Ten pounds

	through a ricer. Pack into hot sterilized jars, allowing one-inch head space. Finger tighten lids.				Ten pounds
Relish	Ladle your hot cooked product into hot sterilized jars, allowing one inch of head space. Finger tighten lids.	Ten min.	15 min.	Pints ten min. Quarts 15 min.	Ten pounds
Salsa	Ladle your hot cooked product into hot sterilized jars, allowing one inch of head space. Finger tighten lids.	Ten min.	15 min.	Pints ten min. Quarts 15 min.	Ten pounds
Tomatoes	Blanch, cold water dip, peel, core. Pack into hot sterilized jars and add hot tomato juice. Finger tighten lids.	30 min.	35 min.	Ten min.	Ten pounds

- **Crystalizing:** This preservation method is used primarily for edible leaves and flowers, and the finished project is used to decorate cakes and other dessert goods.

Ingredients:
Two large egg whites at room temperature
One teaspoon water
One cup (250 ml.) super fine sugar (not icing sugar) If

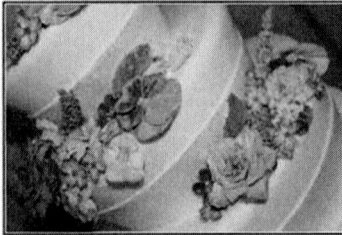

you can't find fine sugar, blitz regular granulated sugar in a blender or food processor.

Directions:

1. Combine egg whites and water in a small bowl and beat with a fork or a whisk.
2. Dip a new, unused paint brush in egg-white mixture and gently paint flower petals thoroughly on front and back.
3. While still wet, gently sprinkle with sugar.
4. Place on a parchment or wax paper lined with baking sheet and allow to dry at room temperature for 12–24 hours.
5. Once thoroughly dry, store at room temperature on paper towel in an airtight container.

- **Dehydrating and Drying:**

- Drying: Most herbs can be dried by securing a good-sized handful with twine, elastic, or zip ties and hanging them upside down in a warm, dry, ventilated area out of the weather. They usually take two–four weeks to dry. Once dry, slip a paper bag over them to keep the dust off or crumble them and pack in glass or plastic containers and label. Dried herbs store in the same warm, dry conditions as garlic and onions.

- Dehydrating is using heat and air movement to remove the moisture from your product, leaving the pulp, flavor and, if done correctly, most of the nutrition, up to 97% of it. Things like the thickness determine the time it will take to remove the moisture as will the temperature and humidity. There are several ways to dehydrate foods. They are:

- Using nature: This method can be used only for fruits with a high acid content. Lay your evenly sized produce outside on stainless steel or plastic racks and cover with a lightweight cloth to avoid insects and bird droppings. The conditions required for this method are temperatures of at least 85 degrees F. (29 degrees C.), a breezy weather with a humidity of 60% or lower lasting for several days. In many areas, even in desert areas, these optimal conditions are hard to come by.

- The oven method: Some ovens have a low enough setting to do a pretty good job of dehydration, the ideal temperature being 110 degrees F. (45 degrees C.). Temperatures higher than that will start to cook the food. The drawback to using this method is it can be expensive running an electric or gas range for hours at a time. The oven door has to stay ajar so the moisture from the food escapes which causes the house to heat up.

- Using a portable readymade dehydrator or making your own: There are quite a few manufacturers of dehydrators on the market. Some are round, some square, some with the mechanical parts at the bottom, some on the top. Some have plastic racks, some stainless-steel racks. They range in price from about $50.00 to almost $500.00. All you really need is for it to create heat and have air movement. I have an electric Nesco Gardenmaster food dehydrator that cost a little over $40.00 that works great. Extra trays can be purchased, as can fruit roll sheets. The advantage to this lightweight machine is it is portable and I can place it outside so it doesn't heat up the house. As mentioned, you can build your own dehydrator, and there are many, many plans on the internet for making one, from using a cardboard box to an old refrigerator conversion.

The benefits to dehydrating are:

- It is a safe method to use.
- You get a concentrated flavor.
- There are no preservatives added.
- It is relatively economical.
- The finished product is lightweight and doesn't take up a lot of storage area.
- The finished product doesn't require electrical costs to store.
- You can use your dehydrator over and over again.

Try to slice your produce as thinly as possible to cut down on the dehydration time. Although a little pricey, a mandolin slicer is perfect for the job. Some vegetables need to be blanched prior to dehydrating them. Blanching helps to preserve the flavor, color, and vitamin content. The blanching time will vary depending on the thickness of your produce. Whatever dehydration method you use, keep in mind the various factors of thickness, temperature, and humidity, which will determine the time it takes to completely remove the moisture. The following chart is a guide only; all produce should be checked on a regular basis.

PRODUCT	BLANCHING TIME	DEHYDRATION TEMP. DEGREES FARENHEIT	DEHYDRATION TIME	REHYDRATION AMOUNT TO 1 CUP OF PRODUCT	SOAKING TIME
Basil		90–100 F.	1–4 hours		
Green beans	Two minutes	125–135 F.	8–12 hours	2 ½ cups	60 minutes
Beets	Four minutes	125–135 F.	8–12 hours	2 ¾ cups	90 minutes
Blackberries		135–145 F.	12–16 hours		
Blueberries		135–145 F.	12–16 hours		
Carrots	Four minutes	125–135 F.	12–14 hours	2 ¼ cups	60 minutes
Cilantro		90–100 F.	1–3 hours		
Corn	four–six minutes	125–135 F.	8–12 hours	2 ¼ cups	30 minutes
Cucumbers (seasoned)		125–135 F.	4–6 hours		
Currants	30 seconds	90–100 F.	10–12 hours		
Dill		90–100 F.	1–3 hours		
Garlic		125–135 F.	10–12 hours		
Gooseberries		135–145 F.	24–48 hours		
Grapes		135–145 F.	24–48 hours		
Kale		125–135 F.	2–3 hours	1 cup	30 minutes

Leeks		125–135 F.	6–8 hours	3 cups	30 minutes
Lovage		90–100 F.	1–3 hours		
Marjoram		90–100 F.	1–3 hours		
Mint		90–100 F.	1–3 hours		
Onions		125–135 F.	8–12 hours	2 cups	30 minutes
Oregano		90–100 F	1–3 hours		
Parsley		90–100 F	1–3 hours		
Parsnip	four minutes	125–135 F	12–14 hours	2 ¼ cups	60 minutes
Pea	three minutes	125–135 F	12–14 hours	2 ½ cups	30 minutes
Pepper		125–135 F	4–12 hours		
Raspberry		135–145 F	12–16 hours		
Rosemary		90–100 F	1–3 hours		
Squash	two minutes	125–135 F	12–14 hours	2 cups	60 minutes
Strawberry		135–145 F	8–18 hours		
Summer Savory		90–100 F.	1–3 hours		
Thyme		90–100 F.	1–3 hours		
Tomato		135–145 F.	6–12 hours	2 cups	40 minutes
Turnip	three minutes	125–135 F.	4–6 hours	2 ¼ cups	30 minutes

- **Freezing and Blanching**: Freezing is probably the most common method of preserving foods in our modern times. Freezing food stops the growth of microorganisms which cause spoilage. It also stops oxidation which cause spoilage and alters the color, flavor, and vitamin content of foods. Thirdly, freezing stops the enzyme action which in turn stops the produce from growing and over maturing. Many of the foods that we freeze also require a blanching time which helps them last longer in a frozen state. Blanching is the process of dipping certain foods in boiling water or steam for a certain period of time. This stops the enzyme action in the foods which helps to preserve the taste, texture, appearance, and most of the nutritional values. If you choose, you can purchase a blanching pot, but I just use a large stock pot and fish my produce out with a sieve. This method has worked just fine for me for years. After blanching your produce, it is important to place these items in ice water to stop the cooking process. This is called icing. After they have chilled sufficiently, allow them to drain and then place them in bags or containers designed specifically for frozen food to prevent freezer burn. Freezer burn is a condition that occurs when frozen food has been damaged by dehydration and oxidation. Try to remove as much air as possible from the containers or use a vacuum sealer. I simply place a straw in the freezer bag and suck the air out. It is equally important to date and label all of your foods designated for the freezer.

The benefits to freezing are:

- Freezers are readily available and are inexpensive.
- It is much less time consuming to freeze foods, rather than can or dehydrate them.
- Freezing your own foods is cost effective.
- Frozen foods retain their color, flavor, and nutrient content.
- As your crops ripen, you can freeze small bits at a time.
- There are no preservatives when you freeze your own produce.
- Frozen foods are available to you all year long.
- Having a freezer full of foods is a convenient way to plan your meals.
- Frozen foods are safe to use.

The drawbacks to freezing are:

- There is an electrical cost to running a freezer
- A freezer breakdown can cause a great loss, unless you have a backup generator or auxiliary solar panel backup plan.
- The texture of frozen foods is often altered.
- A large freezer takes up floor space.
- Frozen foods usually start to break down after being in a frozen state for a year.

BLANCHING AND ICING TIME TABLE

PRODUCT	PREPARATION	BLANCHING TIME		ICING TIME
		WATER	STEAM	
Asparagus	Snap off the tough white end of the stalk. Wash and sort into equal size lengths and thicknesses.	2–3 min.	4 min.	4 min.
Beans (Snap)	Wash and slice or leave whole.	2–3 min.	3 min.	4 min.
Beets	Wash, leaving 1–1½ inches of leaf stems and root intact. Cook until tender. Plunge in ice water. When cool, slip skins off. Slice or dice as preferred.	N/A	N/A	10 min.
Blackberries	Wash and gently pat dry. Place in a single layer on parchment-lined baking trays and freeze. Once frozen, place them in airtight freezer containers.	N/A	N/A	N/A
Blueberries	Wash and gently pat dry. Place in a single layer on parchment-lined baking trays and freeze. Once	N/A	N/A	N/A

	frozen, place in an airtight freezer containers.			
Borage Flowers	Fill ice-cube trays with water and place a flower in each cube space. Once frozen, place in airtight freezer containers to use in cocktails or juice drinks.	N/A	N/A	N/A
Broccoli	Wash and cut into uniform pieces. Soak in saltwater for 30 minutes to remove insects.	3 min.	5 min.	5 min.
Brussels Sprouts	Wash and remove damaged outer leaves.	4 min.	5 min.	5 min.
Cabbage	Wash and remove damaged and insect-infested leaves. Remove leaves from the core to use for cabbage rolls. Slice or dice the remainder into uniform pieces to use in soups and stews.	3 min.	4 min.	4 min.
Carrots	Remove tops. For small tender carrots, scrub clean. Older mature carrots peel, slice, or dice into uniform pieces.	Small whole 5 min. Sliced 2 min.	5 min. 4 min.	5 min. 5 min.
Cauliflower	Wash and break into florets. Soak in saltwater for 30 minutes to remove possible insects.	3 min.	4 min.	4.min.
Chard	Wash and chop.	2 min.	3 min.	3 min.
Chives	Wash and pat dry. Chop into uniform pieces. Place in a single layer on parchment-lined baking trays and freeze. Once frozen, place in airtight freezer containers. Or	N/A	N/A	N/A

	once chopped, freeze in ice-cube trays. Once frozen, place the ice cubes in an airtight container.			
Cilantro	Wash and blanch whole stems. Place in freezer bags. Or chop and freeze in ice-cube trays. Once frozen, place ice cubes in airtight freezer containers *Note: Blanching helps to retain the color of cilantro.	15 seconds	N/A	30 sec.
Corn	Husk and remove silks. For freezing kernels, cut from the cob after the blanching and icing period.	Cob 7 min. Kernels 3 min.	N/A	5 min.
Currants	Wash and gently pat dry. Place in a single layer on parchment-lined baking trays and freeze. Once they are frozen, place them in airtight freezer containers.	N/A	N/A	N/A
Dill	Wash and pat dry. Chop and freeze in ice-cube trays. Once frozen, place ice cubes in airtight freezer containers.	N/A	N/A	N/A
Eggplant	Wash and slice uniformly.	4 min.	6 min.	5 min.
Gooseberries	Wash and gently pat dry. Place in a single layer on parchment-lined baking trays and freeze. Once frozen, place in airtight freezer containers.	N/A	N/A	N/A
Horseradish	Wash, peel, and grate. Place small usable amounts in airtight freezer containers.	N/A	N/A	N/A

Lemon Balm	Wash and pat dry. Chop and freeze in ice-cube trays. Once frozen, place ice cubes in airtight freezer containers.	N/A	N/A	N/A
Lettuce	Wash and pat dry whole leaves. Place in airtight freezer containers.	N/A	N/A	N/A
Melons	Wash the whole melon, quarter it, and remove seeds and rind. Then slice thinly or use a melon scoop to form balls. Place in a single layer, not touching each other, on parchment-lined baking trays and freeze. Once frozen, place in airtight freezer containers.	N/A	N/A	N/A
Mint	Wash and pat dry. Chop and freeze in ice-cube trays. Once frozen, place ice cubes in airtight freezer containers.	N/A	N/A	N/A
Oregano	Wash and pat dry. Chop and freeze in ice-cube trays. Once frozen, place ice cubes in airtight freezer containers.	N/A	N/A	N/A
Parsnip	Remove tops. Wash, peel, and slice into uniform pieces. Parsnip can also be fully cooked and frozen.	2 min.	3 min.	3 min.
Pea	Shell and discard immature and overripe seeds. Wash. For snow peas, wash and remove stem, string, and tail end.	1 ½ min	1 ½ min.	2 min.

Peppers	Wash, remove stem, and cut in half. Remove seeds and membrane. Slice or dice. Place the pieces in a single layer, not touching each other, on parchment-lined baking trays and freeze. Once frozen, place in airtight freezer containers.	N/A	N/A	N/A
Potatoes	Wash, scrape, or peel if preferred. Slice, cube, or dice.	3–5 min.	5–7 min.	10 min.
Raspberry	Wash and gently pat dry. Place in a single layer on parchment-lined baking trays and freeze. Once frozen, place in airtight freezer containers.	N/A	N/A	N/A
Rhubarb	Remove leaf and bottom end. Wash and cut into one-inch pieces. Place in a single layer on parchment-lined baking trays and freeze. Once frozen, place in airtight freezer containers.	N/A	N/A	N/A
Rosemary	Wash and pat dry. Strip leaves from the branches. Chop, place in freezer bags. Or freeze in ice-cube trays. Once frozen, place ice cubes in airtight freezer containers.	N/A	N/A	N/A
Sage	Wash and pat dry. Strip leaves from the branches. Chop, place in freezer bags. Or freeze in ice-cube trays. Once frozen, place	N/A	N/A	N/A

	ice cubes in airtight freezer containers.			
Spinach	Wash and chop.	2 min.		3 min.
Squash (Summer)	Wash and cut off stem and blossom ends. Grate, slice, or dice.	Grated 2 min. Sliced or diced 3 min.	Sliced or diced 4 min.	3 min.
Squash (Winter)	Wash and quarter. Remove seeds. Peel using a potato peeler and slice or cube.	7–10 min.	10–15 min.	10 min
Strawberry	Wash, pat dry, and hull. For small whole berries, place in a single layer on parchment-lined baking trays and freeze. Once frozen, place in airtight freezer containers. For larger berries, slice and pack in freezer bags.	N/A	N/A	N/A
Summer Savory	Wash and pat dry. Strip leaves from the branches. Chop, place in freezer bags. Or freeze in ice-cube trays. Once frozen, place ice cubes in airtight freezer containers.	N/A	N/A	N/A
Tarragon	Wash and pat dry. Strip leaves from the branches. Chop, place in freezer bags. Or freeze in ice-cube trays. Once frozen, place ice cubes in airtight freezer containers.	N/A	N/A	N/A
Thyme	Wash and pat dry. Strip leaves from the branches. Chop, place in freezer bags. Or freeze in ice-cube trays. Once frozen, place	N/A	N/A	N/A

	ice cubes in airtight freezer containers.			
Tomato	Wash and remove stem end. Blanch to remove skins. Once blanched, they can be halved or quartered and placed in a single layer on parchment-lined baking trays. Once frozen, place in airtight freezer containers.	1–2 min.	3 min.	1–2 min.
Turnip	Remove tops. Wash, peel, and slice or cube into uniform pieces. Turnip can also be fully cooked and frozen.	2 min.	3 min.	3 min.

- **Fruit Leather:**

Ingredients:

Two cups (500 ml.) fresh berries (a combination or individual varieties)
Three tbsp. granulated white sugar
Half lemon (juiced)

Directions:

1. Blend all ingredients until the sugar is dissolved and well combined. Taste and add more sugar if desired. Blend until dissolved.
2. Line dehydrator trays with parchment paper or use a fruit roll-up tray.
3. Spread the mixture evenly over trays and replace the lid.
4. Set the dehydrator to 140 degrees F. (60 degrees C.) and run anywhere between 4–12 hours depending on the number of trays you have in the machine and the thickness of the leather.
5. When dried, not at all tacky, allow it to cool, cut, and roll up in parchment paper and store in an airtight container in fridge.

*Note: If you have a problem with the leather sticking to the tray, give the tray a very light coating of olive oil.

- **Freeze Drying**: I have to admit that this method of preserving is a new one for me. I have no experience and no knowledge, so everything I am writing is based on a bit of research. Freeze drying actually dates back to the 15th century when the Incas stored their harvested crops at the top of Machu Picchu. The freezing-cold temperature combined with the low air pressure slowly vaporized the water from their food stash.

Experimentation of freeze drying began in earnest during WW2 where blood and medicines were needed for medical use for wounded soldiers. It was found that by freeze drying these items, they could be shipped without spoilage, saving many lives. Since then, this method has been perfected and is used to preserve many items. It became a common-place method of preservation for the foods the astronauts required for long periods of time in outer space. In a nutshell, this is how it works (taken from the Harvest Right website):

- Fresh or cooked foods are placed in the dryer where they are frozen to -40 degrees Fahrenheit (-40 C.) or colder.
- Once the food is frozen, the freeze dryer creates a powerful vacuum around the food. Then, as the food is slightly warmed, the ice transitions into vapor and evaporates.
- The freeze-dried food is then sealed in moisture and oxygen-proof packaging (Mylar bags, mason jars, or cans) along with an oxygen absorber to ensure freshness until opened.
- When water is added to the food, it regains its original fresh flavor, aroma, and appearance!

This truly sounds like the ultimate preservation method, but in looking into the cost of around $3500.00 for a home-based machine, I will be sticking to my freezing and canning methods for some time to come.

- **Jam, Jelly, Sauce, and Syrup**: All of these products, once made, must be preserved, either by freezing or water-bath canning. The method for making all four of these sweet treat products is similar, using the open-kettle method of cooking. Jam and sauce use the fruit pulp, and jelly and syrup use the fruit juice. To make jelly and syrup, the juice from the pulp needs to be extracted. This is done by hanging the mashed fruit in a jelly bag or in several layers of cheese cloth and allowing it to drip into a glass container. For a clear product, allow it to drip without squeezing. (Do not use juice extractors for making jelly.) Follow the steps below for the cooking method.
- Wash jars, rings, and lids. Rinse well. Sterilize in a boiling water bath for 15 minutes or in the oven at 225 degrees F. (107 C.) for ten minutes. Keep warm until ready for use.
- Prepare fruit or juice as directed in the following chart.
- Measure prepared pulp or juice into a large saucepan. Add lemon juice if listed in the recipe. The pan should be only half full to allow mixture to reach a full rolling boil without overflowing. To reduce foaming, add half tsp. butter.
- Measure the exact amount of sugar specified. Add to pulp or juice and mix well.
- Place pot over high heat and bring to a full boil, stirring constantly. Boil hard for one minute. Remove from heat.
- Immediately stir in liquid fruit pectin.
- Stir and skim for five minutes to prevent floating fruit.
- Pour quickly into hot sterilized jars to within half inch (1.25 cm.) from rim.
- Wipe the top of the jar with a clean, damp paper towel to remove any seeds or pulp.
- Place the hot sealing lid, rubber side down, on the rim of the jar and screw on the band until it is finger tight. Do not use too much force.
- Place jars in simmering canner and return to boil, being sure one–two inches (2.5–5 cm.) of water is covering the jars.
- Process ten minutes in water-bath canner.
- Remove jars from the canner. Do not tighten the lids or press down on the sealing lid. Place jars on a dry thickness of cloth two–three inches

(5–7.6 cm) apart from each other out of a draft. Do not cover them. As they seal, you will hear a clicking sound.

- Once the jars are cool, test for a seal by tapping the lid with a spoon. A clear ringing sound means a seal. The sealing lid will also be concaved when a seal has been achieved.

JAMS, JELLIES, SAUCES, AND SYRUPS

FRUIT	PREPARATION	QUANTITIES IN CUPS	METHOD
Blackberry	Jam: Wash berries and crush one layer at a time.	4 c. fruit 7 c. sugar 1 pouch pectin	Combine crushed fruit and sugar. Boil hard one min. Remove from heat, add pectin.
	Jelly: Extract juice from crushed fruit.	3 ¾ c. juice ¼ c. lemon juice 7 c. sugar 2 pouch pectin	Combine juices and sugar. Boil hard one min. Remove from heat, add pectin.
	Sauce: Wash and crush one layer at a time.	4 c. fruit 1 c. sugar 1 tbsp. lemon juice 1 tbsp. corn starch	Combine crushed fruit and sugar. Boil hard three min. Combine lemon juice and corn starch, add to fruit. Cook until thickened.
	Syrup: Wash and crush one layer at a time. Cook over med. heat 10–15 min. Extract juice from cooked fruit.	3 c. juice 1 tbsp. lemon juice 2 ½ c. sugar 2 tsp. powder pectin	Combine juices and sugar. Boil hard three min. Remove from heat, add pectin.
Blueberry	Jam: Wash berries and crush one layer at a time.	4 ½ c. fruit	Combine crushed fruit and sugar. Boil

		2 tbsp. lemon juice 7 c. sugar 2 pouch pectin	hard one min. Remove from heat, add pectin.
	Jelly: Extract juice from crushed fruit.	4 c. juice 7 c. sugar 2 pouch pectin	Combine juices and sugar. Boil hard one min. Remove from heat, add pectin.
	Sauce: Wash and crush one layer at a time.	2 c. fruit 1/3 c. water ¼ c. sugar 2 tbsp. lemon juice 1 ½ tbsp. corn starch	Combine crushed fruit, water, and sugar. Boil hard three min. Combine lemon juice and corn starch, add to fruit. Cook until thickened.
	Syrup: Wash and crush one layer at a time. Cook with one c. water over med. heat 10–15 min. Extract juice from cooked fruit.	3 ½ c. fruit 2 ½ c. water 1 ½ c. sugar 2 tsp. lemon juice	Combine juice, 1½ c. water, sugar, and lemon juice. Boil five min.
Currant	Jelly: Stem and thoroughly crush two quarts berries. Add one c. water. Bring to a boil and simmer, covered for ten min. Extract juice.	5 c. juice 7 c. sugar 1 pouch	Combine juices and sugar. Boil hard one min. Remove from heat, add pectin.
Gooseberry	Jam: Remove blossom and stem ends and finely chop.	3¾ c. fruit ¼ c. lemon juice 6 c. sugar 1 pouch pectin	Combine crushed fruit and sugar. Boil hard one min. Remove from heat, add pectin.
Grape	Jelly: Stem and thoroughly crush three quarts fruit. Add three c. water. Bring to a boil and simmer, covered for ten min. Extract juice.	4 c. fruit 7 c. sugar 1 pouch pectin	Combine juice and sugar. Boil hard one min. Remove from heat, add pectin.

Mint	Jelly: Wash 1½ c. mint leaves. Add 2¼ c. water. Bring to a boil. Remove from heat, cover, and let stand ten min. Strain and measure mint infusion into a saucepan.	1 ¾ c. infusion 2 tbsp. lemon juice 3 ½ c. sugar 1 pouch pectin Few drops green food color	Combine juices and sugar. Boil hard one min. Remove from heat, add pectin and color.
Pepper (Hot)	Jelly: Grind peppers till liquefied. Place in pot with sugar and vinegar.	2 c. ground red bell pepper ½ c. ground chili pepper 6 c. sugar 1½ c. apple cider vinegar 2 pouch pectin	Combine liquefied peppers, sugar, and vinegar. Bring to a boil, add pectin, and boil hard one min.
Raspberry	Jam: Wash berries and crush one layer at a time.	4 c. fruit 7 c. sugar 1 pouch pectin	Combine crushed fruit and sugar. Boil hard one min. Remove from heat, add pectin.
	Jelly: Extract juice from crushed fruit.	3 ¾ c. juice ¼ c. lemon juice 7 c. sugar 2 pouch pectin	Combine juices and sugar. Boil hard one min. Remove from heat, add pectin.
	Sauce: Wash and crush one layer at a time.	4 c. fruit 1 c. sugar 1 tbsp. lemon juice 1 tbsp. corn starch	Combine crushed fruit and sugar. Boil hard one min. Combine lemon juice and corn starch, add to fruit. Cook until thickened.

	Syrup: Wash and crush one layer at a time. Cook over med. heat 10–15 min. Extract juice from cooked fruit.	3 c. juice 1 tbsp. lemon juice 2 ½ c. sugar 2 tsp. powder pectin	Combine juices and sugar. Boil hard three min. Remove from heat, add pectin.
Rhubarb	Jam: Thinly slice or chop two pounds unpeeled rhubarb. Add ¾ c. water; bring to a boil and simmer, covered five min.	3 c. cooked fruit 5 ½ c. sugar 1 pouch pectin	Combine cooked fruit and sugar. Boil hard one min. Remove from heat, add pectin.
Strawberry	Jam: Hull and thoroughly crush one layer at a time.	3 ¾ c. fruit 7 c. sugar 1 pouch pectin	Combine crushed fruit and sugar. Boil hard one min. Remove from heat, add pectin.
	Syrup: Wash and crush one layer at a time. Cook over med. heat 10–15 min. Extract juice from cooked fruit.	3 ½ c. juice 1 ½ c. water 1 ½ c. sugar 2 tsp. lemon juice	Combine juice, 1½ c. water, sugar, and lemon juice. Boil give min.

- **Pickling**: Pickling is basically preserving fruits and vegetables in a mixture of vinegar, salt, water, and sometimes spices and sugar. The process of pickling alters the taste and texture of the product, and it also causes a lot of the nutritional valve to be lost. However, pickling is a tasty way to preserve vegetables, such as cucumbers, that can't otherwise be frozen, canned, or put in cold storage. The vinegar's acetic acid acts in conjunction with the natural acid in the foods which kills any existing microorganisms that cause spoilage. The best vinegars to use for pickling are ones with a minimum of 5% acidity. Commonly used are distilled white vinegar, white-wine vinegar, and apple-cider vinegar. Salts used should be free of anti-caking ingredients and minerals which can cause cloudiness and discoloration to the product. Commonly used are Pickling Salt, Kosher Salt, and Sea Salt. Hard water and chlorinated water can also cause discoloration to your pickled product, so it is worth purchasing a jug or two of reverse osmosis water to use. Pickling should be done in glass sealing jars and processed in a water-bath canner to lengthen the shelf life.

- **Storage:** Some of our garden crops store in their natural state, while others have to be preserved, altering their natural state. Prior to electricity, many pioneers and early settlers used root cellars to store their produce. They didn't have the luxury of driving to the supermarket and purchasing their groceries on a weekly basis. They had to find a means to keep their garden produce for many months until the next

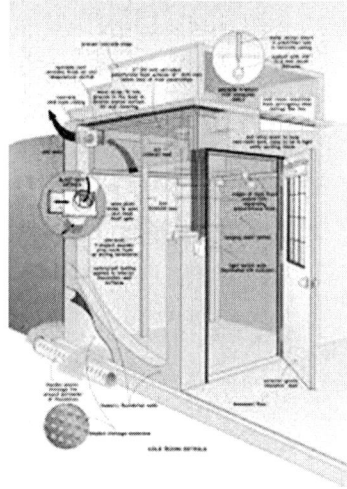

summer when they would plant and harvest again. A root cellar is a structure that is built fully or partially underground in order to keep produce cold and dark. It is highly unlikely you have a root cellar, unless you live in an old farmhouse. We can however improvise and create a similar storage area in our modern abodes. One very good way to create a cold storage area is in a basement or crawl space, preferably with one wall being an outside one. In the home I grew up in, our cold storage area was under the stairs leading to the basement. This housed all of the canning and produce that we harvested from the garden. It is important to store individual varieties of food in their own storage containers. Keep the containers on pallets or on shelving to allow for air circulation. Cabbage, squash, and pumpkins do well sitting on open shelving. Things like potatoes, beets, carrots, parsnip, and turnip keep well in wooden boxes lined with burlap or landscape fabric and filled with slightly moist, horse-bedding chips. Some people use fallen leaves to store their produce in, but dead leaves can also bring disease and insects inside that can harm your fruits and vegetables. Other people use moist sand, but I find sand is heavy and messy. The horse-bedding chips are lightweight, clean, and can be slightly moistened by using a misting bottle. They are also reusable by spreading them out on a tarp outside in the summer on a calm, hot, sunny day and letting the sun sterilize and dry them. Load them back into the wooden crates and they are ready for the next storage season. Plastic storage containers are not recommended, as they don't breathe well. A cold storage room is also a great place to store your canning, wine, orchard fruits, dried beans, onions, garlic, and your heirloom seeds.

A cold storage area requires:

- Two ventilation pipes (one to vent off the ethylene gas that foods give off and one fresh air vent).
- Cool temperatures (generally between 32–40 degrees F.) (0–4.5 C.).
- Darkness.
- Humidity (generally between 90–95% relative humidity).
- Shelving.
- A thermometer.
- A hygrometer (reads the percentage of relative humidity).
- Sometimes a fan for air circulation.

My storage area is in my windowless laundry room where I have blocked the heat source and keep the inside door closed most of the time to block out light. My canning is kept in there in a closet, and the freezer is also in there. I keep the potatoes and squash on the top shelf and hang the onions and garlic in mesh bags from shelving.

CROPS SUITABLE FOR COLD STORAGE			
CROP	METHOD	TEMP. (F)	HUMIDITY
Beets	Dig before a hard frost. Don't wash but gently brush soil off without damaging the skin. Cut stems down to about one inch and leave the roots intact. Place a layer of horse-bedding chips in the bottom of a wooden crate and give them a very light misting. Lay down a layer of beets on the chips, making sure they don't touch each other. Repeat this process, discarding any that maybe damaged.	32–40 F.	90–95
Brussels Sprouts	Just before you are expecting a heavy snowfall, pull the plant out by the roots and hang it upside down, or pick the sprouts off and store in perforated plastic bags.	32–40 F.	90–95
Cabbage	Pull the whole plant out of the ground, leaving the root intact. Remove the outer leaves and check carefully for bugs. Wrap each individual head in burlap or landscape fabric and place on an upper shelf.	32–40 F.	90–95
Carrots, Parsnips and Turnip	Dig before a hard frost. Don't wash but gently brush soil off without damaging the skin. Cut stems down to about one inch. Place a layer of moistened horse-bedding chips in the bottom of a wooden crate. Lay down a layer of produce on the bedding chips, making sure they don't touch each other. Repeat this process, discarding any that maybe damaged.	32–40 F.	90–95
Garlic and Onion	Hang the braided dried stems in the driest area of your storage area. Or	35–38 F.	60–70

	cut off the dried stems and store the bulbs in a mesh bag on a top shelf.		
Potato	Dig before a frost, wash, allow to dry, and place in paper bags or a cardboard box at 65 degrees F. for two weeks to cure them. Then place them in burlap bags in the warmest area in your cold storage area. Note: When potatoes are stored in temperatures 45 degrees F. or lower, the starches change to sugars, making them very sweet.	38–45 F.	80–90
Pumpkin and Winter Squash	These squash like a warmer and drier area for storage, so place them on the top shelf of your storage area.	50–55 F.	60–75
Tomato	Pick your unripe tomatoes before a frost. Place a layer of them on newspaper in a cardboard box and repeat; don't build any more than two layers. Bring a few at a time into a bright warm area to ripen for use.	40–50 F.	60–70

- **Wine**: Making wine is also an excellent way to preserve an excess of fruit. I don't profess to be a 'from scratch' winemaker, preferring to have my wine made at a U-brew. Winemaking is also a vast topic and, for that reason, I have chosen to copy 'HOW TO MAKE HOMEMADE WINE' from WikiHow to do anything website.

➤ How to Make Homemade Wine?

If you're a wine lover, you've probably dreamed of making your own wine right at home. Luckily, with the right tools and ingredients, you can! Once you get the hang of it, you can experiment with different fruits until you find the wine that's right for you. People have been making wine for thousands of years, and they've learned a few tricks along the way. Keep the following in mind as you make your own wine for the first time:

- Use very clean equipment to prevent bacteria from spoiling your wine.
- Keep your first ferment covered, but allow for ventilation.
- Keep all bottles full to minimize oxygen in the bottle.
- Keep red wines in dark bottles so they don't lose their appearance.
- Make wines too dry instead of too sweet. You can add sugar later.
- Taste the wine at intervals to make sure the process is going well.

Ingredients:

16 cups (4 lt.) fruit
2 cups (500 ml.) honey
1 packet wine yeast
Filtered water

Preparing Supplies and Ingredients:

GATHER SUPPLIES: In addition to the wine ingredients, you'll need a few basic supplies to ensure that your wine can age without being affected by bugs or bacteria. Home winemaking shouldn't be expensive, so it's not necessary to splurge on special equipment. You will need the following supplies:

- A two-gallon (7.6 l.) crock or glass jar (you can often find these at yard sales or secondhand stores. However, be advised that many used crocks may have been used for sauerkraut or pickles and could contaminate your wine).
- A one-gallon (3.6 l.) carboy (a glass container with a small neck).
- An airlock.
- A thin plastic tube to be used for siphoning.
- Clean wine bottles with corks or screw caps.
- Campden tablets (optional).

Pick Out Your Fruit: Wine can be made with any type of fruit, though grapes and berries are the most popular choices. Choose fruit at the peak of its flavor. It's best to choose organic fruit that hasn't been treated with chemicals, since you don't want these to end up in your wine. If possible, use fruit you've picked yourself, or buy some from a farmer's market. Some retailers also specialize in providing wine grapes to home winemakers, which is great if you don't live near vineyards.

Clean the Fruit: Take off the stems and leaves and make sure the fruit doesn't have particles of dirt or grit. Rinse the fruit thoroughly and place it in your crock. You can peel the fruit before crushing, but much of the flavor of the wine will come from its skin. Peeling it will result in a much milder wine. Some winemakers choose not to wash the fruit before crushing. Since fruit has natural yeasts on its skin, it's possible to make wine using only the yeast from the fruit's skin and the air. However, washing the fruit and controlling the yeast you add allows you to ensure that the flavor of the wine will be to your liking. Allowing wild yeast to grow can produce foul flavors. If you're up for an experiment, you could make two batches of wine, one with controlled yeast and one with wild, to find out which you like best.

Crush the Fruit: Using a clean potato masher or your hands, crush and squeeze the fruit to release its juices. Keep doing so until the level of the fruit juice is within 1½ inches (3.8 cm.) of the top of the crock. If you don't have enough fruit and juice to fill the crock almost to the top, top it off with filtered water. Add a Campden tablet, which releases sulfur dioxide into the mixture, killing wild yeast and bacteria. If you're making wild yeast wine, don't take steps to kill the yeast. As an alternative to using a tablet, you can pour two cups of boiling water over the fruit. (Using tap water can affect the taste of your wine, since it contains additives. Be sure to use filtered or spring water.)

Stir in the Honey: Honey provides food for the yeast and sweetens your wine. The amount of honey you use will directly affect the sweetness of your wine. If you prefer sweeter wine, add more honey. If you don't like it as sweet, limit your honey to two cups. Take the type of fruit you're using into account as well. Since grapes have a high sugar content, you don't need to add a lot of honey to grape wine. Berries and other fruits with lower sugar content will need a little more honey. You can add white sugar or brown sugar instead of honey if you like. You can always add more sweetener later if your wine doesn't come out as sweet as you like.

Add the Yeast: If you're using your own wine yeast, now is the time to add it. Pour it into the crock and stir it into the mixture with a long-handled spoon. This mixture is called a must. If you're making wild yeast wine, you can skip this step.

Fermenting the wine:

Cover the Crock and Store Overnight: IT'S important to use a cover that will keep bugs out but allow air to flow in and escape the crock. You can use a crock lid designed for this purpose or stretch a cloth or t-shirt over the opening and secure it in place with a large rubber band or twine. Place the covered crock in a warm area with a temperature around 70 degrees F. (20 C.) overnight. Putting the crock in a cool place won't facilitate the growth of the yeast. Storing it in a place that's too warm will kill the yeast. Find a good in-between place in your kitchen.

Stir the Must a Few Times Per Day: The day after you make the mixture, uncover it and stir it thoroughly, then recover. Do this every four hours or so the first day, then keep stirring a few times per day for the next three days. The mixture should start bubbling, as the yeast moves into action. This is the fermentation process that will lead to delicious wine.

Strain and Siphon the Liquid: When the bubbling slows down, about three days after it begins, it's time to strain out the solids and siphon the liquid into your carboy for long-term storage. Once you've siphoned it into the carboy, affix the airlock to the opening to allow for the release of gas while preventing oxygen from coming in and spoiling your wine. If you don't have an airlock, you can use a small balloon placed over the opening with about five pin-sized holes in it. Secure it with tape or an elastic band. This will let the gas escape but not let in oxygen.

Let the Wine Age for at Least One Month: It's better if you can let it age for up to nine weeks, during which time the wine will age and mellow, resulting in a much-improved taste. If you used extra honey in your wine, it's better to age it on the longer side, or else it will taste too sweet when you drink it.

Bottle the Wine: To prevent the wine from catching a bacterium that could cause it to turn to vinegar, add a Campden tablet to the mixture as soon as you remove the airlock. Siphon the wine into your clean bottles, filling them almost to the top, and cork them immediately. Allow the wine to further age in the bottles or enjoy it immediately. Use dark bottles to preserve the color of red wines.

➢ Proven Winning Recipes

Some of these recipes have been passed down in my family from generation to generation. Others are made from my annual harvested goods that I have won prizes for at our local Interior Provincial Exhibition.

Pickled Asparagus

4 lb. (1.8 kg.) untrimmed asparagus spears
1 lemon
3 garlic cloves
15 peppercorns
1 tsp. red pepper flakes
4 cups (1 lt.) pickling vinegar
2½ cups (625 ml.) dry white wine
1½ cups (375 ml.) water
2 tbsp. sugar
1 tbsp. pickling or kosher salt
Pickle Crisp

Wash asparagus and cut into six-inch (15.25 cm.) spears (freeze remaining pieces to extract the flavor for soups throughout the winter months). Slice lemon and set aside. Bring vinegar, wine, water, sugar, and salt to a boil. Place a lemon slice, a garlic clove, five peppercorns, and a pinch of pepper flakes and a quarter tsp. of Pickle Crisp in the bottom of each clean, hot, sterilized quart jar. Place asparagus spears in jars and fill with hot liquid to within half inch (1.25 cm.) of jar top. Wipe the jar rims with a clean, damp paper towel. Place lids on jars and screw on the bands finger tight. Process for 15 minutes in a water-bath canner. Makes three quarts (three liters).

Hot Pickled Beans

3 pounds green beans
2 cups pickling vinegar
2 cups water
5 tbsp. pickling salt

3 garlic cloves

6 sprigs fresh dill weed

¾ tsp. hot pepper flakes

Pickle Crisp

Wash beans, remove stem and tail ends, and cut into size to fit jars. Bring vinegar, water, and salt to a boil. Place one garlic clove, two sprigs of dill, quarter tsp. hot pepper flakes, and quarter tsp. Pickle Crisp in the bottom of each hot, sterilized jar. Place beans in jars and fill with hot liquid to within half inch (1.25 cm.) of jar top. Wipe the jar rims with a clean, damp paper towel. Place lids on jars and screw on the bands finger tight. Process for 15 minutes in a water-bath canner. Makes three quarts (three liters).

Leather Britches (as taken from Joan Wells's recipe in Organic Gardening Harvest Book)

"Just thread a fairly large needle with heavy thread or string, knotted at the end, and string your fresh picked beans as you would a necklace. Do enough for one good meal, plus a few more…you'll taste why…and repeat. Hang them in a warm, dry place like attic rafters.

"Then some cold midwinter day, prepare the feast as follows: remove (beans) from string, and soak overnight; the next day, boil slowly for three hours. An hour before supper, add a hunk of bacon rind (or pork sausage, ham hock, bacon, salt pork) and boil together the next hour until there's just enough liquid left to barely cover them. Serve juice and all. We've found we can make a whole meal of these alone, especially with a pan full of plump, homemade biscuits on the side for sopping."

Mom's Pickled Beets

10 lb. (4.5 kg.) small, young beets

2 cups sugar

2 cups water

2 cups pickling vinegar

1 tbsp. cinnamon

1 tsp. each cloves and allspice

Select small, young beets and cook until tender. Dip into ice-cold water and peel off skins. Fill clean, hot, sterilized jars with the beets to within half inch (1.25 cm.) of the top. Pour in the spicy, boiling brine. Wipe the jar rims with a clean, damp paper towel. Place lids on jars and screw on the bands finger tight. Process for 15 minutes in a water-bath canner.

Blueberry/Scallion Vinegar

50 Blueberries
6 scallions (green onions)
Clear decorative glass bottles
White vinegar
Corks

Mash 30 berries and strain. Put juice in a bottle and add three scallions; add vinegar. Cork and place on a window ledge for several weeks. Strain, reserving the vinegar. Place the remaining berries in a fancy, decorative jar. Add three scallions and fill with the reserved vinegar. Cork and seal with wax and decorate with raffia.

Hot Dog Relish

4 cups (1 lt.) seeded chopped cucumbers
1 cup (250 ml.) chopped red bell pepper
1 cup (250 ml.) chopped onion
2 tbsp. kosher salt
½ cup (125 ml.) apple-cider vinegar
1½ tsp. corn starch
¾ cup (175 ml.) sugar
½ tsp. each celery seed and mustard seed
¼ tsp. each of turmeric and nutmeg
Pepper to taste

Chop cucumber, pepper, and onion in a food processor. Put in a large bowl and mix in salt. Cover and leave in fridge for 24 hours. Next morning, rinse with cold water and allow to drain. Whisk together vinegar and cornstarch, stir in sugar and spices. Bring to a boil, stirring constantly. Once the cornstarch is cooked and thickened, add drained vegetables. Simmer for ten minutes. Fill clean, hot, sterilized half pint jars to within half inch (1.25 cm.) of the top. Wipe the jar rims with a clean, damp paper towel. Place lids on jars and screw on the bands finger tight. Process for ten minutes in a water-bath canner. Makes 3½ pints.

Hamburger Relish

1 cup (250 ml.) chopped, unpeeled cucumbers
1½ cup (375 ml.) chopped red bell pepper
½ cup (125 ml.) chopped celery
1 cup (250 ml.) chopped onion
2 tbsp. pickling or kosher salt
2 cups (500 ml.) chopped tomatoes
1 cup (250 ml.) apple-cider vinegar
½ cup (125 ml.) white vinegar
1 tbsp. mustard seed
1 tbsp. Dejon mustard
1 tsp. turmeric
½ tsp. each cinnamon and allspice
¼ tsp. cayenne pepper
1 cup (250 ml.) sugar
2 tsp. corn starch
1 cup tomato paste or tomato ketchup

In a large bowl, combine cucumbers, peppers, celery, onion, and salt. Cover and let stand in fridge for 24 hours. Next morning, rinse with very cold water and allow to drain. Bring to a boil tomatoes, vinegars, and spices. Reduce heat and allow to simmer for 30 minutes. Stir in sugar and drained vegetables. Simmer for 20 minutes. Stir in tomato paste or ketchup and cook five minutes more. Fill clean, hot, sterilized half pint jars to within half inch (1.25 cm.) of the top. Wipe the jar rims with a clean, damp paper towel. Place lids on jars and screw on the bands finger tight. Process for ten minutes in a water-bath canner. Makes 3½ pints.

Cucumber Relish

6 large, unpeeled cucumbers chopped
2 large onions chopped
2 green peppers chopped
1 red pepper chopped
1 tbsp. pickling or kosher salt
3 cups (750 ml.) white vinegar
3 cups (750 ml.) sugar
1 tsp. each celery seed and mustard seed
½ tsp. turmeric
Couple drops of green food color (optional)

In a large bowl, combine cucumbers, onions, peppers, and salt. Cover and let stand in fridge for 24 hours. Next morning, rinse in cold water and allow to drain. Place in a large cooking pot and add other ingredients. Bring to a boil and simmer for 30 minutes. Fill clean, hot, sterilized half pint jars to within half inch (1.25 cm.) of the top. Wipe the jar rims with a clean, damp paper towel. Place lids on jars and screw on the bands finger tight. Process for ten minutes in a water-bath canner. Makes 4½ pints.

Aunt Avis's Fresh Kosher Style Dill Pickles

30-36 small cucumbers
3 cups (750 ml.) pickling vinegar
3 cups (750 ml.) water
6 tbsp. pickling or kosher salt
Fresh dill (flowers and leaves)
Garlic cloves
Mustard seed
Pickle Crisp

Wash cucumbers. Make a brine of the vinegar, water, and salt. Bring to a boil. Place a generous layer of dill, one–two garlic cloves, half-tbsp. mustard seed, and quarter-tsp. Pickle Crisp in the bottom of each clean, sterilized quart (liter) jar. When the jars are half filled with cucumbers, add another layer of dill and complete packing the cucumbers in the jars. Fill clean, hot, sterilized jars to within half inch (1.25 cm.) of the top with the boiling brine. Wipe the jar rims with a clean, damp paper towel. Place lids on jars and screw on the bands finger tight. Process 15 minutes in a boiling water-bath canner.

Bread and Butter Pickles

3 lb. (1.36 kg.) crisp cucumbers
1 medium onion
¼ cup (125 ml.) pickling or kosher salt
1½ cups (500 ml.) pickling vinegar
½ cup (125 ml.) apple cider vinegar
½ cup (125 ml.) water
1 cup (250 ml.) sugar
2 tbsp. mustard seeds
1 tbsp. pickling spice
1 tsp. celery seed
1 tsp. turmeric
1/8 tsp. cloves
Pickle Crisp

Thinly slice cucumbers and onion and place in a colander resting in a large bowl or in the sink. Toss with the salt and let stand for one–two hours. (The cucumbers will release a lot of water during this salting process.) Rinse well and place in a single layer on a couple of sheet pans lined with paper towels. Cover with another layer of paper towels and let dry overnight. Next day, combine vinegar, water, sugar, and spices in a large cooking pot. Bring to a boil. Fill clean, hot, sterilized jars with the cucumbers and onions and quarter-tsp. Pickle Crisp to within half inch (1.25 cm.) of the jar top. Pour in the boiling brine. Wipe the jar rims with a clean, damp paper towel. Place lids on jars and screw on the bands finger tight. Process ten minutes in a boiling water-bath canner. Makes three pints.

Horseradish Sauce

1 cup (250 ml.) minced horseradish root
2 tbsp. white wine vinegar
1 tbsp. sugar
1 tsp.

Peel and chop horseradish pickling salt root into one-inch (2.5 cm.) pieces. Place in a food processer and mince. Add vinegar, sugar, and salt. Carefully remove the lid, as this mixture is hot and can burn the eyes. Store in a sealed container in the fridge, or it can be processed in a water-bath canner ten minutes for half a pint. If canning, add a pinch of ground up ascorbic acid (Vitamer C) to prevent decolorization.

Rhubarb Custard Pie

PASTRY:

1½ c. (375 ml.) all-purpose flour
1 tbsp. sugar
1 tsp. salt
½ c. (150 ml.) butter
6–8 tbsp. ice-cold water

Mix flour, salt, and sugar in a bowl. Cut in butter with a pastry blender until mixture is crumbly. Add water using just enough to bind mixture so that dough can be patted lightly to form a ball. Add more water if needed. Form dough into two flattened balls. Handle as little as possible. Roll dough out on a floured surface. Start rolling from the center outward with light, even pressure to form a circle 1/8 inch thick and one inch (2.5 cm.) larger than your inverted pie plate. Fold double and lift gently into pie plate. Unfold and fit loosely in place. Do not stretch.
FILLING:

4 cups (1 lt.) rhubarb cut into half-inch (1.25 cm.) pieces
1/3 cup (75 ml.) flour
1½ cup (375 ml.) sugar

¼ tsp. nutmeg

2 eggs, slightly beaten

1 tbsp. milk

1 tbsp. butter

Fill unbaked pastry-lined pie plate with rhubarb. Combine flour, sugar, and nutmeg in a bowl. Add beaten eggs and milk. Mix well. Pour evenly over rhubarb and dot with butter. Place rolled-out pastry top-over filling, make slits in top to allow steam to escape. Bake in a preheated 400 degree F. (204 degree C.) oven for 50–60 minutes.

Marinara Sauce

4 lb. (1.8 kg.) ripe Roma tomatoes

2–14 fl. oz. (398 ml.) cans tomato paste

¼ cup (50 ml.) each of fresh chopped parsley, oregano, basil, rosemary, and sage

2 garlic cloves (crushed)

2 onions (finely chopped)

Salt and pepper to taste

2 tsp. brown sugar

10 tbsp. olive oil

1 cup (250 ml.) white or red wine vinegar

Put tomatoes through a press to extract the juice and pulp. Bring to a boil and reduce to half the initial amount. Add all other ingredients and continue to cook until it has reached a sauce consistency. Fill clean, hot, sterilized pint jars to within half inch (1.25 cm.) of the top. Wipe the jar rims with a clean, damp paper towel. Place lids on jars and screw on the bands finger tight. Process in a water-bath canner for 15 minutes. Makes five pints. Note: About 10 lb. (4.5 kg.) of tomatoes makes 5.25 pints (3 lt.) of juice and pulp.

Fire Truck Salsa

4 lb. (1.8 kg.) ripe Roma tomatoes

3 large onions (chopped)

1 each sweet red, orange, and yellow pepper

2 black Hungarian hot peppers

8 garlic cloves

1–48 oz. (1.4 lt.) can tomato juice

4 tbsp. white vinegar

4 tbsp. brown sugar

1 tbsp. kosher salt

1 tbsp. hot pepper flakes and seeds

1 tbsp. cayenne pepper

¼ c (50 ml.) each chopped basil, oregano, parsley, cilantro

Blanch and peel tomatoes. Slightly chop in a food processor. Place in a colander and gently press out excess liquid. Place in a large stainless-steel cooking pot. Slightly chop peppers and onions in food processor. Place in a colander and gently press out excess liquid. Add to tomatoes. Chop hot peppers, garlic, and herbs in food processor and add to cooking pot. Bring to a boil. Add all other ingredients and reduce heat to low. Simmer for 1½ hours or until mixture becomes thick. Fill clean, hot, sterilized pint jars to within half-inch (1.25 cm.) of the top. Wipe the jar rims with a clean, damp paper towel. Place lids on jars and screw on the bands finger tight. Process in a water-bath canner for 15 minutes.

Makes nine pints.

And so ends this book with facts and my personal experiences that I hope and wish will help all of you readers and your families to have the most productive and awesome gardening experience ever!

Marian Prince

Index